IMAGES
of America

TAVARES

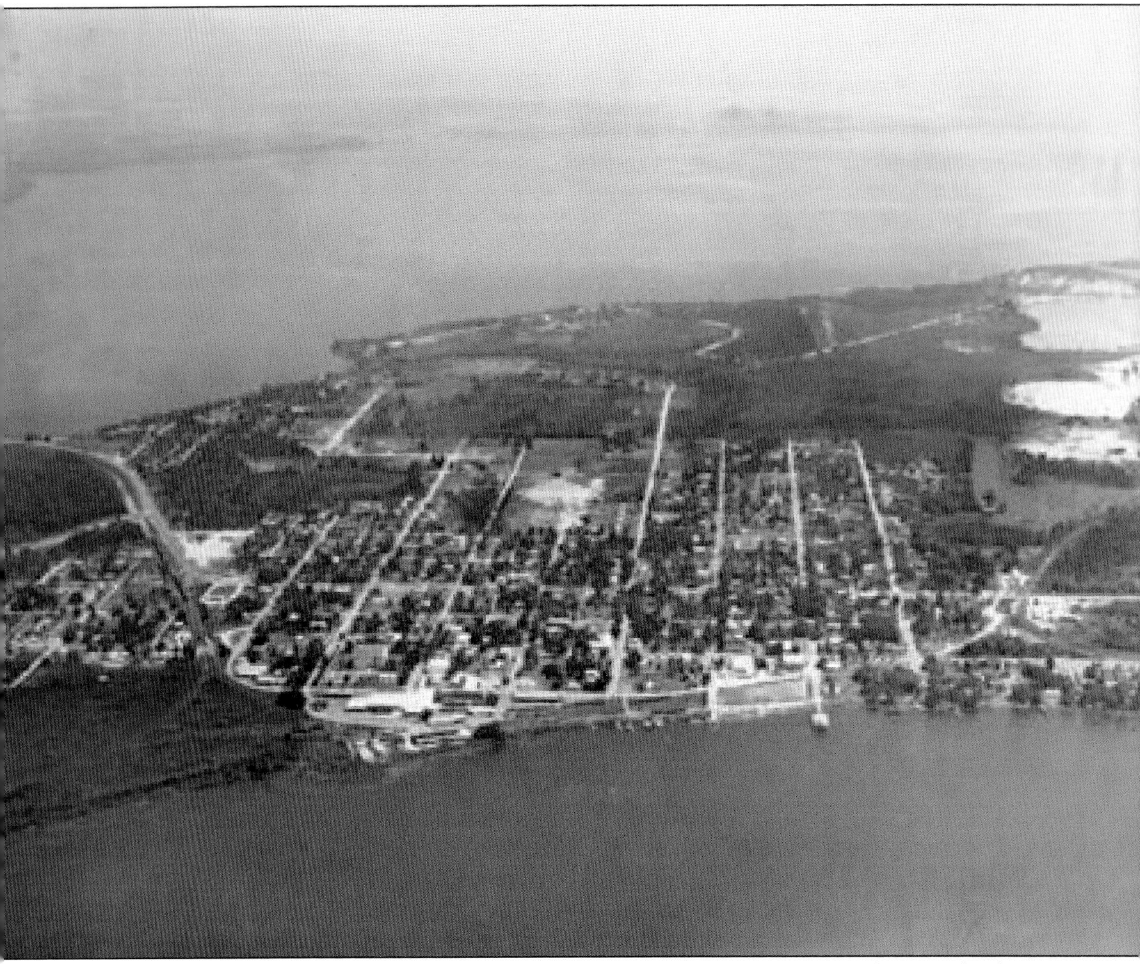

On Friday, September 25, 1953, this aerial photograph of Tavares was spread across the front page of the *Lake County Citizen* with the headline, "The Town of Tavares . . . The City of the Future." The newspaper wrote, "We invite you to come to Tavares to live, to play, to work, to enjoy life at its best." (Courtesy of the Lake County Historical Society; photograph by Glenn Bolles.)

ON THE COVER: Tavares residents, along with friends from Leesburg, hold a picnic to celebrate the opening of the Dead River trestle that linked their two towns in the mid-1880s. The engineer of this Tavares & Gulf Railroad wood-burning locomotive posed the train and joined the party. (Courtesy of the Lake County Historical Society.)

IMAGES
of America

TAVARES

Bob Grenier

ARCADIA
PUBLISHING

ISBN 978-0-7385-9107-0

Published by Arcadia Publishing
Charleston, South Carolina

Printed in the United States of America

Library of Congress Control Number: 2011932109

For all general information, please contact Arcadia Publishing:
Telephone 843-853-2070
Fax 843-853-0044
E-mail sales@arcadiapublishing.com
For customer service and orders:
Toll-Free 1-888-313-2665

Visit us on the Internet at www.arcadiapublishing.com

Dedicated to my family, the Tavares Historical Society, and the citizens of Tavares.

Contents

Acknowledgments

When I moved to Tavares in 1998, my introduction to the people of this city came by way of an old wooden house sitting on the shore of Lake Harris. My desire to preserve this old Tavares home, known as the Woodlea, was the beginning of a wonderful friendship with the Tavares community. Through the years, Tavareans have opened their homes and hearts and have shared their memories with me. This photographic journey through Tavares history was made possible by the following people and organizations, for which I am truly grateful: Bernice Odums, Charlene King, Harryette Anne Duncan, Lura Hall, Bettye Wilcox, Betty Burleigh, Brenda Smith, Doris Ragan, Yvette Young, Jane Whaley, Rick Reed, Martha and Bill Burleigh, Sue Nunes, Jackie Kinsler, Bob and Kathy Cook, Judy Rainey, Lurlene Lawton, Lila Lee Buckbee, Susan Caddell, Imogene Wigglesworth, Jean Miller, Glorianne Fahs, Nancy Clutts, John Drury, Glenda LaRoe, Mary Glover, Billy Powell, Lavonda Morris, and the legendary Clayton Bishop. Everyone worked diligently to identify faces from long ago and to spell the names correctly.

There are many outstanding organizations to thank, including the Tavares Historical Society, Lake County Historical Society, Sons of Confederate Veterans, Leesburg and Tavares Masonic Lodges, Tavares Woman's Club, Tavares African American Heritage Organization, Tavares Chamber of Commerce, Tavares City Council, and the Tavares city staff.

Publications, journals, and letters were a great resource for this book, including Major St. Clair Abrams's *Memoranda on Tavares*, Annie Burleigh's memoirs, Emmett Peter's *Lake County, Florida: A Pictorial History*, Prof. William Kennedy's *History of Lake County*, and my *Woodlea: Life on the Lake of the Dancing Sunbeams*. My appreciation goes to the Arcadia Publishing team, especially Lindsay Carter, Caitrin Cunningham, and Laura Saylor. I wish to thank Betty Ann McClellan and Doris Bloodsworth, who are also Arcadia Images of America authors, for their assistance. My sincerest appreciation to Kathy Carter for proofreading and editing the entire manuscript and also adding valuable historical insight.

And finally, this book was truly made possible by the support and encouragement of my Mom and Dad, Dave Clevinger, Patrick Adams, Wahine, Flash, Capt. Melton Haynes, and of course God!

Introduction

In 1875, ten years after the end of the War Between the States, Maj. Alexander St. Clair Abrams first came upon what is now Tavares. A man named Steeley occupied the Lake Dora section of the town. The land northwest of Steeley to Lake Eustis was homesteaded by the M.V. Hull family. Hull and his wife lived in a log cabin surrounded by a small grove of sweet orange trees. He was a hunter and trapper who traded with the Seminoles and the soldiers stationed along the Little Ocklawaha, now known as the Dora Canal. By June 1880, St. Clair Abrams had acquired the Hull homestead from L.P. Westcott, the new owner of the property, and subsequently bought out the prime Steeley land along Lake Dora. Within two years, St. Clair Abrams had the land surveyed and platted.

He immediately set out to bring the railroads to Tavares. The first line into Tavares was a 10-mile extension of the Florida Railway and Navigation Company, running from Leesburg to Tavares. This extension was completed in June 1885, with St. Clair Abrams investing $30,000 of his own money. Over the next three years, he succeeded in bringing several more railroads into Tavares.

Throughout the 1880s, St. Clair Abrams built Tavares at a rapid rate. First he built the Peninsular Hotel, intending to make Tavares a tourist resort. He then built a double-deck sawmill, a planing mill, several large stores, two warehouses, a cigar factory, cottages, a tramway from Lake Dora to Lake Eustis, and much more. From the time he purchased the land in 1880 until the double freeze of 1894 and 1895, St. Clair Abrams spent more than half-a-million dollars of his own money in constructing Tavares. After the freezes, St. Clair Abrams decided to move to Jacksonville and reopen his law practice.

Annie Burleigh was one of the first in a long line of remarkable women of Tavares. From teachers to technicians, mothers to mayors, and librarians to legislators, from generation to generation, these women have played an active and leading role in the Tavares community.

In her memoirs, Annie Burleigh described when she first learned that she was moving to Tavares. In 1885, her husband, Ed, had heard about Major St. Clair Abrams, who had started a town located between lovely Lake Dora and beautiful Lake Eustis. The town had railroads, which provided an excellent opportunity for machinists, Ed's trade. According to Annie, it was a beautiful moonlit night when Governor Sinclair drove her husband to Tavares with a span of horses and a wagon. Annie said the moon, the lake, and St. Clair Abrams won her husband over so much that the next day, Ed bought seven lots in Tavares. He started a machine shop on the Lake Dora shore, on the line of a little railroad that was being built from Astor to Lane Park, three miles from Tavares on Lake Harris. Unfortunately, the machine shop was not a success, so Ed and a business associate named Whitley started the Lake Abstract Company.

Legend has it that in April 1888, as the business section of Tavares was ablaze, Annie Burleigh performed a heroic feat. As the legend goes, when the train started out of the station at 9:00 a.m., sparks from the engine ignited some paper that had blown under the stores. Although someone thought the fire had been extinguished, more papers had blown under the stores and began to burn. Soon, with a stiff breeze blowing in from the lake, the three-story hotel, two boardinghouses, the drugstore, grocery, meat market, saloon, hardware store, and the abstract office were burning out of control. Annie, seeing the blaze rising high, ran into the barn, harnessed Dolly, and drove her buggy into the heart of the fire. She rode up to the Lake Abstract building, helped her husband load up the books and papers, and then courageously drove Dolly beyond the burning buildings into Lake Dora to preserve the abstract books. Annie, in her memoirs, says the true story is a tad different, but we'll print the legend.

After the formation of Lake County in 1887 came the task of choosing the county seat. The two frontrunners, Tavares and Leesburg, were battling feverishly to claim that title. During the first election, Major St. Clair Abrams hosted an extravagant barbecue in Tavares to sway voters. With the first election ending in a tie, there were two subsequent elections held, each fraught with accusations on both sides of fraud and the purchasing of votes. In July 1888, three months after the devastating fire and three highly contested and controversial elections, Tavares would claim victory and become the county seat.

Three miles southwest of downtown Tavares is Lane Park, named for Capt. A.J. Lane. In 1883, Lane had plans for developing a town on this distinctive peninsula of land that extended into Lake Harris. When he arrived, there were already more than 100 people homesteading the area growing oranges and pineapples. Also located in Lane Park was a terminus of the St. Johns & Eustis Railroad.

In a 1923 newspaper interview, Isabella May Keeling, nearing 71, reminisced about her father, Capt. Melton Haynes, who was the first settler in the Lane Park region in 1868. She recalls that even after moving to their Woodlea homestead, they were isolated. M.V. Hull, four miles distant, was their nearest neighbor, and to the east, there were no settlers between Lake Harris and Apopka. In 1875, Colonel Blackman came and settled a mile from the Haynes farm, and Col. Daniel Troy of Alabama came and developed Oxmoor. In 1892, Amos Wakelin arrived from Philadelphia and purchased the Woodlea property from Isabella May.

One of Tavares's most scenic geographic features is the Dora Canal. The famous sportswriter Grantland Rice called the Dora Canal the most beautiful mile of waterway in the world. The Dora Canal has been the center of many social events since the 1880s. Even today, the Dora Canal is a popular tourist attraction featuring fishing and leisurely cruises.

Sadly, some of the old familiar buildings are no longer standing. With the decline in the citrus industry, the Lake Region Packing Plant on Lake Dora was bulldozed in 2005, opening the lakefront for development. The Opera House, the Osceola Hotel, the Pioneer Building, and the Pavilion on Lake Dora are no more. But all was not lost. In 2006, the people of Tavares established community-wide priorities that resulted in a vision statement for the city's future. A master plan was designed to reinvigorate the downtown area, with special emphasis on building on Tavares's historic foundation.

May these vintage photographs and captured moments in time bring back fond memories of days gone by. Enjoy your journey!

One

A Capital Idea

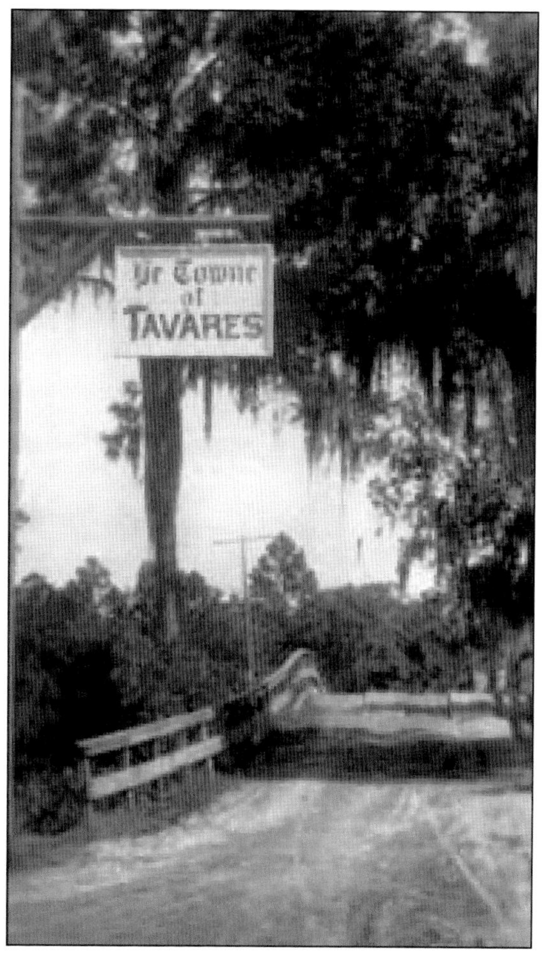

In the 1920s, this wooden bridge crossing over the Dora Canal welcomed travelers into "Ye Towne of Tavares." In 1882, Maj. Alexander St. Clair Abrams boasted at the town's grand opening, which included special guest Gov. William Bloxham, that he intended to make Tavares the seat of a new county and that he ultimately expected the town to become the capital of the state. (Courtesy of the Tavares Historical Society.)

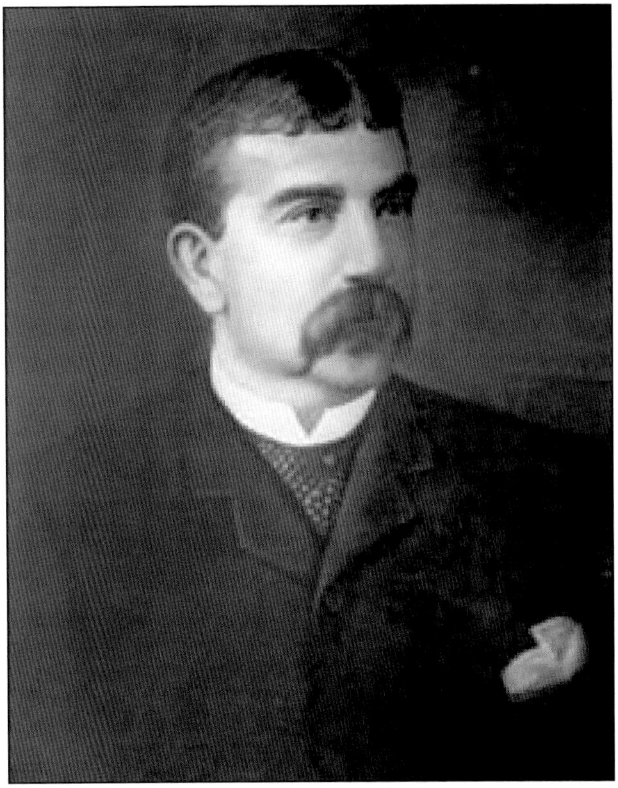

Alexander St. Clair Abrams was born on March 10, 1845, in New Orleans. He was educated in private schools and was a law student when the War Between the States broke out in 1861. He served as aide-de-camp to two Louisiana infantry commanders. He died in Jacksonville on June 5, 1931, after a brilliant career as a soldier, lawyer, newspaper editor, and public servant. (Courtesy of the Tavares Historical Society.)

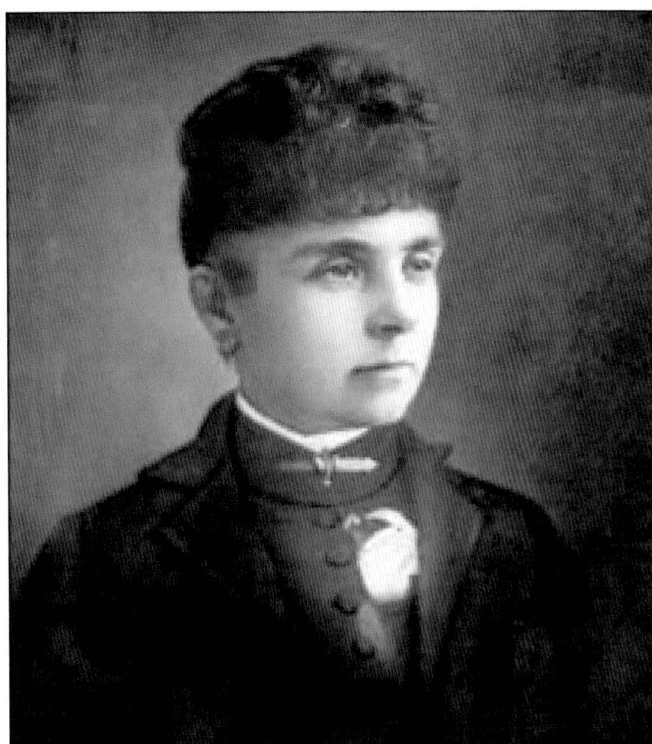

Joanna Immel St. Clair Abrams was born on February 22, 1848, in Atlanta. She was the daughter of a prominent manufacturer. She married Alexander on August 24, 1864, and they had four children. Joanna died on October 7, 1901, from the direct effects of shock sustained shortly after the great Jacksonville fire of 1901. The flames surrounded her home for several hours. (Courtesy of the Tavares Historical Society.)

The St. Clair Abrams home is under construction in 1881. It was his family home until they moved to Jacksonville in 1895. From 1907 to 1927, it was the family home of Harry Cottrell Duncan and for a while the Keister family. Since 1945, this house has been the home of the Kenneth and Harriet Sears family. (Courtesy of the Tavares Historical Society.)

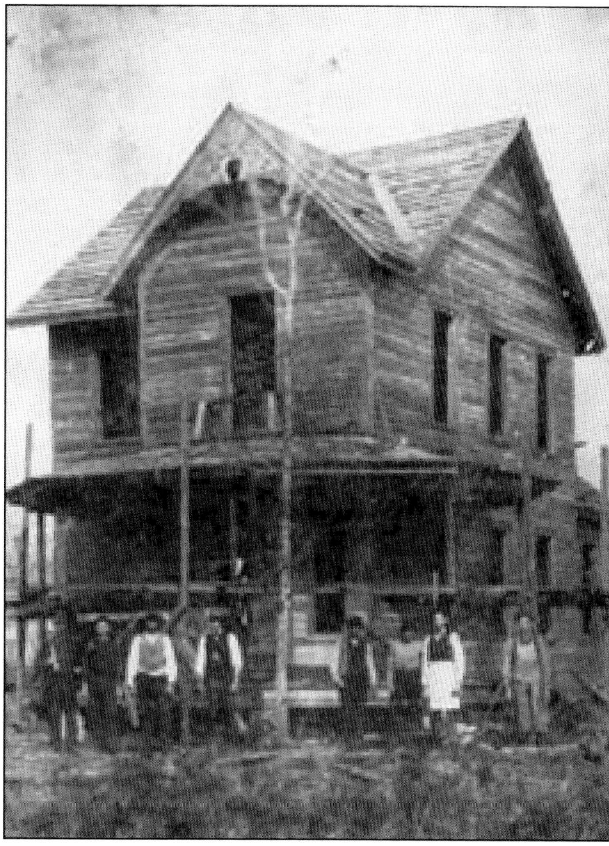

This house on Rockingham Avenue, built in the mid-1880s, was the home of Judge James Milam. In 1899, Gov. Edward Perry appointed him county judge, a position Milam held until his death in 1910. This home served as Lake County's first courthouse. Emmett Tally was appointed by Gov. Albert Gilchrist to fill Milam's unexpired term. Emmett and Lucille Tally purchased the Milam home in 1911. (Courtesy of the Tavares Historical Society.)

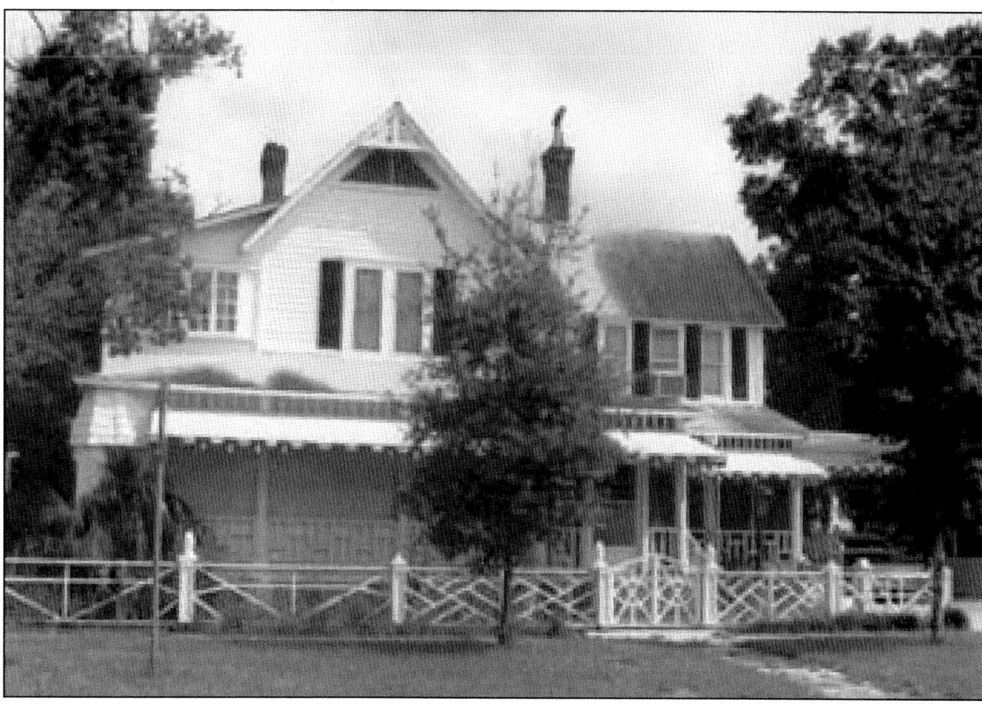

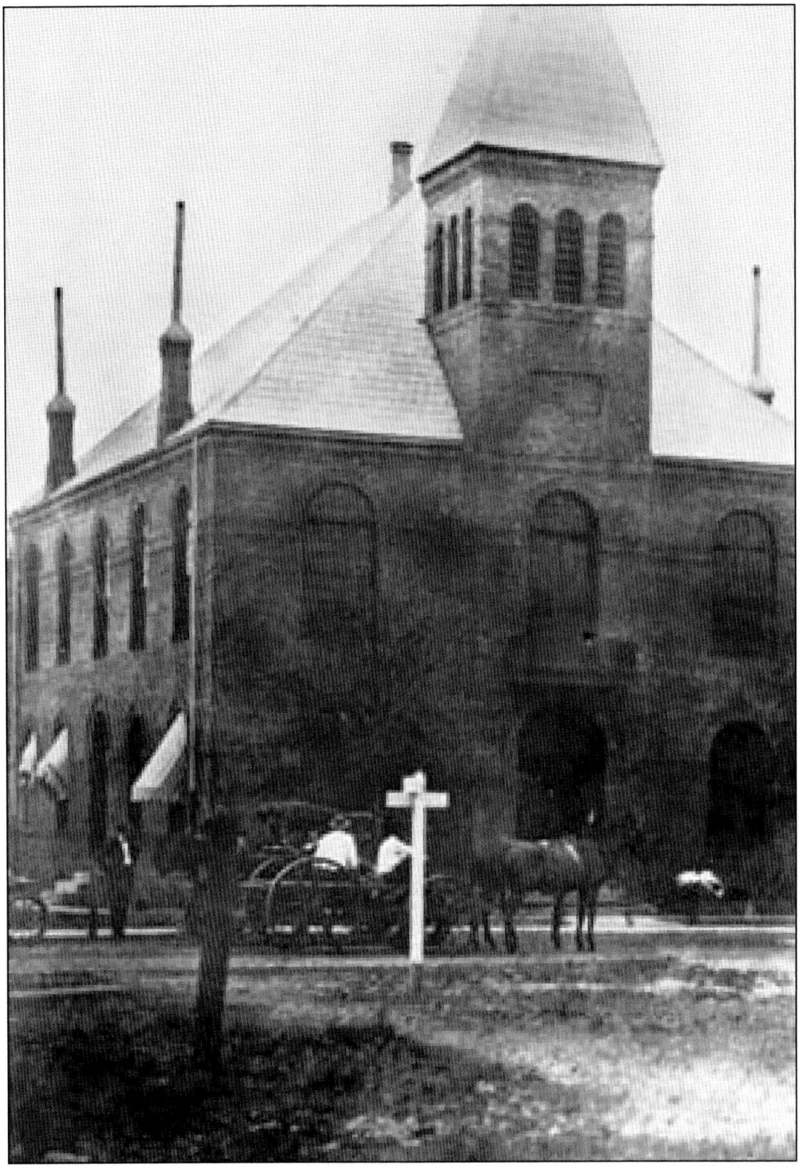

Immediately following the fire of 1888 that destroyed a large section of Tavares, rebuilding began. In 1890, with financial help from Alexander St. Clair Abrams, construction of Lake County's first official courthouse was completed. This new two-story structure, built at a cost of nearly $10,000, was dubbed the Pioneer Building and served as the courthouse for 34 years until 1924. When construction of a new courthouse began in 1923, the Pioneer Building was moved across the street. After the new courthouse opened, the Pioneer Building became home to the Civil Defense, Veterans Services, driver's license offices, the county agricultural agents, and the Lake County School Board. In 1975, Tavareans, county employees, and reporters watched as the Fort Lauderdale Wrecking Company began to raze the Pioneer Building. This valiant building did not succumb easily to the bulldozer and battering rams. Efforts to demolish the building continued into the night when finally the building appeared to self-destruct as one of its own support beams suddenly gave way and the building began to tumble. (Courtesy of the Tavares Historical Society.)

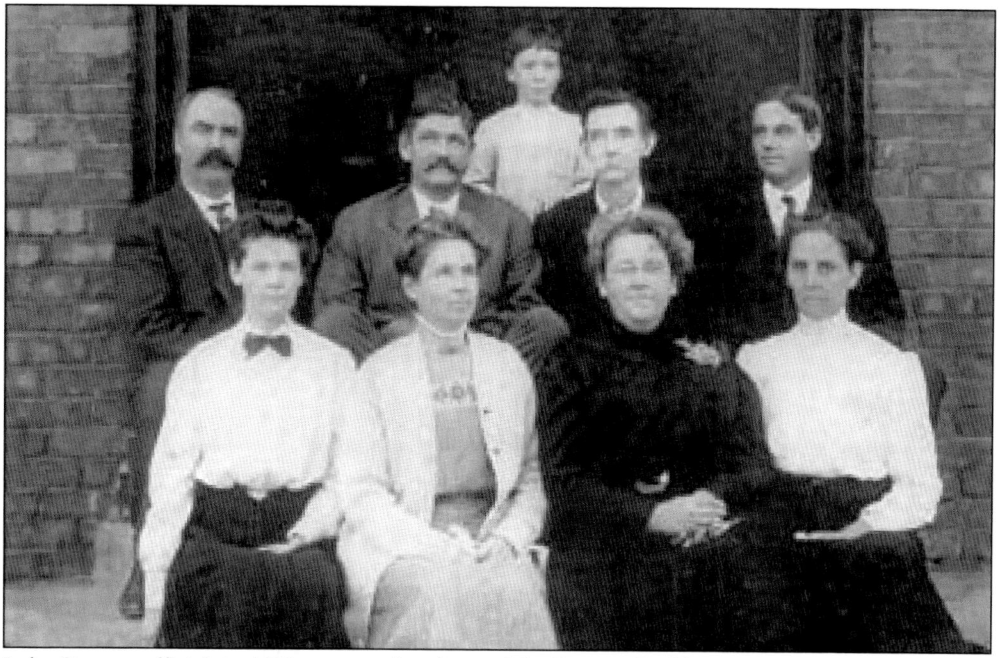

Lake County officials in 1910 are seated in front of the Pioneer Building. From left to right are (first row) Beth Burleigh, Annie Burleigh, Cora Peet, and Kate Lacey; (second row) tax assessor Robert Lee Nutt, tax collector William Long, clerk of court Henry Duncan, and Judge Emmett Tally. Young Banks Duncan is standing behind his father. (Courtesy of the Lake County Historical Society.)

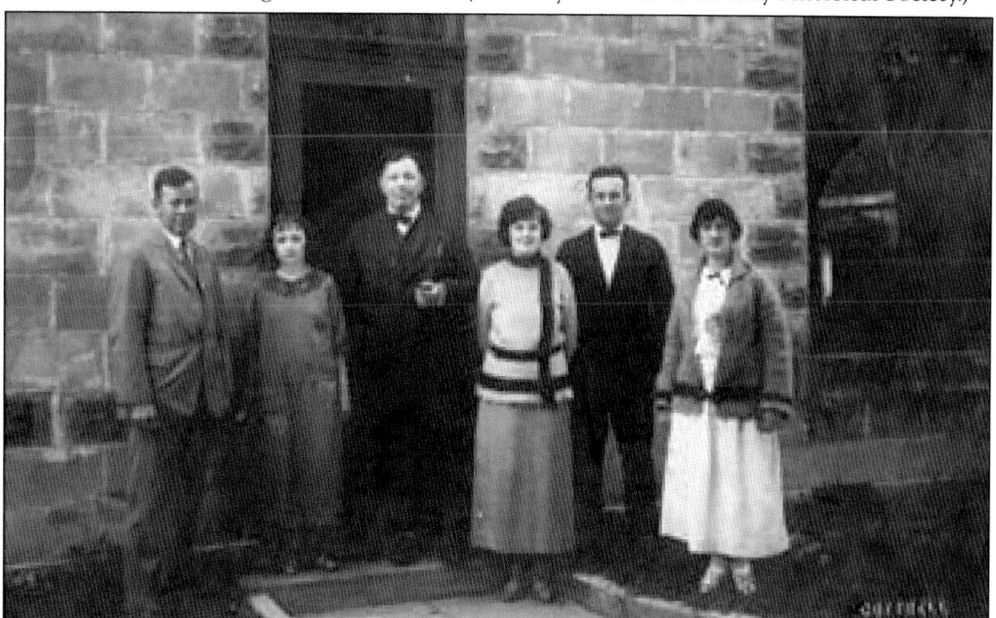

This c. 1925 picture was taken at the front entrance of the Duncan, Hamlin, and Duncan law firm on West Main Street. From left to right are Roy Hamlin, secretary Mary Jane Cassady, Harry Duncan, an unidentified secretary, Carl Duncan, and an unidentified secretary. Roy Hamlin and Harry Duncan received their law degrees from Stetson University in DeLand and Carl Duncan from the University of Florida. (Courtesy of Harryette Anne Duncan.)

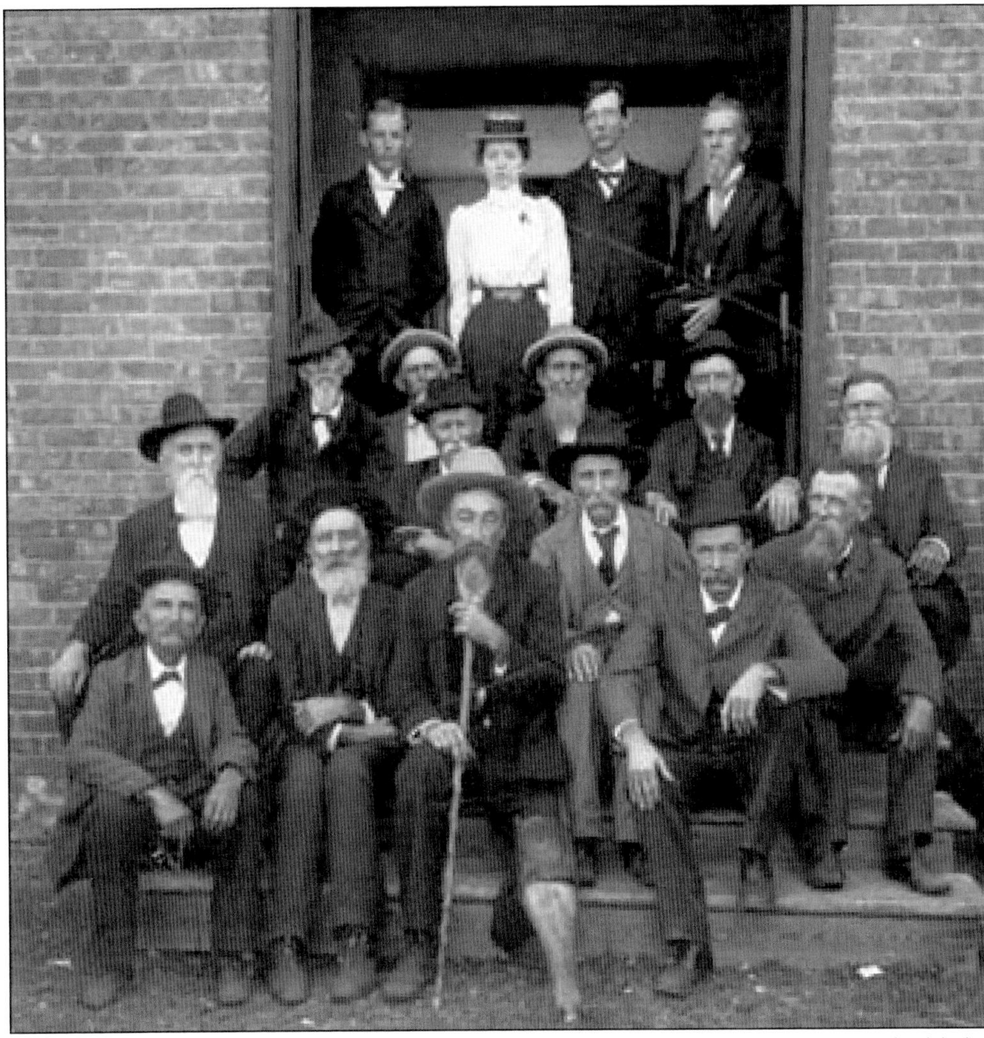

Marian D. Duncan, the eldest daughter of Henry H. Duncan and Marian Peet Duncan, highlights this group photograph of Lake County Confederate veterans. This photograph was taken at the Pioneer Building in the late 1890s. Henry H. Duncan, standing to Marian's left, was born in Springfield, Illinois. Henry was a lad of 16 when he mustered into Company C, 45th Alabama Infantry. In 1863, he survived an apparent mortal wound to his left lung from a musket ball in the Battle of Stones River in Murfreesboro, Tennessee. In 1864, Henry was captured at the Battle of Franklin and sent to the infamous Camp Douglas prison in Chicago, Illinois, where he had only a thin blanket to survive the bitter cold of winter. Another notable is Sgt. Thomas Kennedy Hall, seated first row, fourth from the left. Hall, born in Columbia, South Carolina, enlisted on April 16, 1864, in Company E, Third Georgia Volunteers. Hall's company assignments included guard duty at Andersonville prison in Georgia. In 1868, Hall moved to the Leesburg area. (Courtesy of the Lake County Historical Society.)

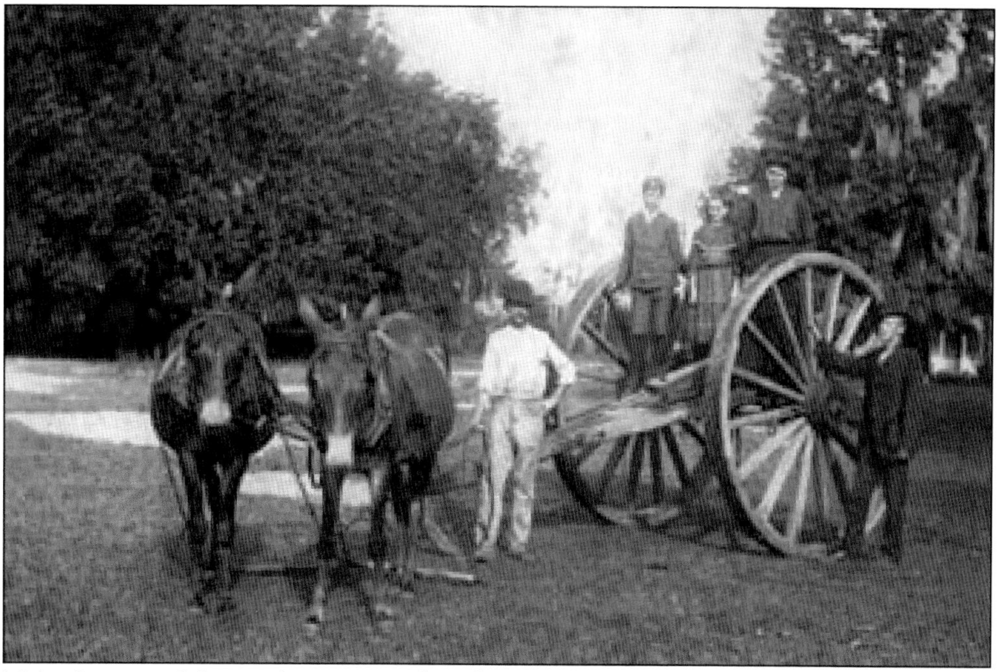

Mules, because of their endurance, sure-footedness, and strength, were the tow trucks of pioneer times. Big two-wheel carts, like the one being pulled by Uncle Joe's mules in the photograph above, were capable of transporting heavy loads. A matched pair of mules was extremely valuable and was utilized daily for pulling out stumps and hauling away brush. In the early 1920s, when the Pioneer Building was moved to Texas Avenue to make room for the new courthouse, mules were used. The building was placed on rollers; then, using mules, a winch, and lever (similar to that used for sugarcane mills), the courthouse easily rolled to its new location. This move was done in two phases as the building first was moved off to the side and then later rolled onto its new foundation. (Both, courtesy of Clayton Bishop.)

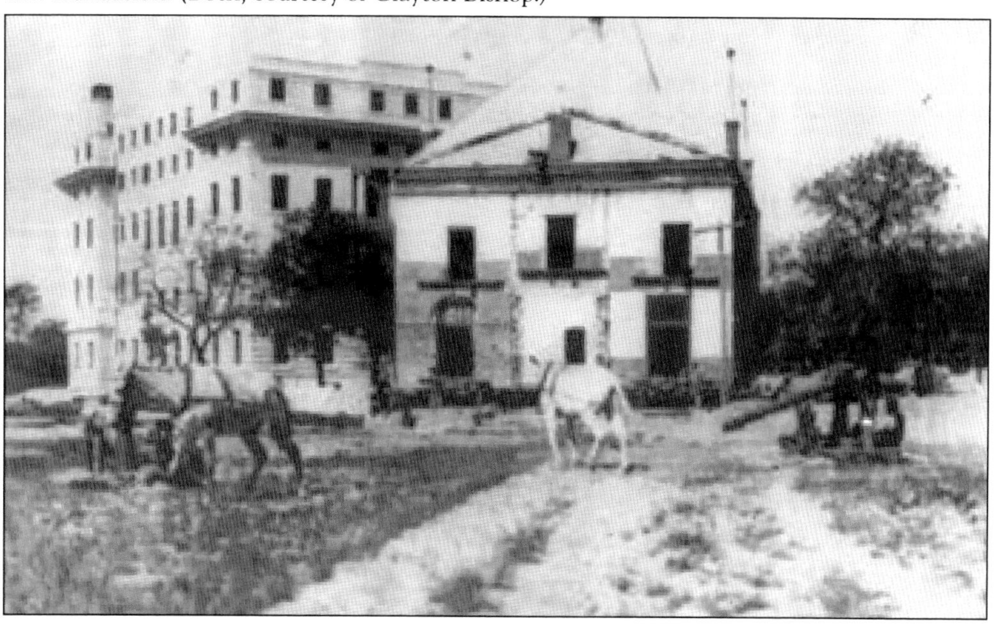

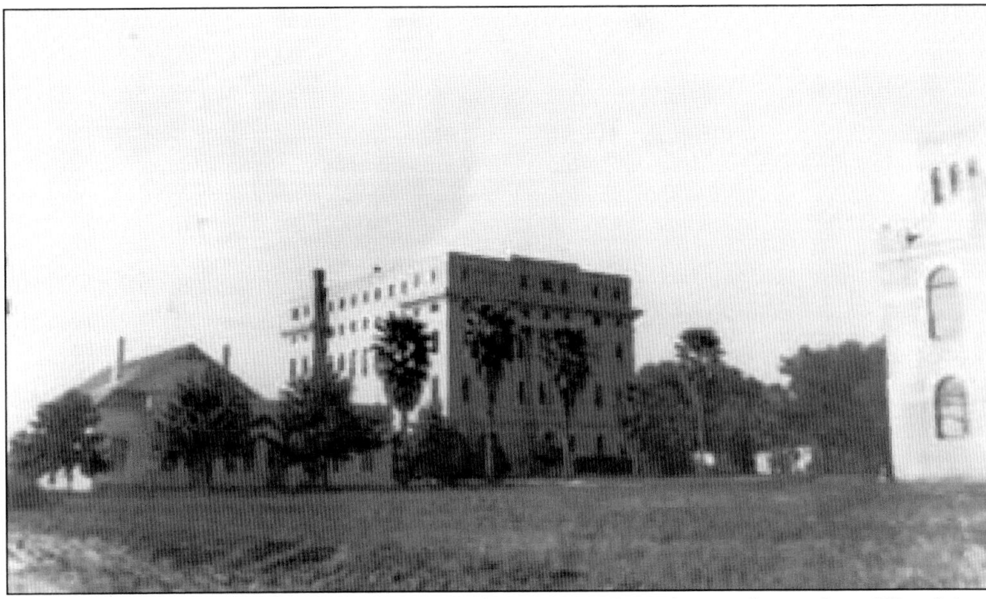

In 1923, construction began on the new Lake County Courthouse, located on West Main Street. It was completed in 1924. The five-story building was designed by Eustis architect Alan J. MacDonough, in the Classical Revival style featuring Ionic columns, pilasters, and parapet. It cost $250,000 to build. The jail was located on the fifth floor. The old courthouse was placed in the National Register of Historic Places in 1998. (Courtesy of the Lake County Historical Society.)

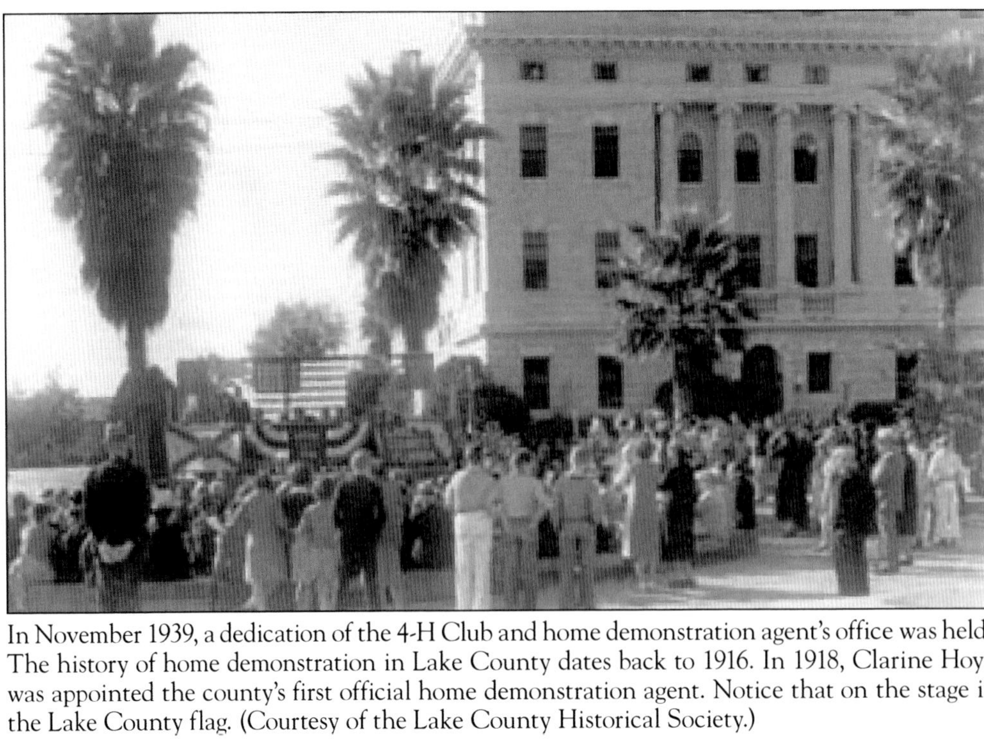

In November 1939, a dedication of the 4-H Club and home demonstration agent's office was held. The history of home demonstration in Lake County dates back to 1916. In 1918, Clarine Hoyt was appointed the county's first official home demonstration agent. Notice that on the stage is the Lake County flag. (Courtesy of the Lake County Historical Society.)

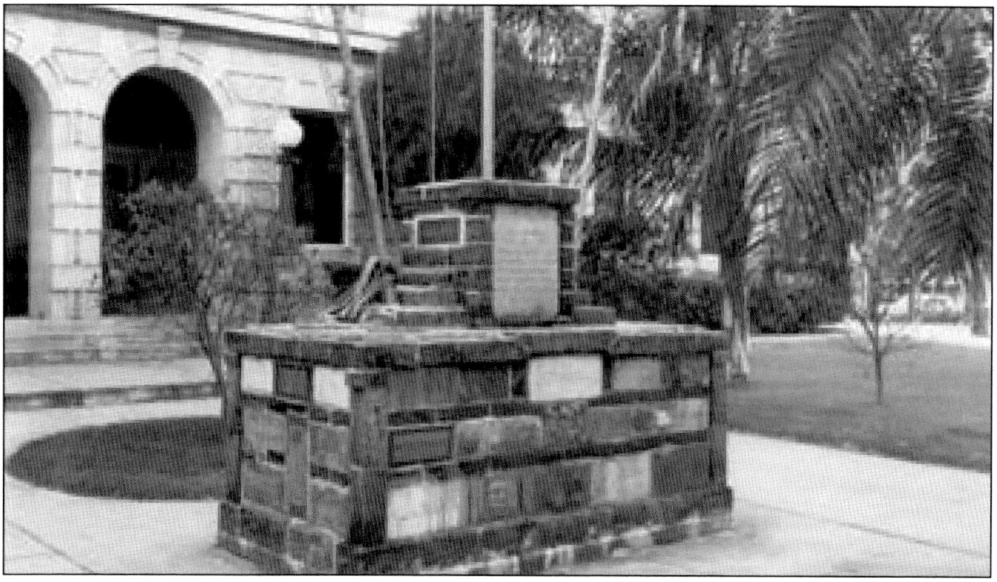

Lake County was the first county in the nation to have its own flag. A contest was held in 1936 to select the official flag. Eighteen designs were submitted, with Mrs. E.G. Owens of Leesburg being awarded the winning design. The flag was raised for the first time on March 5, 1937, at Lake County's semicentennial celebration and dedication of this flagpole base. (Courtesy of the Lake County Historical Society.)

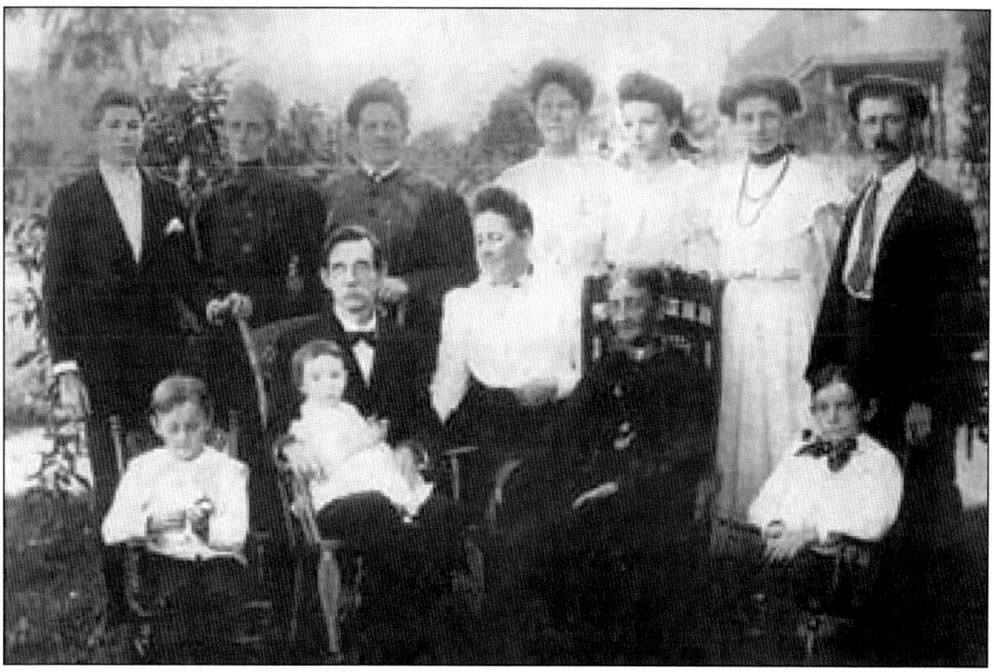

A 1904 family portrait of the Henry Duncan family was taken at the Duncan home in Tavares. From left to right are (first row) Carl Duncan, Henry H. Duncan with Banks Duncan on lap, Marian Peet Duncan (Henry's wife), Harriett Paul Peet (Marian's mother), and Wyeth Duncan; (second row) Duncan Peet, Sue Cotrell Peet, Hattie Peet, Cora Peet, Dorothy "Dolly" Peet, Marian "Nannie" Duncan, and Edwin Peet. (Courtesy of Harryette Anne Duncan.)

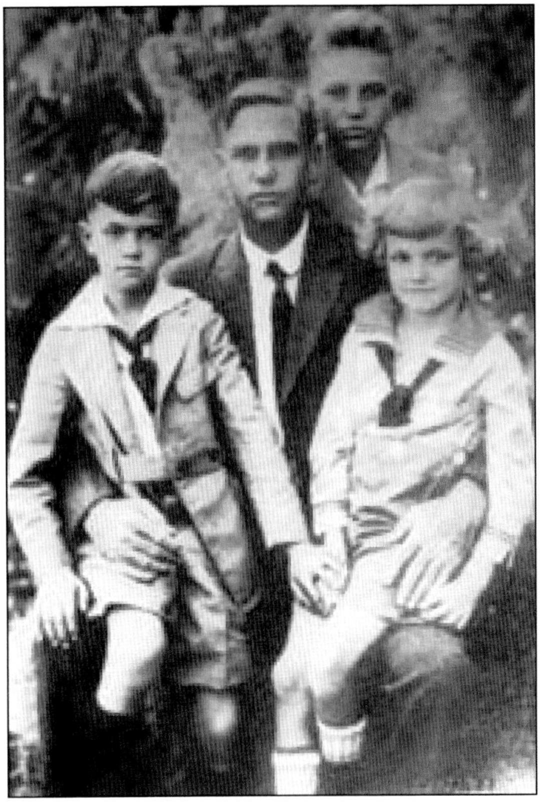

Emmett Murchison Tally, pictured here with his sons, (from left to right) Emmett Jr., Cottrell, and Sydney, was born in 1877 and arrived in Lake County in 1906. He was appointed Lake County judge in 1910 and was reelected five times. In June 1911, he married Lucille Cottrell. Lucille was a leading businesswoman, owning the Tally Insurance Agency. Judge Tally gained notoriety when he apprehended an escaped convict in 1933, shooting and wounding the escapee. (Courtesy of the Tavares Historical Society.)

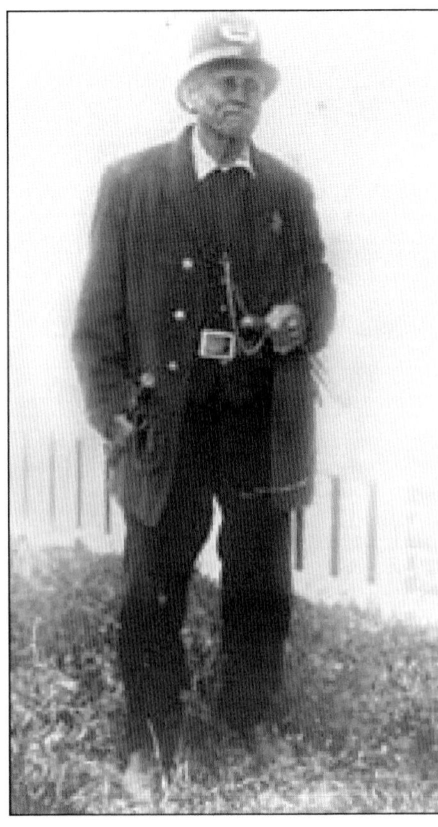

Charlie Loper, born in 1846, was Tavares's first town marshal. He was a Confederate veteran who had served in the Second Florida Cavalry. Loper's regiment participated in battles throughout Florida, including Olustee, Gainesville, and Braddock's Farm. In the early 1900s, he was known for spinning tall tales and telling war stories to the children. Loper died in 1926 and is buried at the Tavares cemetery. (Courtesy of the Tavares Historical Society.)

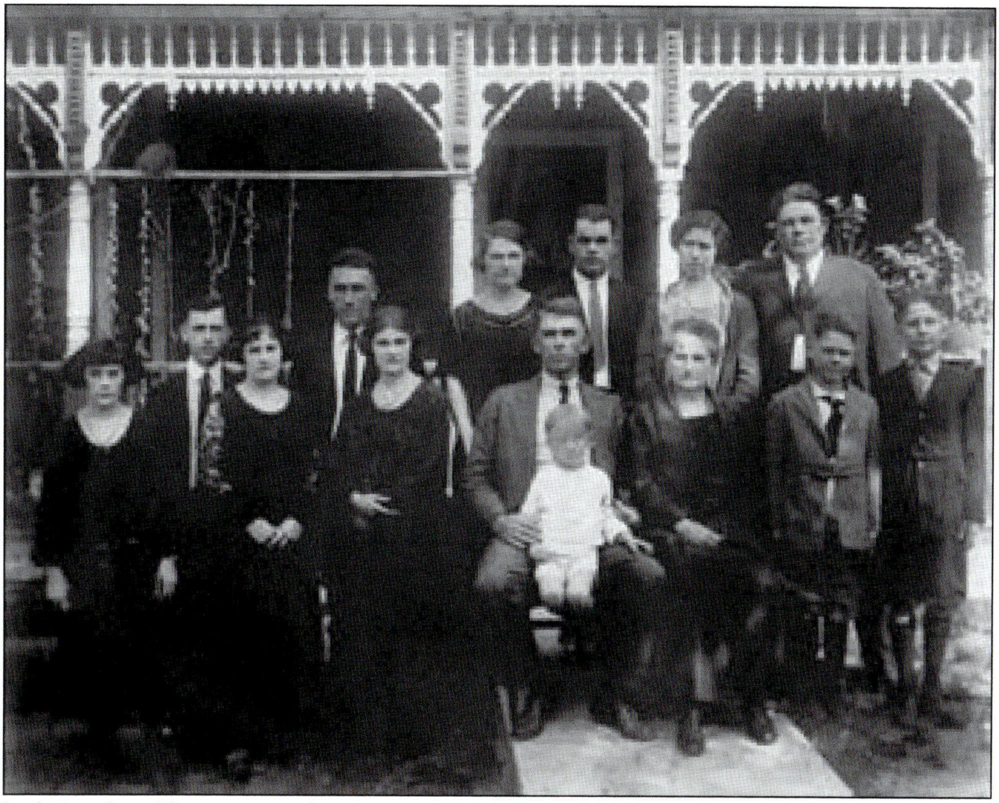

Joel Napoleon Flowers arrived in Tavares in 1920 and became the town marshal. In 1929, he became the town's first police chief. Fines imposed by Chief Flowers included paying $10 for selling moonshine and $2 for using profanity. During this time, he was also the outhouse, plumbing, and septic inspector. Chief Flowers is seated with grandson Lucious Clark on his lap and his wife, Sophia, to his left. (Courtesy of the Tavares Historical Society.)

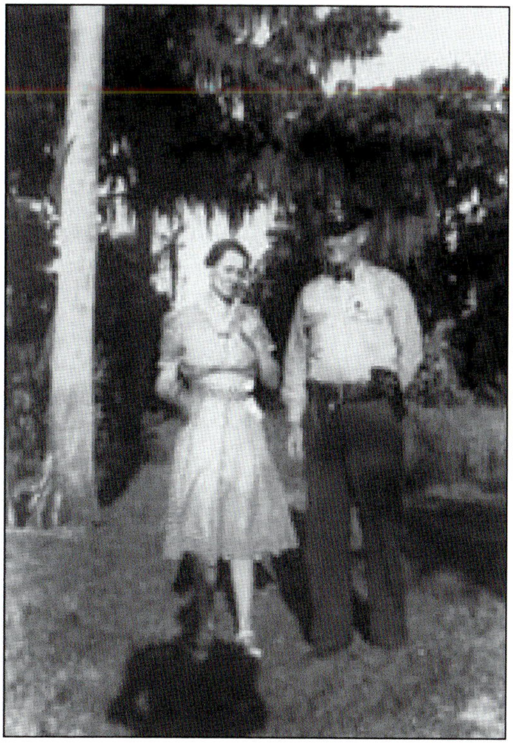

Chief Geanous Messer, pictured with Margie Entz at Summerall Park, was the whole Tavares police force when he was hired by Mayor J.B. Prevatt in 1937. Messer patrolled on a red-and-cream-colored bicycle. He rigged a yellow light on the telephone pole by his home so that when calls came in, his wife, Zula, could let him know by turning on the light. Messer served until 1948. (Courtesy of Lura Messer Hall.)

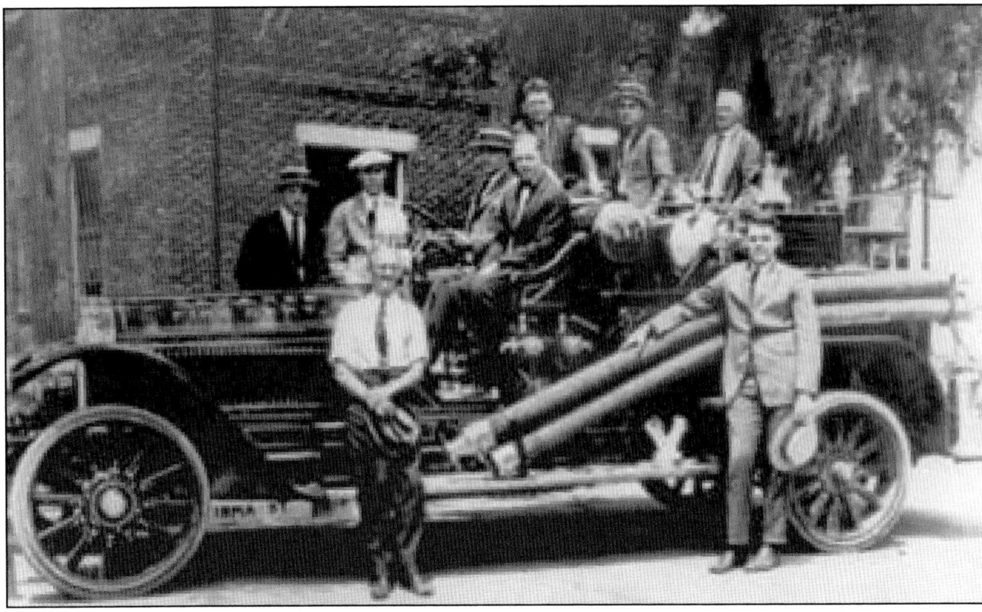

In 1924, Tavares purchased a new American LaFrance fire engine (above) with a rotary gear pumper, hoses, and soda acid chemical tank. Soon after the purchase of this fire truck, all the local departments were called to a burning hotel surrounded by citrus groves. The new Tavares truck never made it to the fire because its wheels were stuck deep into the soft sand of the groves. From left to right are (first row) fire chief ? Montgomery and Bill Feagle; (second row) unidentified, Dr. Sanford C. Colley, Jesse Hunter (driver), Ed Burleigh, Russ Peeples, Chester Treadway, and Thomas A. Hux. Below, Chief Lansing Taylor, standing in the truck, was very active in the education of fire prevention. In this c. 1950 photograph, Billy Hill is the boy on crutches, and the girl in shorts is June Taylor, Chief Taylor's daughter. (Courtesy of the Tavares Historical Society.)

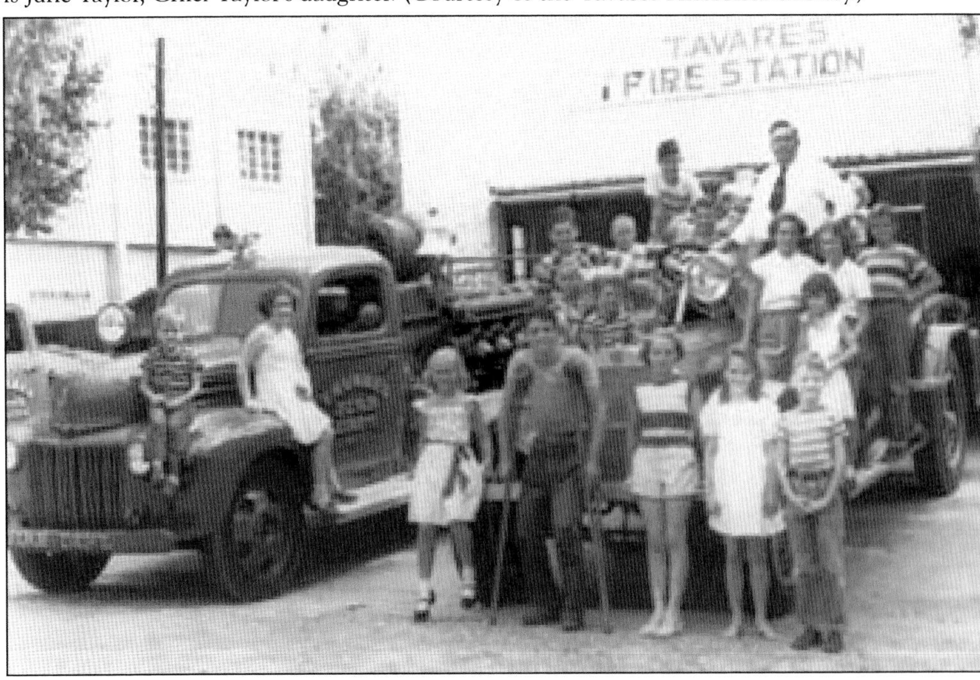

Jesse Walton Hunter was born in Naylor, Georgia, in 1879. In 1913, Hunter passed the bar exam and opened a law practice in Tavares, eventually becoming the Tavares city attorney. He was elected mayor in 1925 and 1927. In 1920, he became the attorney for the Lake County Board of County Commissioners, holding that position for 24 years. Hunter served as state attorney from 1925 to 1953. (Courtesy of the Tavares Historical Society.)

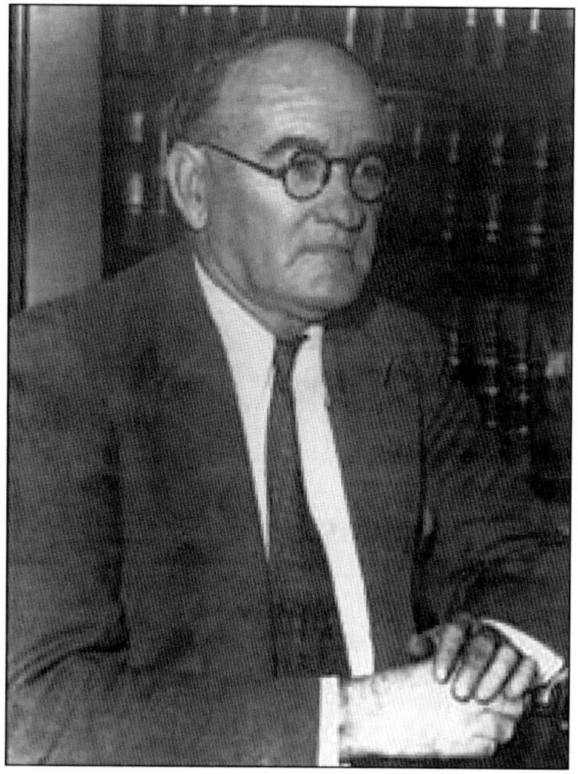

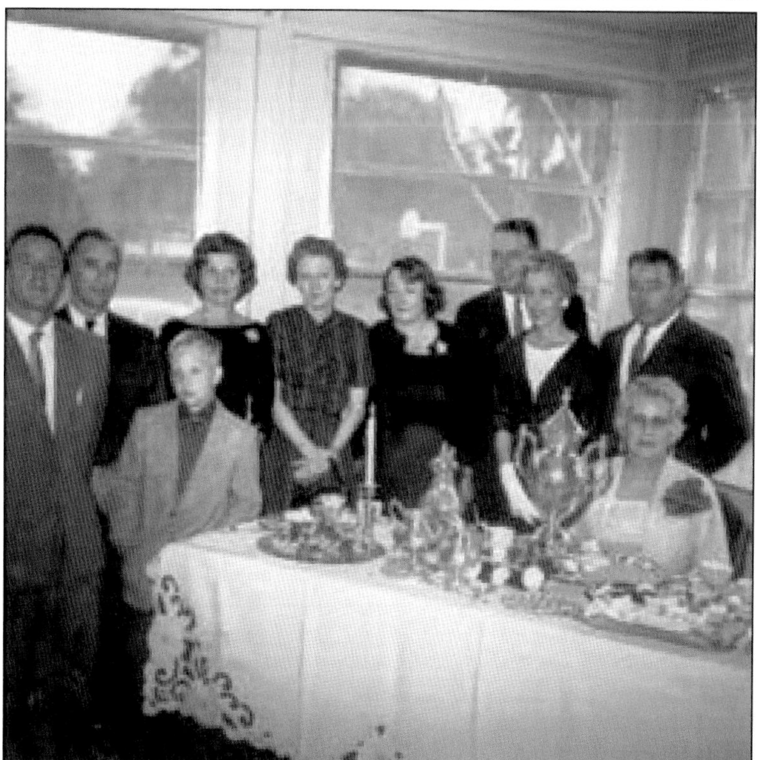

This c. 1957 photograph of the Jesse Hunter family was taken at the family home on New Hampshire Street. Jesse Hunter died on February 3, 1956. Nettie Morin Hunter, seated at the table, was married to Jesse on Thanksgiving Day 1904. Nettie's parents arrived in Eustis, Florida, in 1875 and settled on a hillside overlooking a lake later named for Nettie. (Courtesy of the Lake County Historical Society.)

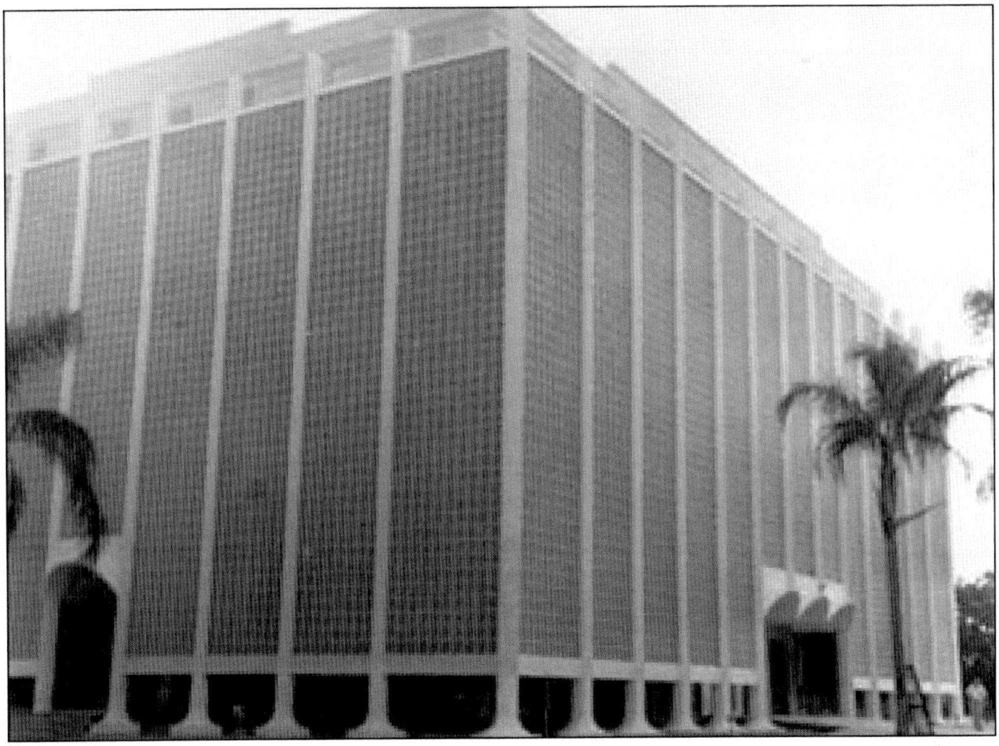

What could they have been thinking? This photograph of the 1924 Lake County Courthouse (above) was taken in July 1964. For more than two agonizing decades, this stone filigree facade covered the Classical Revival architecture, including the cornerstone, which was laid on May 24, 1923, by the Grand Lodge of Free and Accepted Masons of the State of Florida. This facade, once thought of as modern and fancy, was finally removed in 1989. On a positive note, air-conditioning was added during this time. A new Judicial Center, as seen in this 1991 architectural rendering (below) opened in 1992 at 550 West Main Street. In 2010, construction began on a 150,000-square-foot expansion of the Judicial Center that included additional court rooms, judges' chambers, holding cells, jury assembly space, and court administrative offices. (Both, courtesy of the Lake County Historical Society.)

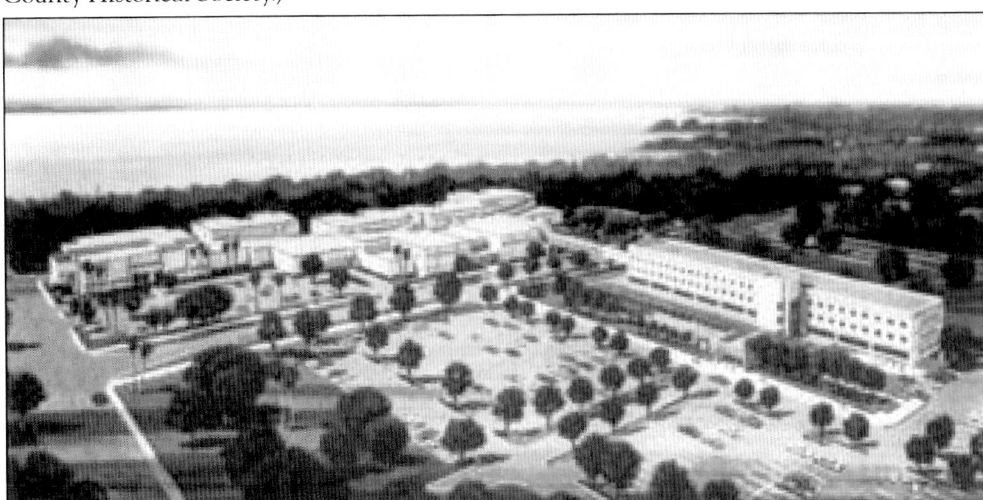

Two

On the Shores of Old Lake Dora

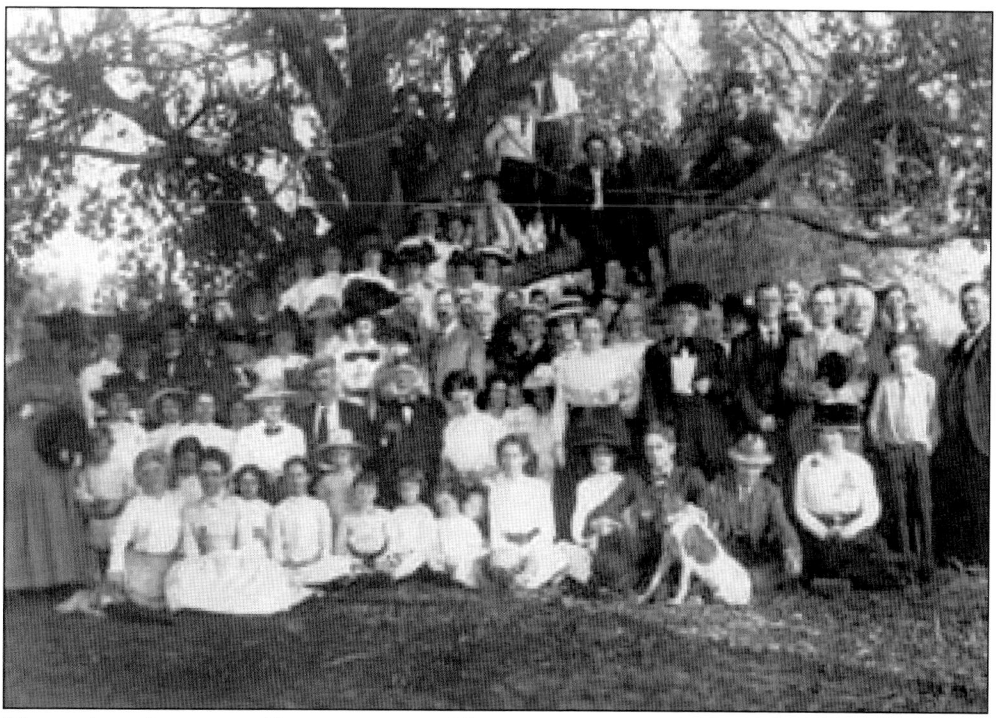

The settlers who came to Tavares originated from many regions of the country. Florida, after the War Between the States, was still a frontier with endless opportunities to start a new life. This 1892 photograph of the entire town celebrating the Fourth of July was taken on the shore of Lake Dora. Notice the dog seems more interested in the man's cigar than getting its picture taken. (Courtesy of the Tavares Historical Society.)

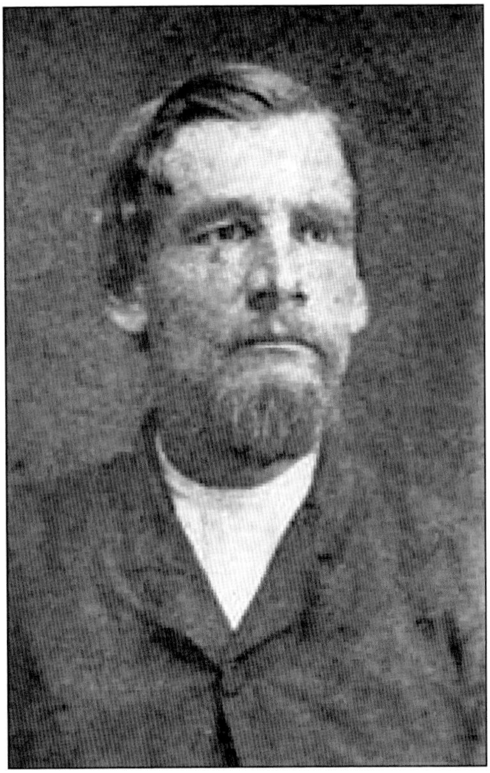

In 1869, Confederate veteran Thomas Asbury Hux settled at Fort Mason, where he married Mary Ballard. In 1912, the Hux family moved to Tavares. In 1936, on the occasion of his 66th wedding anniversary, 95-year-old Hux challenged 96-year-old Adam Hazelwood of Mount Dora to a footrace. Hazelwood responded, "Hux is too young for me to disillusion him and spoil his whole future." (Courtesy of Judy Hux Rainey.)

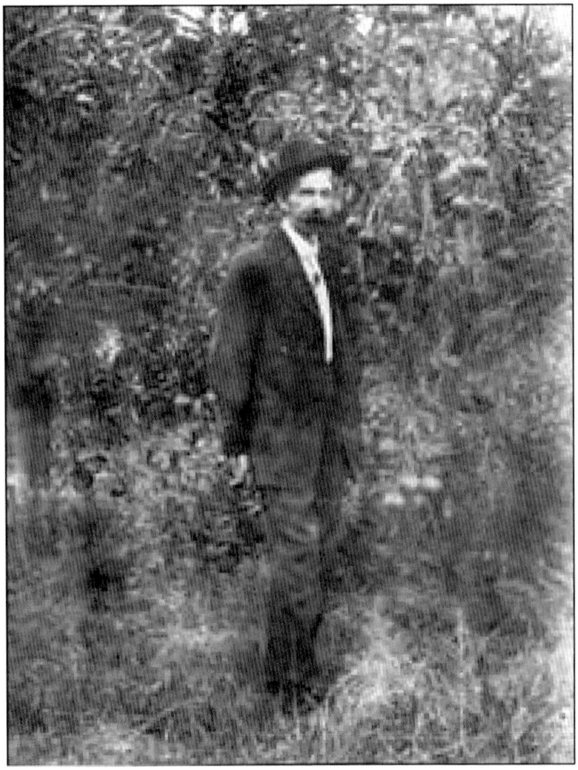

Jeremiah B. Booth was born in 1862. When he was 19 years old, he herded horses from Tennessee to Central Florida. He decided to stay in Florida owning and managing orange groves. His wife's name was Luna, and together the couple built a home on Rockingham Avenue. Booth had suffered a severe stroke that limited his mobility, but he lived several more decades until 1952. (Courtesy of Martha Booth Burleigh.)

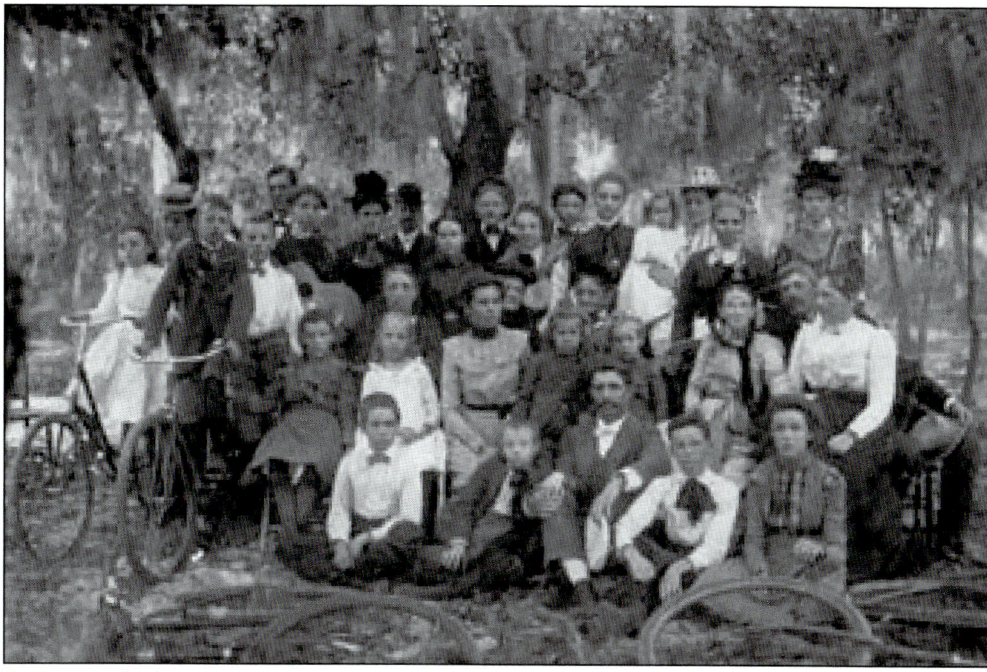

Everyone who knew Annie Burleigh was impressed that she had learned the secret of a successful and happy life. Burleigh is seated in the center of the second row of this c. 1900 photograph of the Burleigh and Duncan families enjoying a picnic on the Dora Canal (above). In her memoirs, Burleigh recalled how lean the years were following the freezes of 1894, 1895, and 1898. "Besides helping in the Abstract office, which remained in our house until March 1913, being the assistant postmaster, keeping house, bearing eight children, making and mending clothes, I got along wonderfully well." Pictured below is the Burleigh family hosting a Thanksgiving Day dinner at their home, which was located at the corner of Disston Avenue and Alfred Street. (Both, courtesy of the Tavares Historical Society.)

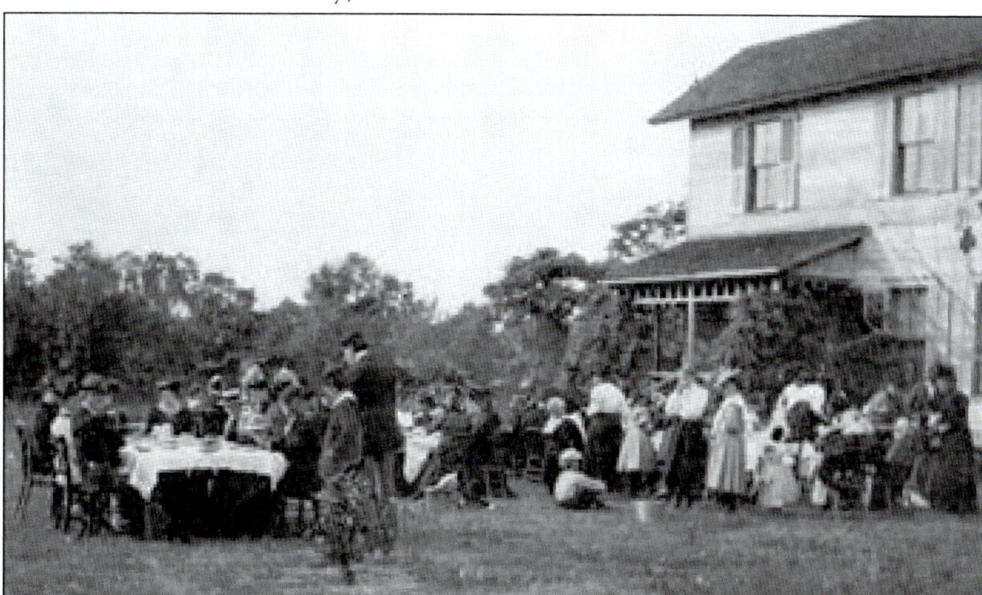

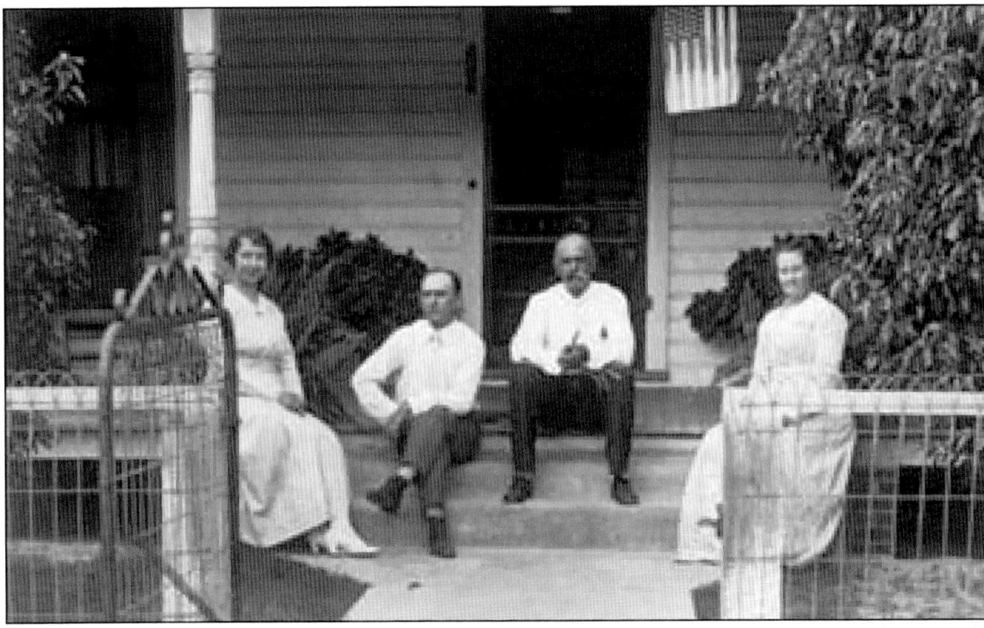

Pictured from left to right are Alice Alberta Bell Getch, Dr. W.A. Getch, J.W. Bell, and Mrs. Bell. J.W. Bell owned the *Tavares Herald* newspaper originally started by Major St. Clair Abrams in 1882. In 1922, A.P. Vaughn, Irving Burleigh's brother-in-law, bought the paper and changed the name to the *Lake County Citizen*. Doctor Getch was born in Altoona in 1885. He attended Southern Dental College and received his degree in 1912. (Courtesy of the Lake County Historical Society.)

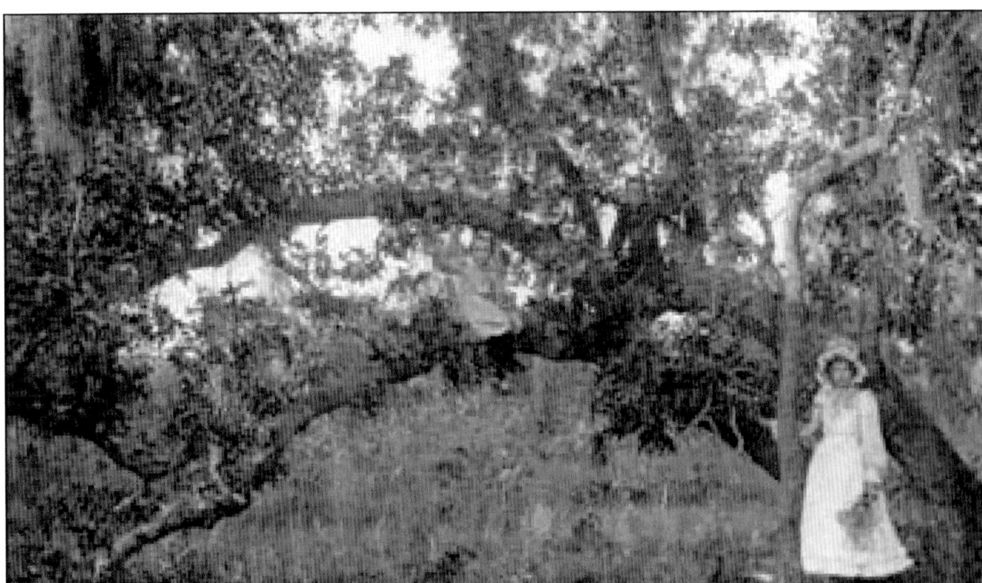

Three of Henry and Marian P. Duncan's children are pictured in this c. 1901 photograph. Dolly Duncan and her brother Leonard are sitting in the big live oak. Marian D. Duncan is holding a bouquet of wildflowers. Marian, whose middle name is her father's surname, Duncan, was born in Yalaha. She is a graduate of Wesleyan Female College in Macon, Georgia. Marian attended the Palmer School of Chiropractic in Iowa. (Courtesy of Harryette Anne Duncan.)

Young Forrest Banks Duncan, the fifth son and youngest child of Henry Holcomb and Marian Peet Duncan, was born in 1904 at the Duncan home on Texas Avenue in Tavares. Banks is featured in these two c. 1908 photographs. On the right, Banks is doing his impersonation of Nipper the dog listening to his master's voice resonating from a Victor Talking Machine Company gramophone. In this September 1908 family photograph, Uncle Banks is playfully holding the foot of his niece Geneva Simpson Duncan. Standing from left to right are Dolly Holcomb Duncan, Marian D. Duncan, and family friend Lucille Tally, who is holding baby Geneva. Baby "Neva" was named for her mother, who had died three months earlier on June 19, 1908. (Both, courtesy of Harryette Anne Duncan.)

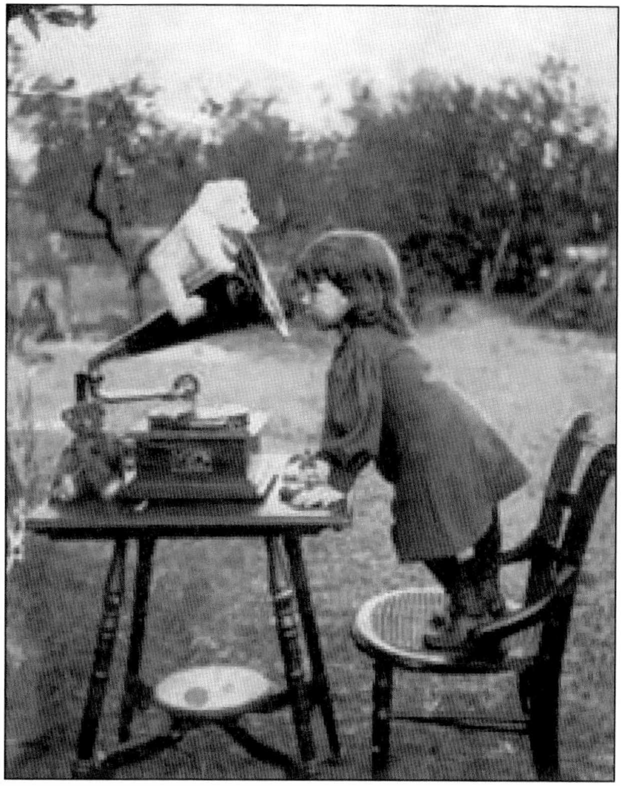

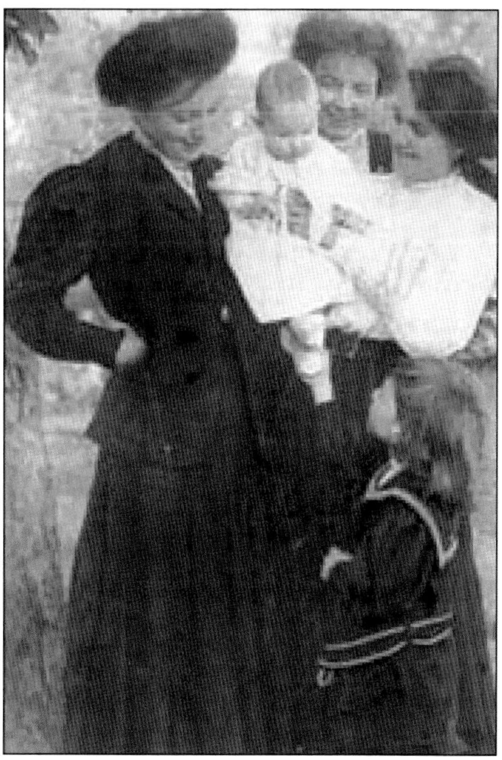

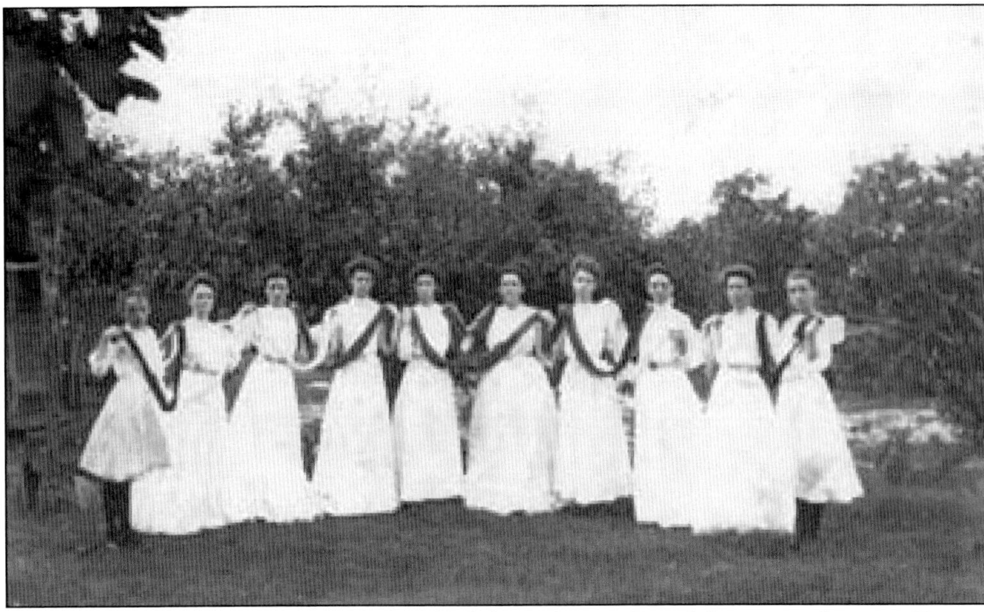

The annual Fourth of July celebration, called the "Glorious Fourth," was a tradition in Tavares that included inviting the whole county for a parade and barbecue at the Courthouse Square. The women preparing to perform the scarf drill in this 1903 photograph are, from left to right, Dolly Duncan, Anice Freeman, Marian Duncan, Beth Burleigh, Frances Burleigh, Cora Peet, Margie Burleigh, Ada Entz, Annie Burleigh, and Ruth Newell. (Courtesy of Harryette Anne Duncan.)

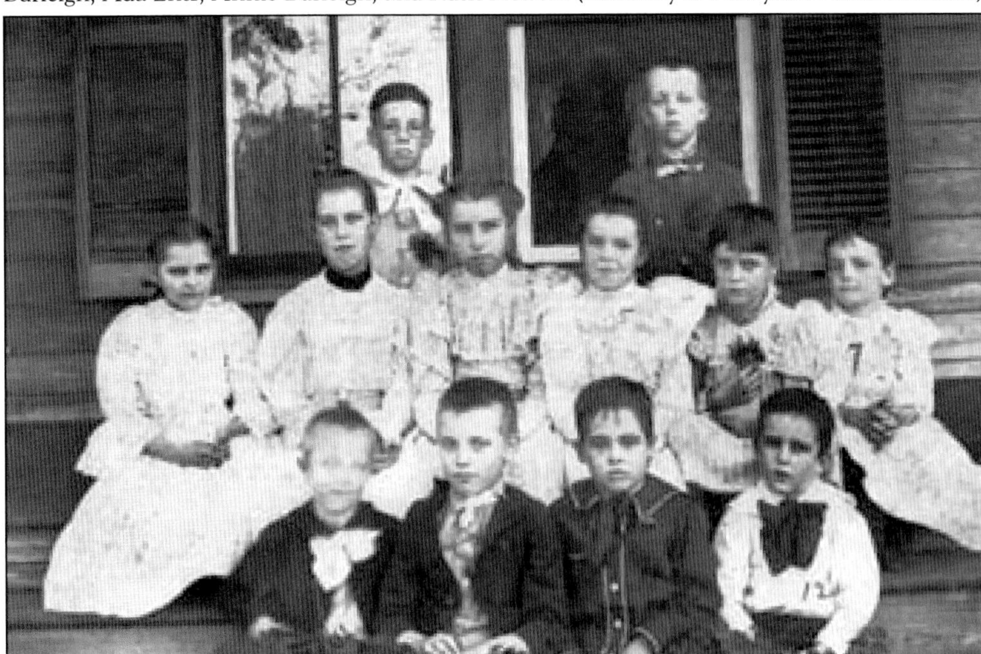

Pictured in this late-1890s photograph from left to right are (first row) Albert Donaldson, Fred Donaldson, Charlie Nutt, and Jeff Caruthers; (second row) Mary Caruthers, Irma Lanier, Margaret "Margie" Burleigh, Frances "Franca" Burleigh, Ruth Newell, and Dolly Duncan; (third row) Leonard Duncan and Gordon Donaldson. (Courtesy of Harryette Anne Duncan.)

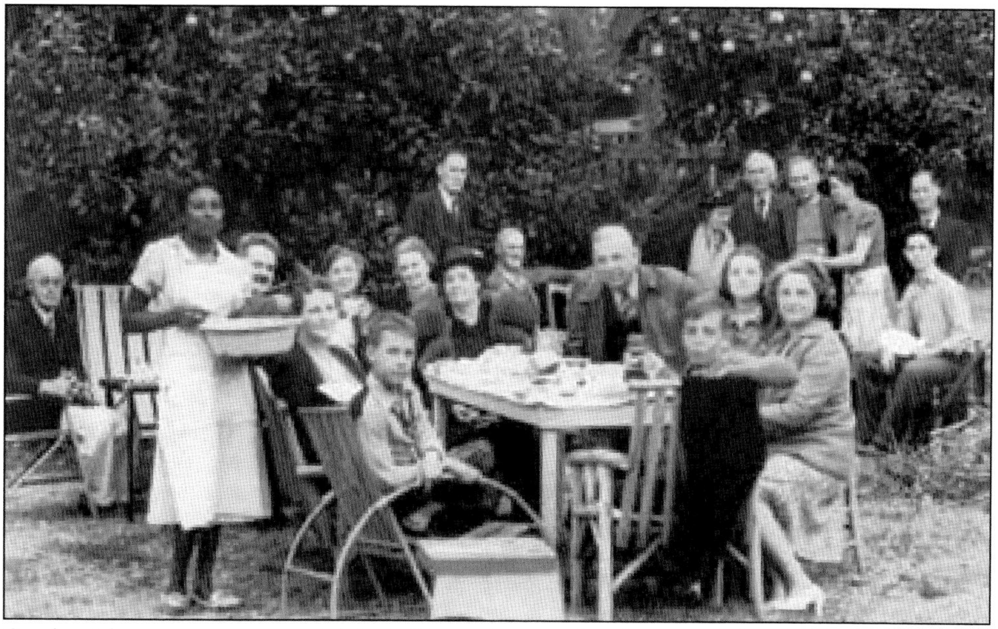

On the right wearing an apron is Marie King, who owned and operated the Tavares Inn on North Rockingham Avenue. In this 1938 photograph, the Bill Rogers family, who lived next door to the Tavares Inn, joins neighbors and inn guests for a picnic. Marie's husband, Jack, is standing in the center of this photograph. The woman on the left serving chicken is Pearl McHorn, who worked for Marie for many years. (Courtesy of Charlene Nichols King.)

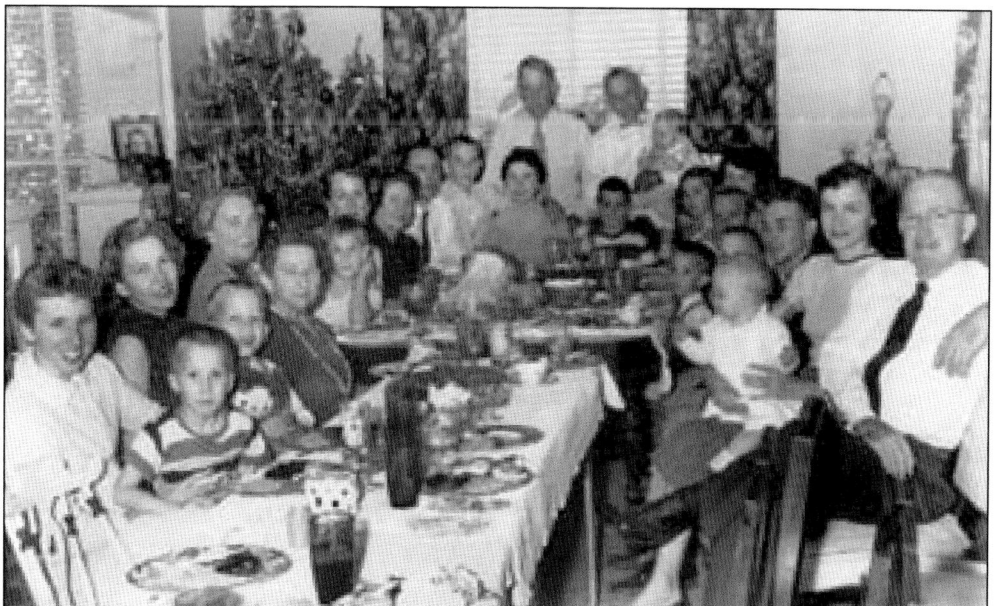

Blanche Sperry, seated on the left wearing a pearl necklace, arrived in Tavares in 1926. For more than 40 years, Sperry was the lunchroom manager for all Tavares schools and cooked for the entire student population of Tavares. In 1939, she was one of the country's early pioneers in school lunch programs. Because of her limited budget for the lunch program, she would buy vegetables from local farmers. (Courtesy of Brenda Kirby Smith.)

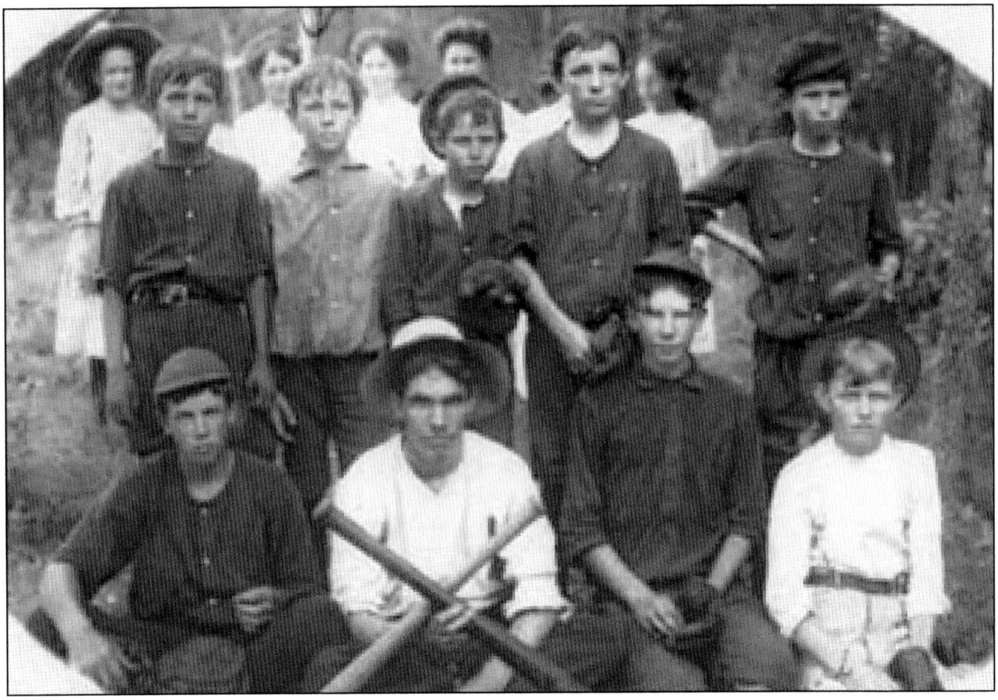

These are not the 1912 World Series champion Boston Red Sox but Tavares's finest in sandlot ball. Team catcher Irving Burleigh (first row, left) is the son of Tavares pioneers Annie and Edward Burleigh. After leaving Tavares to attend high school and college and serve in World War I, Burleigh returned in 1921. He married Dorothy Marsh in 1923. Burleigh served as the mayor of Tavares for 20 years. (Courtesy of Harryette Anne Duncan.)

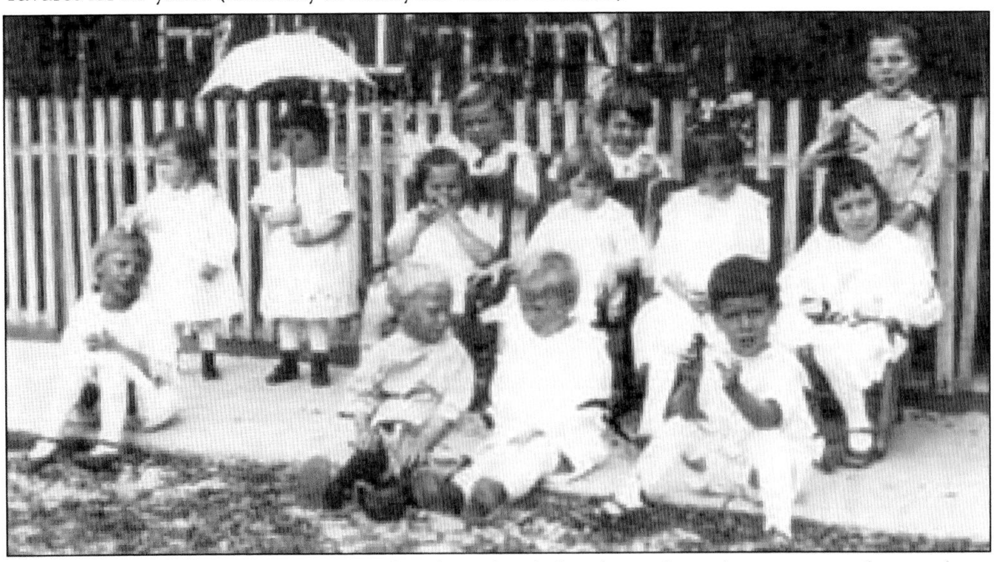

The children of Marian D. Duncan's Sunday school class have their class picture taken in front of the Duncan family home on Texas Avenue and Maud Street. Marian D. Duncan was a lifelong Sunday school teacher. The children are dressed for a party in this c. 1915 photograph. Virginia "Gou" Duncan, Marian's niece, is holding the umbrella. Virginia's sister Neva is sitting in the chair to the far right. (Courtesy of Harryette Anne Duncan.)

These young Tavareans had their picture struck next to an eastern diamondback rattlesnake in 1898. The eastern diamondback is the largest venomous snake in North America and can reach lengths of eight feet, like the one hanging from this street pole on Irma Street (Main Street). The Donaldson brothers (left) are wearing their wide-brim straw hats. Dolly Duncan is the young lady. The tower of the Pioneer Building is seen in the background. (Courtesy of Harryette Anne Duncan.)

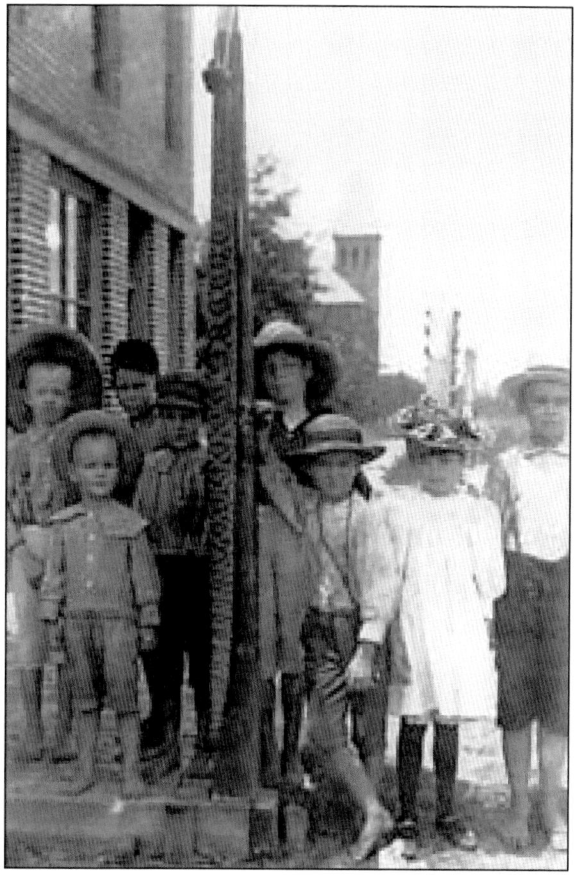

On May 1, 1932, Ira Moorhead (center) shot this 12-foot, 8-inch alligator in Lake Eustis. The gator was dragged using a rowboat through the Dora Canal to a cove at the Summerall Park Bridge. Moorhead's sons, Truman and Bob, helped load the gator on the side of his Studebaker and brought it to their home on Joanna Avenue. Standing with Moorhead are his daughter Susan and friend Paul Daniel. (Courtesy of the Tavares Historical Society.)

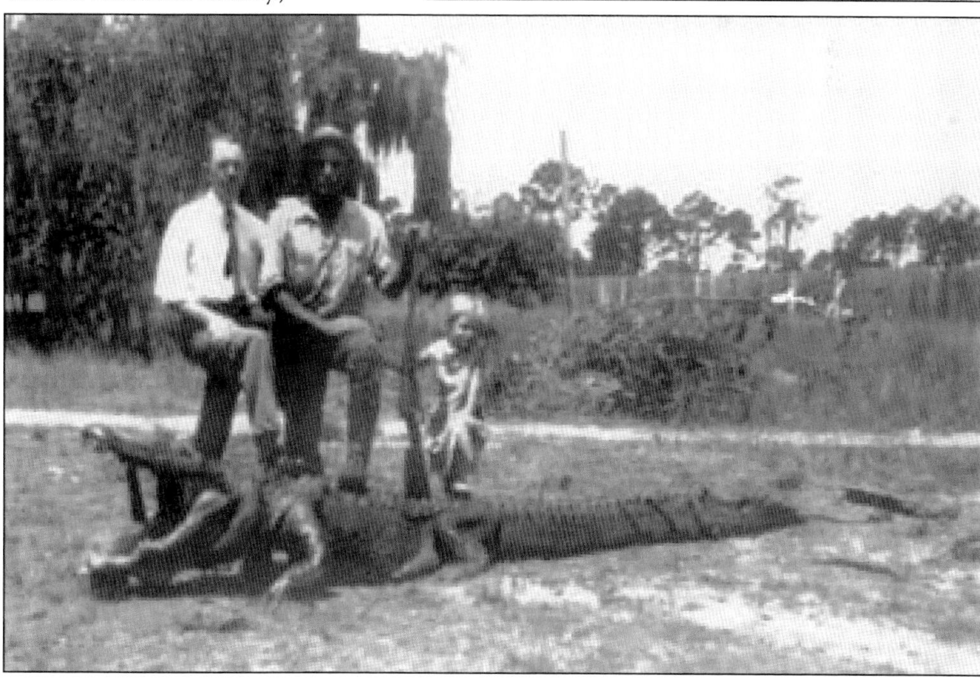

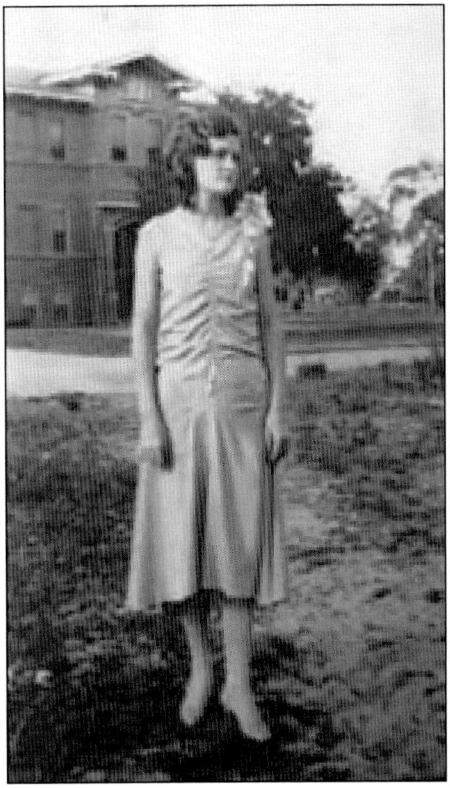

Dorothy Moorhead, pictured here in 1930, was Tavares High School's class valedictorian of 1931. That same year, she received the American Legion Medal of Honor for Outstanding Scholarship. Dorothy received a four-year scholarship to Florida State College for Women in Tallahassee. She was an educator for more than 30 years. (Courtesy of the Lake County Historical Society.)

Henry Gast (left) and Truman Orren Moorhead were Tavares surveyors. Moorhead became a certified surveyor in 1950. In September 1981, he was honored by the Florida Society of Professional Land Surveyors for his efforts in organizing the society in 1955. Moorhead, who died in 1985, said about his profession, "I used a trigonometric function book to figure calculations and double checked them on an adding machine, and now computers tell you everything." (Courtesy of the Lake County Historical Society.)

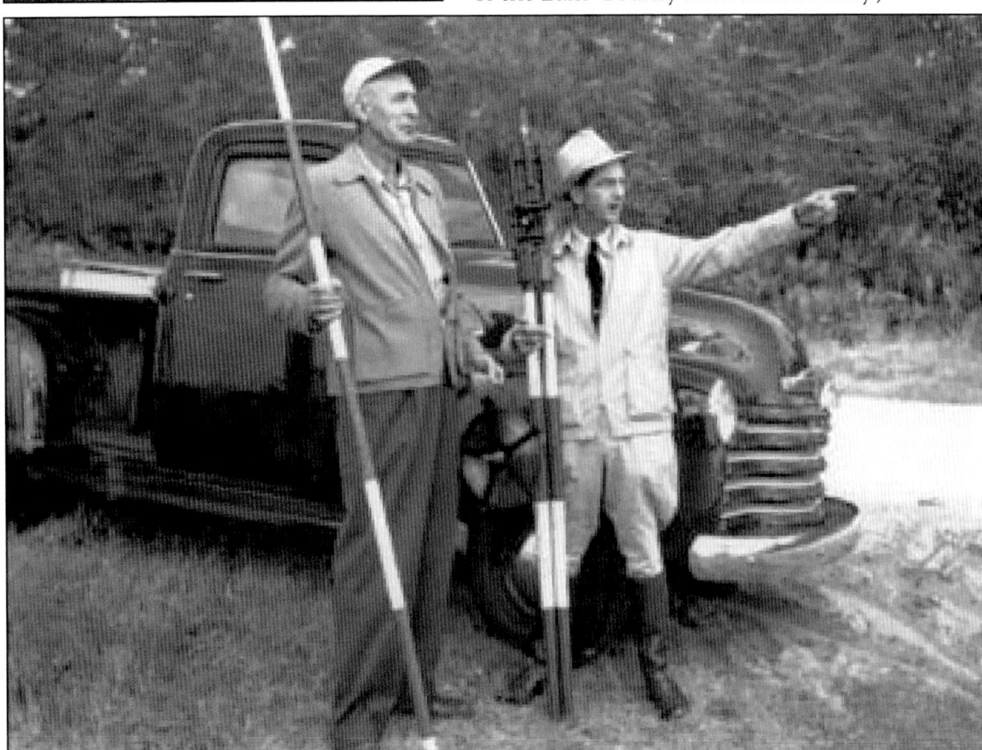

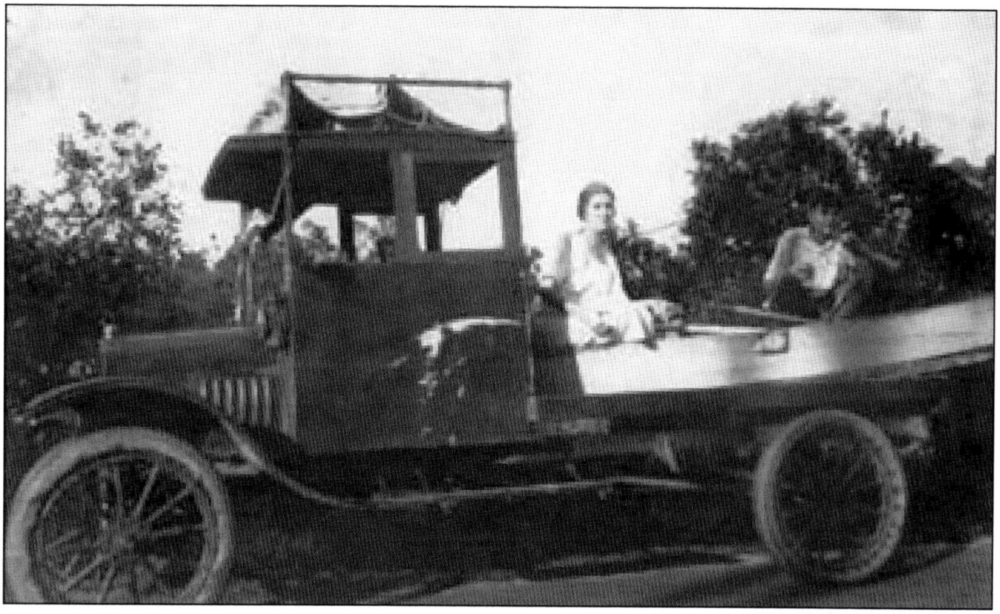

A tourist family from the north on a fishing vacation in Lake County stops alongside a Tavares orange grove on their way home. On the back of this family photograph, the father writes, "Ella and Walter are eating stolen fruit while I snap the picture." (Courtesy of Clayton Bishop.)

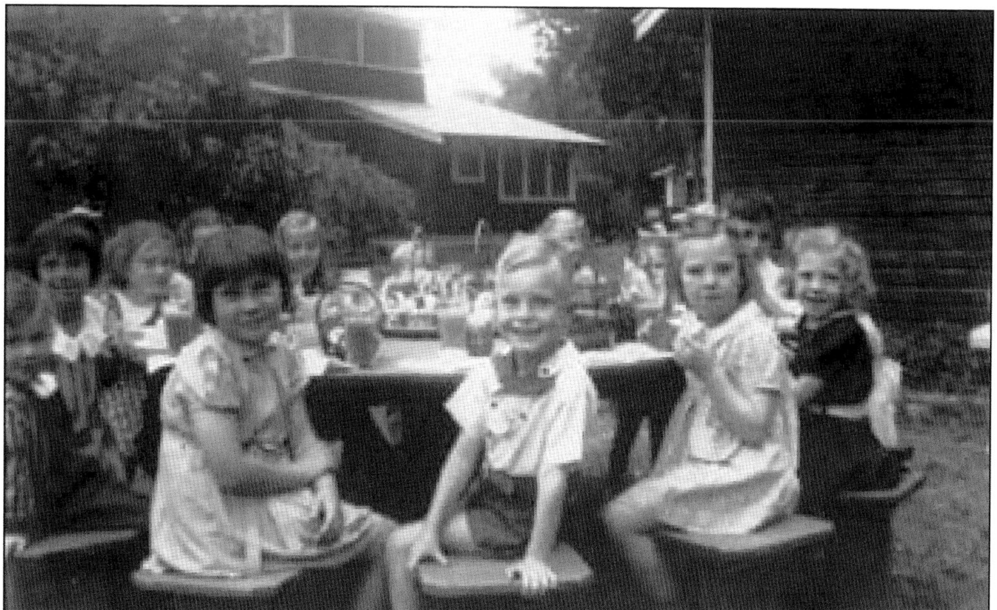

Pictured at this 1941 Easter party for beginners and primary children of the First Baptist Church of Tavares are, from left to right, (first row) Herbert Carden, Lura Messer, Kelly Smith, Elvy Taylor, and Joanne Works; (second row) Lila Lee LeVar, Nancy Lee, Beverly Boulware, Shirley Bassett, Lynda Stone, and Sandra Nutt. Teachers for the primary children were Marie King, Alenia Nutt, and Elizabeth Lacy. (Courtesy of Lura Messer Hall.)

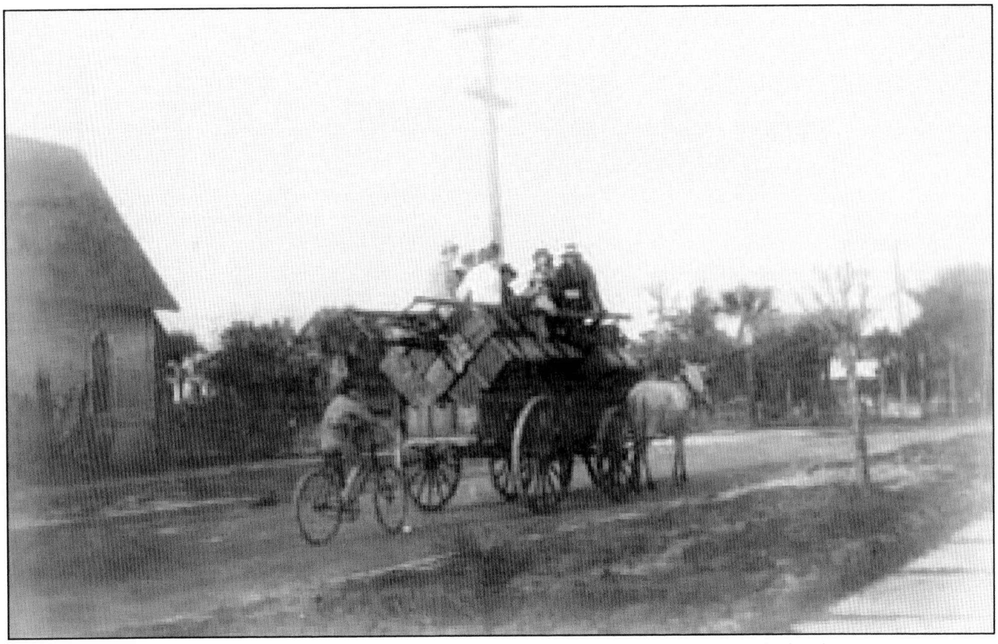

On a cool day in 1922, some of Tavares's leading young women hitch a ride high atop an orange picker's supply wagon loaded with crates and ladders. The ladies are traveling east on Alfred Street. The Union Congregational Church is on the left, and the Annie and Ed Burleigh residence is on the right. (Courtesy of Clayton Bishop.)

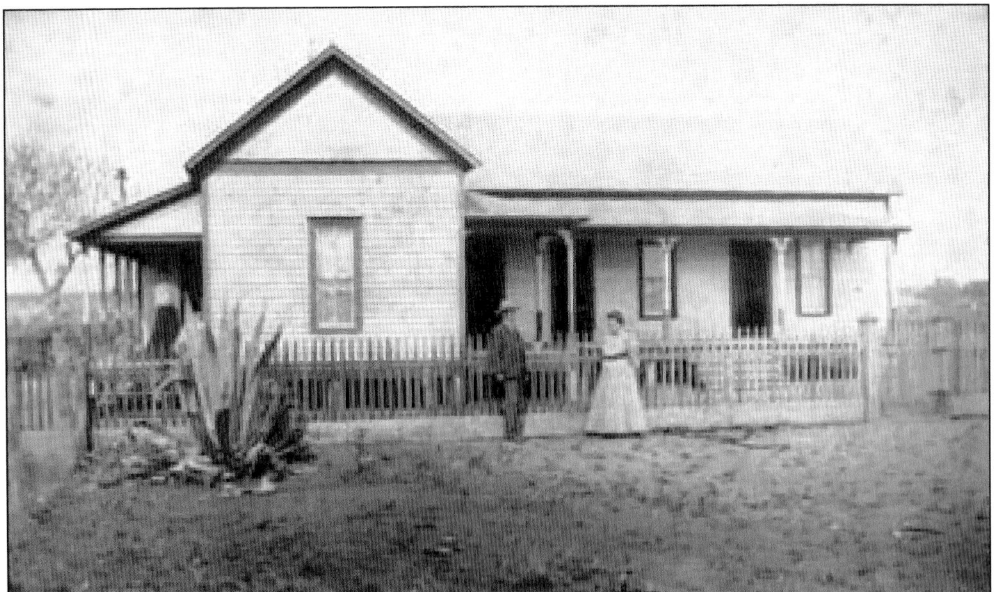

Tavares police chief Joel Napoleon Flowers and his wife, Sophia, lived at this home in Tavares. Sophia was the daughter of James A. Jackson and Minerva Mason. Alice Williams, the Flowerses' granddaughter, recalls the times when her grandfather would sit on the front porch of his home in front of the old Pioneer Building, talk with the children, and watch them play hide-and-seek around the house. (Courtesy of the Tavares Historical Society.)

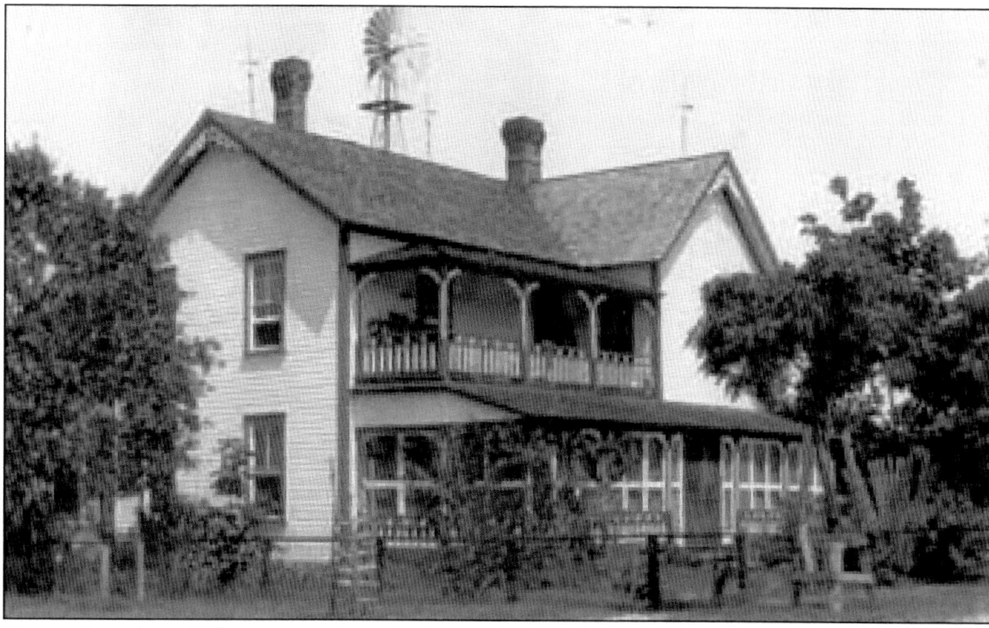

Pictured in this 1908 photograph is the Texas Avenue home of Henry and Marian P. Duncan. Henry Duncan served as Lake County's first clerk of the court, holding that position until he died on January 15, 1920. Maj. Gen. Charles Summerall said of H.H. Duncan, "These characteristics which Mr. Duncan possessed are the characteristics which make the true man, the true soldier, the good citizen, and the best nation." (Courtesy of Harryette Anne Duncan.)

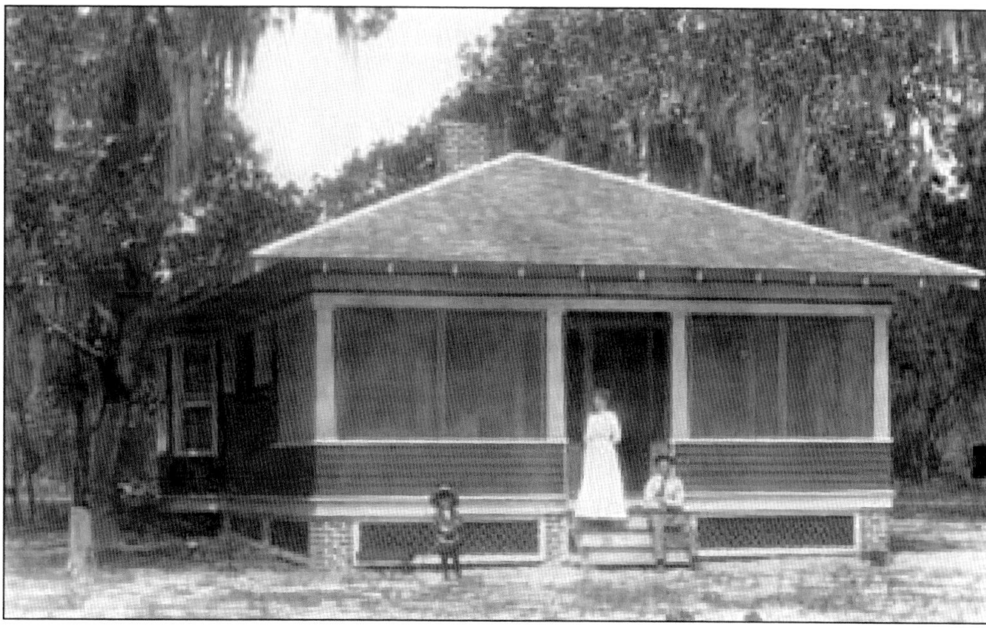

Master craftsman, architect, and builder Leo Coven, with his first wife, Chloe Hewitt, moved from Ohio to this home on Disston Avenue in 1903. They called their home the "Cove-Inn." Leo and Chloe had two sons, Russell, born in 1909, and Lyndon, born in 1914. In 1916, Chloe died of tuberculosis. Pictured in this c. 1912 photograph are (from left to right) Russell, Chloe, and Leo. (Courtesy of Bettye Coven Wilcox.)

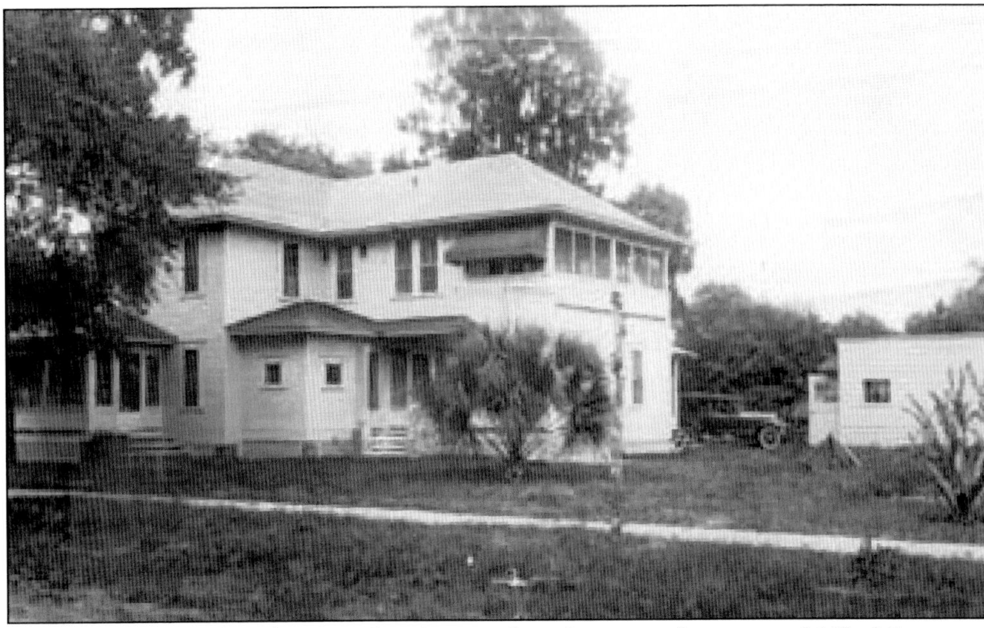

In the 1920s, Leo and Leela Coven bought a rundown house on the corner of Alfred Street and New Hampshire and refurbished it. The family called their home the "Big House." The house, which is still standing today, was used by Leela as a rooming house, mainly for tourists and teachers. Leo built a second floor onto the garage and rented it to laborers at the Lake Region Packinghouse. (Courtesy of Bettye Coven Wilcox.)

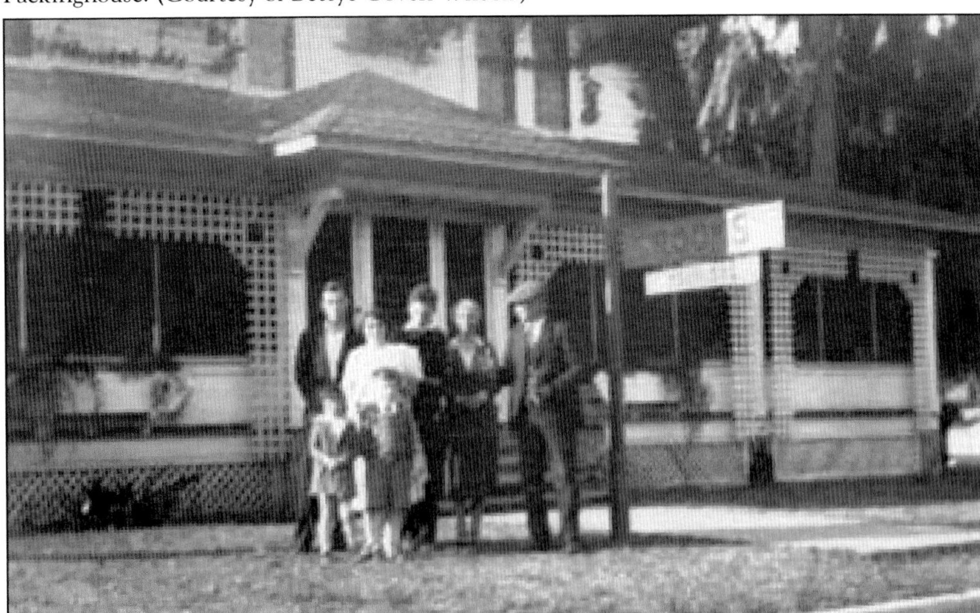

This c. 1930 Coven family picture was taken in front of the "Big House." The two small children are Bettye Faye Coven and her brother Leod Lamar, whom everyone called Babe. Standing are (from left to right) Russell Coven, Leela Coven, Lyndon Coven, Leo Coven's sister Bertha Buckley, and unidentified. Today, Bettye Coven describes herself as a pampered girl who got away with things her brothers never would have. (Courtesy of Bettye Coven Wilcox.)

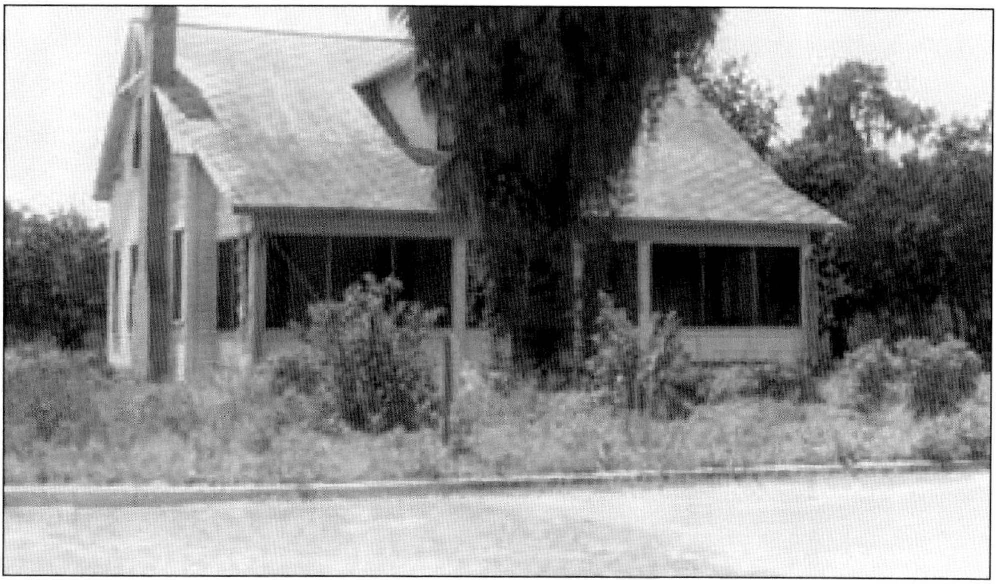

Pictured is the home of Thomas and Mary Hux located on Texas Avenue. In 1872, prior to moving to Tavares, Thomas and Mary homesteaded land south of Tavares raising cotton, sugarcane, and oranges. Game was plentiful, with lots of wild turkeys and bears. The first bear Thomas killed weighed more than 400 pounds. The town of Astatula was established from land owned by Thomas and Mary Hux. (Courtesy of Judy Hux Rainey.)

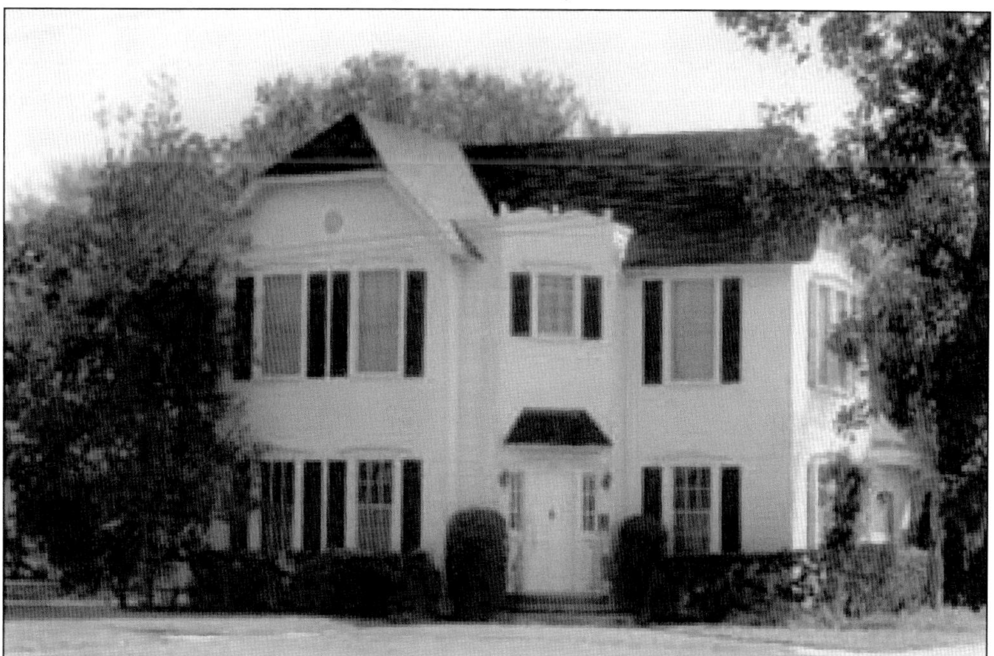

This residence at 204 North St. Clair Abrams Avenue at Maud Street was built for the J.C. Orth family in 1884. In 1923, the house was sold to George Dykes, who served from 1929 through 1953 as Lake County's Clerk of the Circuit Court. C.L. Bassett, who worked at the railroad depot on the corner of Main Street and Barrow Avenue with Bill Edmunds, bought the home in 1943. (Courtesy of the Tavares Historical Society.)

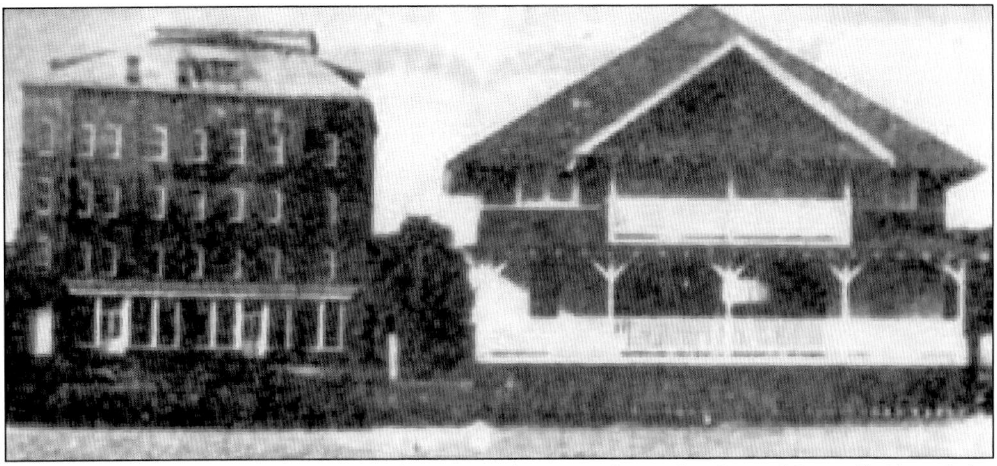

This c. 1915 photograph taken from a boat on Lake Dora shows the Opera House (left) and the Pavilion. The Opera House was built by Major St. Clair Abrams in 1887. In 1917, the top two floors burned down. In 1918, with only two floors remaining, the building reopened as the Lake Building. Through the years, several stores opened inside, including Chases' Fashion Shop and A&P Grocery. In 2011, the building was deemed unsafe and razed. (Courtesy of the Tavares Historical Society.)

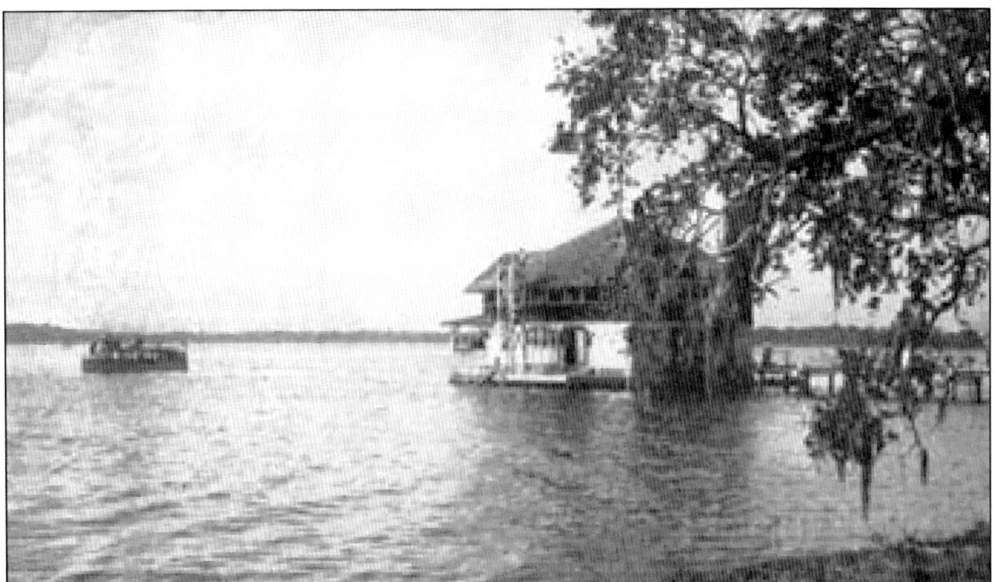

In December 1912, plans were approved for a 40-by-40-foot, two-story pavilion to be built over Lake Dora. The pavilion would be constructed with a 50-foot-long, six-foot-wide pier at a cost of $2,000. A campaign to raise money started, and construction began in 1913. By autumn of 1914, the Pavilion was completed. The Tavares Improvement Association was the first group to hold a meeting there. (Courtesy of Clayton Bishop.)

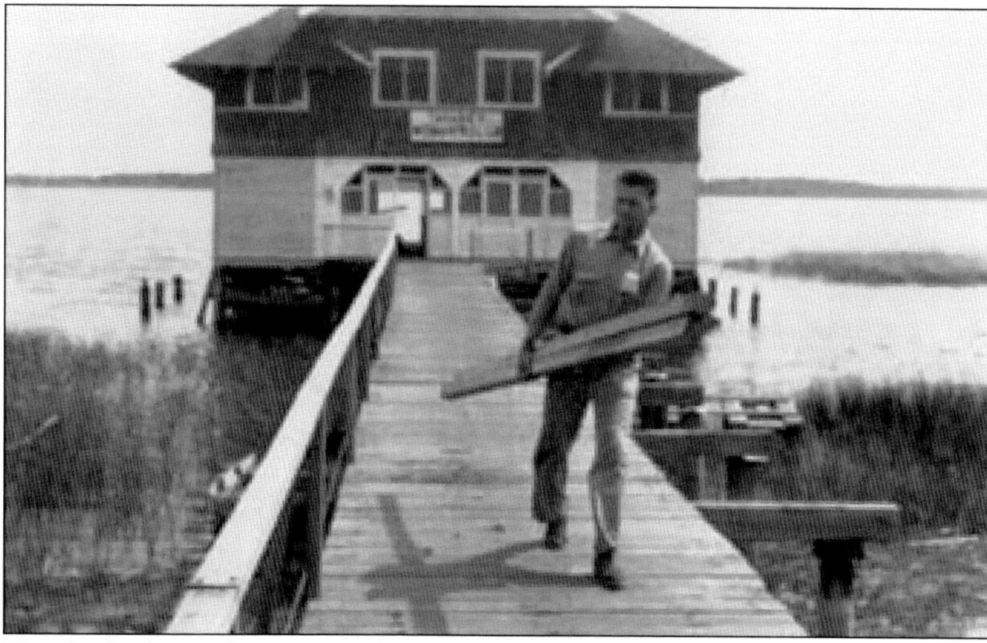

The idea for the Pavilion originated in 1908 with the Tavares Improvement Association. Built by Leo Coven, the Pavilion served as Tavares's foremost community center, hosting almost every social event in town. For more than 50 years, it hosted regular meetings of the Tavares Woman's Club and the Kiwanis Club. In 1961, the Pavilion was demolished in favor of the new Tavares Civic Center that was built at Ridge Park. (Courtesy of the Lake County Historical Society.)

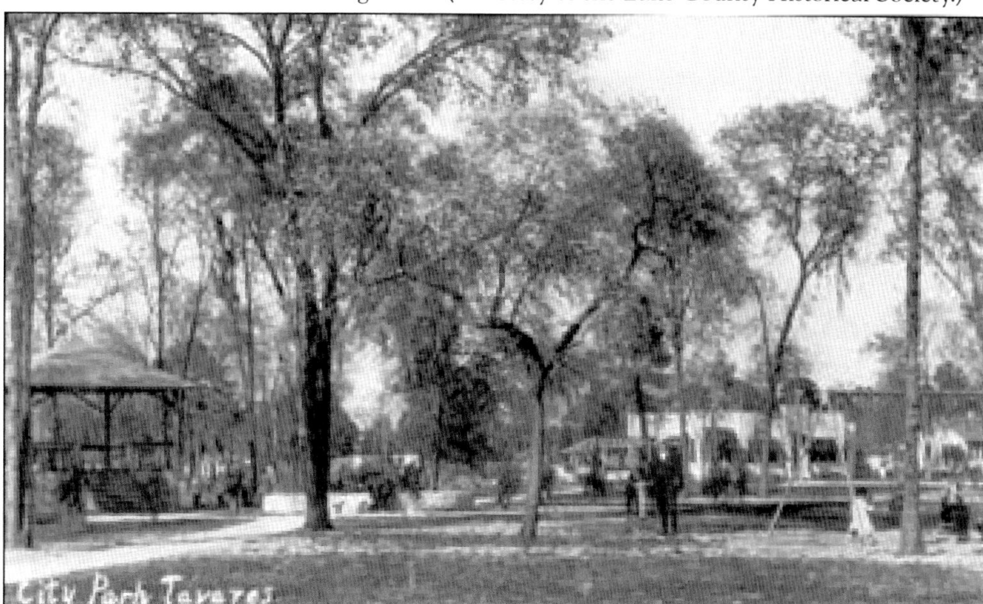

City Park appears here in 1929. The little girl on the swing is Bettye Coven. Her father, Leo Coven, and uncle Orlo Coven installed the playground equipment. Behind the large tree is the fishpond with the band shell on the left. The park had clay tennis courts and croquet courts. Dr. Sanford Colley's home is in the background. Today, the Tavares Civic Center and library stand on this site. (Courtesy of Bettye Coven Wilcox.)

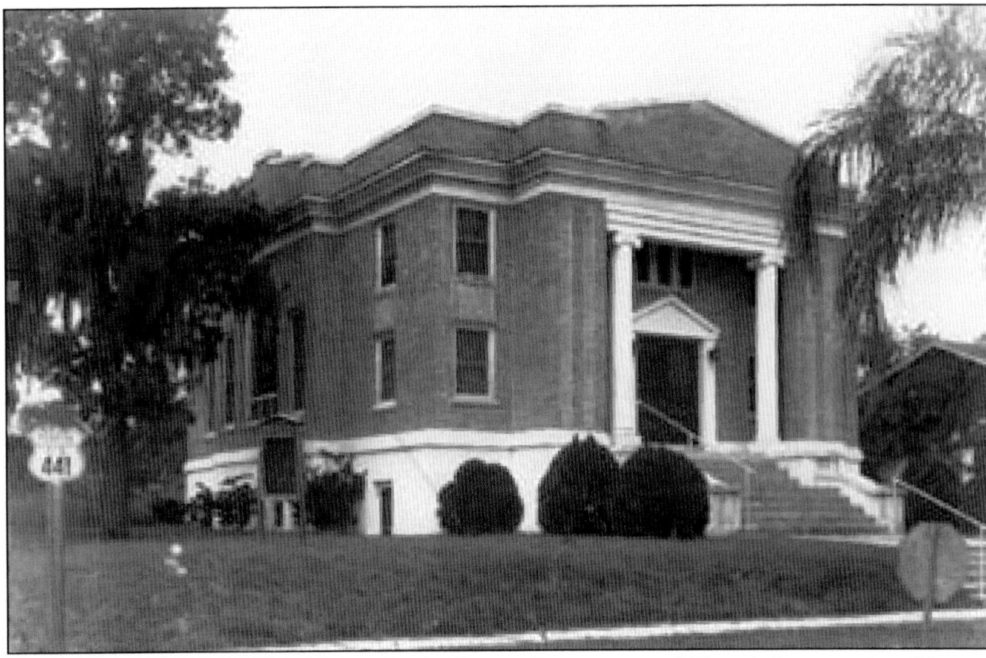

In October 1923, after holding services at the Union Congregational Church for more than 30 years, the Methodists moved into their first church building (above) located at Alfred Street and Joanna Avenue. Today, the church belongs to the Church of Christ. In 1968, the First United Methodist Church opened the doors to its new sanctuary on Alfred Street and Highway 19 (below). On May 9, 1998, an electrical malfunction in the church's kitchen started a fire that destroyed the sanctuary, including a stained-glass window depicting the Ascension of Christ, which was brought over from the original church. In the aftermath of the blaze, Rev. Denman Jones said, "The church is the people. The building is the means through which we express who we are." A new church was built on the same site in 2002. (Courtesy of the Tavares Historical Society.)

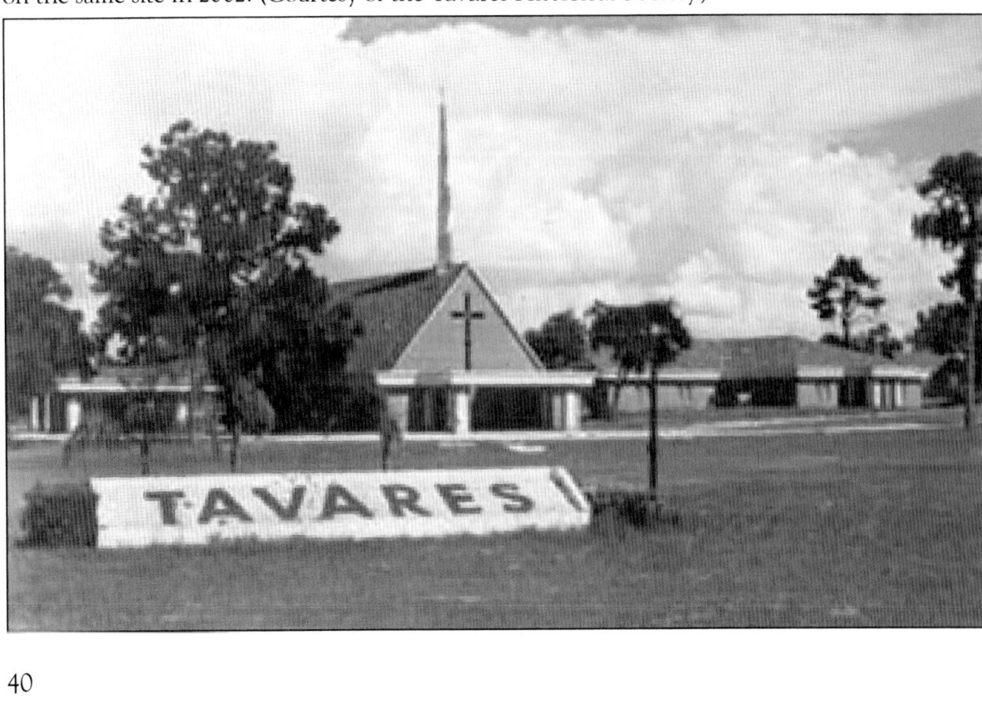

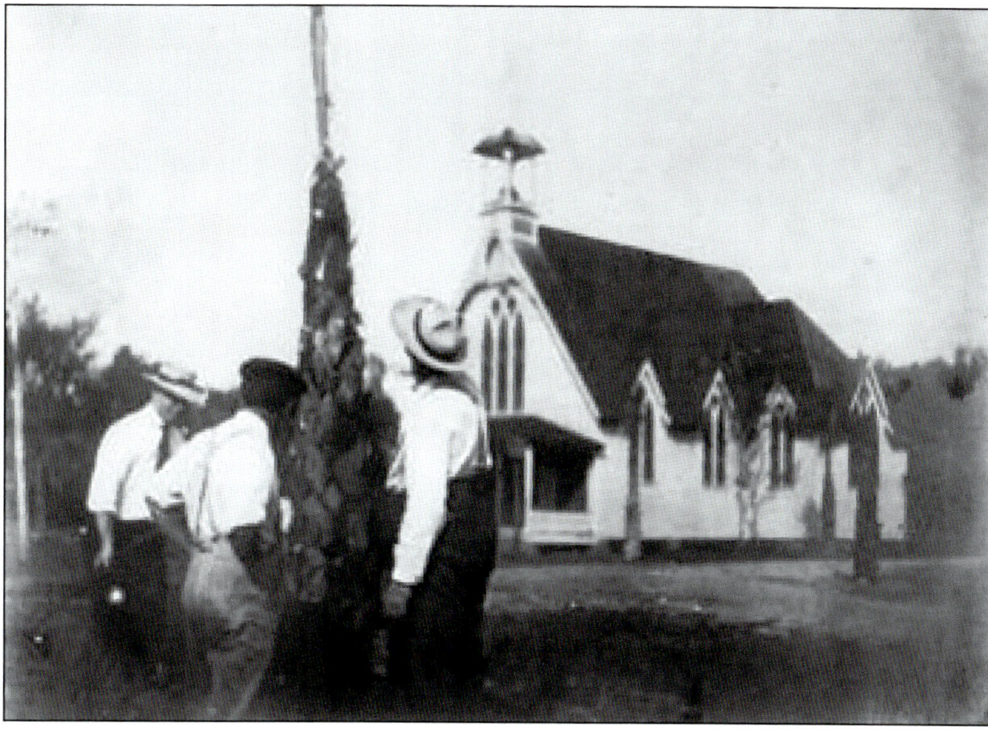

The Union Congregational Church was organized in 1885 by Rev. W.W. Winchester of Mount Dora. In May 1886, with plans submitted by the Honorable John G. Sinclair, church construction began. Jabez H. Sears of Boston was the architect who modeled the church after the Trinity Church built in 1846 in New York City. The estimated cost of the church sanctuary, located at St. Clair Abrams Avenue and Alfred Street, was $3,000. Major St. Clair Abrams donated the land and the lumber. After construction was completed in 1888, the Union Congregational Church was also used by other denominations. This 1903 photograph (below) shows the interior decorated with flags for Tavares's annual Fourth of July celebration, called the "Glorious Fourth." (Courtesy of the Tavares Historical Society.)

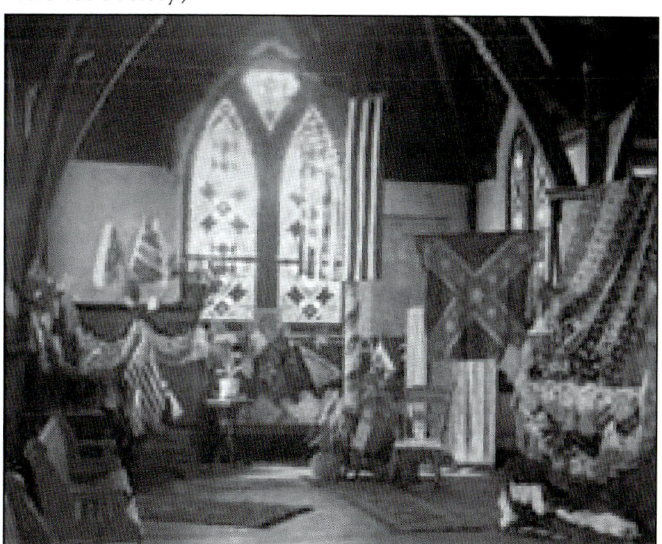

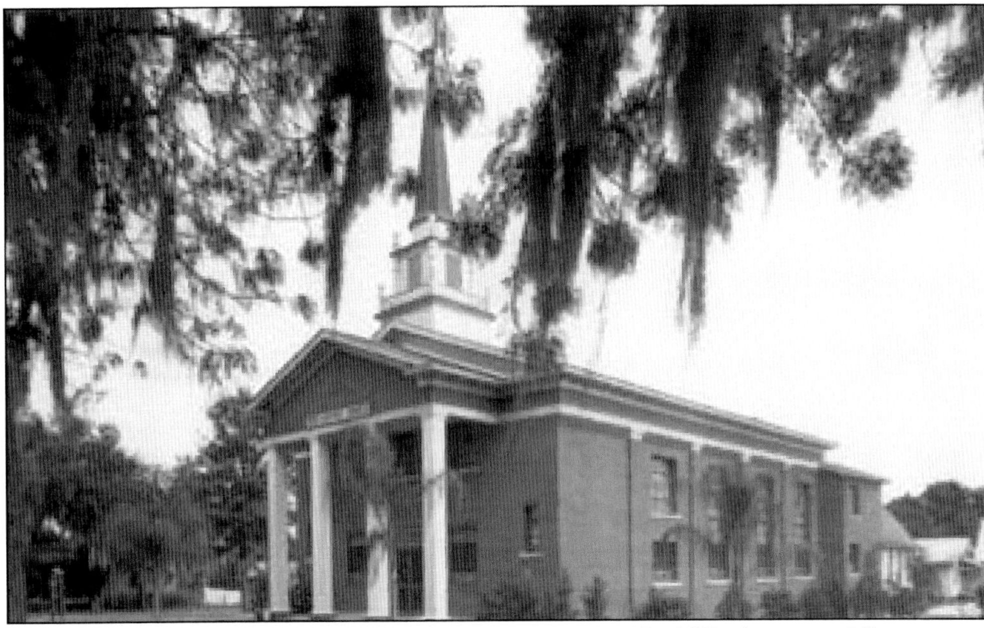

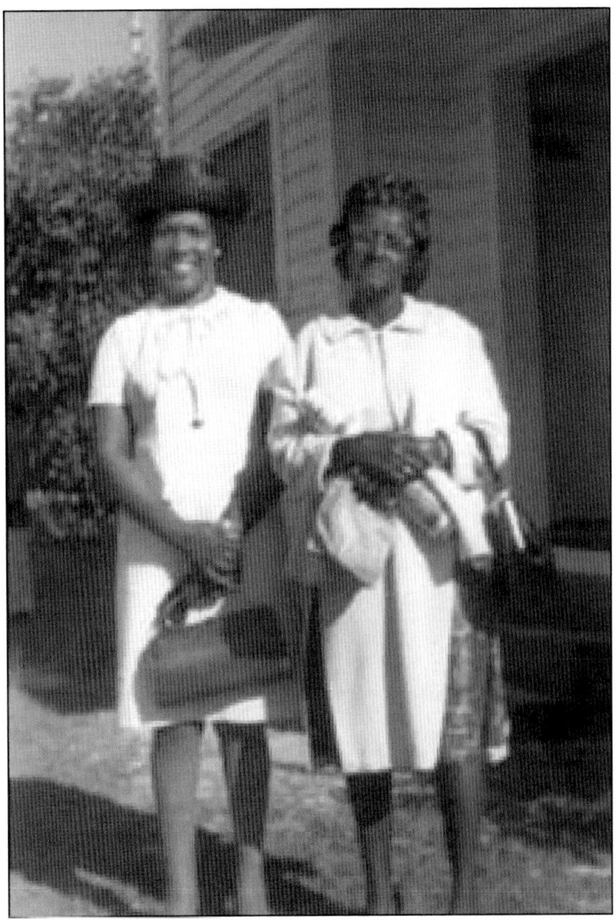

In 1951, the original First Baptist Church was a wooden building on Joanna Avenue. It was relocated to Maud Street and Barrow Avenue to construct the new church pictured here. The old wooden church eventually burned down. In 1952, T. Keith Hall and Lura Messer were the first couple married in the new church building. The First Baptist Church celebrated its 100th anniversary in 2011. (Courtesy of the Tavares Historical Society.)

Mount Moriah Missionary Baptist Church was established in 1885. In 1887, a church was built on a hill near present-day Lane Park Road and Highway 19 in Lane Park. Soon after the church was built, it was used as a school for Tavares's and Lane Park's black children. Atheria Owens and Victoria Bell are pictured here in 1950 attending Mount Moriah Church. (Courtesy of Bernice Shorts Odums.)

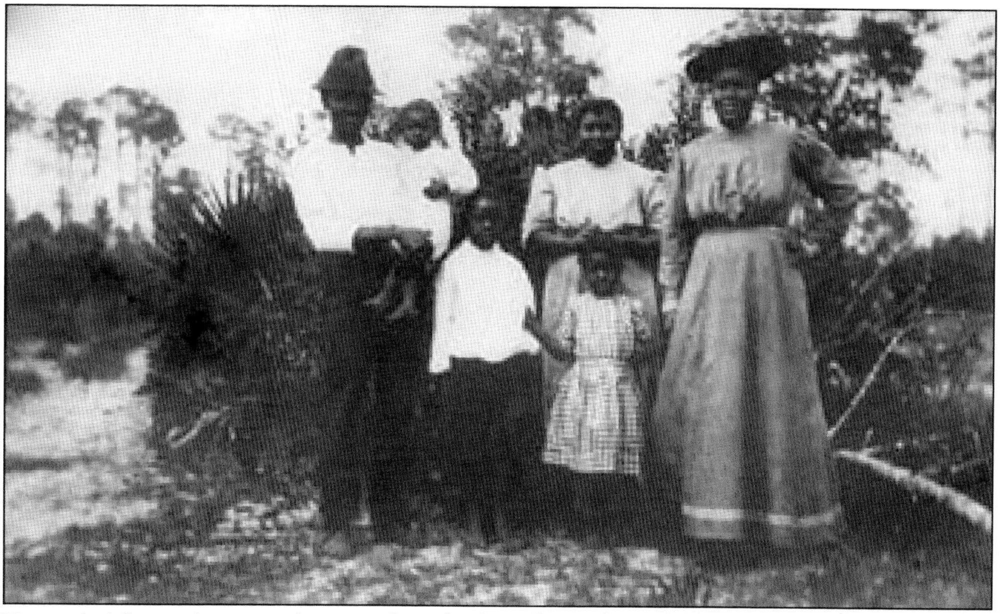

Tavares's African American heritage dates back to the settling of the town in the 1880s. Bob and Lucile Allen (above) were one of the first families to arrive. The Allen children are, from left to right, (first row) Tom and Queen; (second row) Annie and Laura. John Henry Wade (below) was a fireman on a Seaboard Railway freight train that hauled fruits and vegetables. Pictured with Wade are Mamie Lane Warren (left) and Wade's wife, Thelma Cromartie Wade. Thelma's father was William Reed Cromartie, who came to Tavares from North Carolina in 1904. Cromartie, affectionately called "Uncle Reed" by everyone, was very active in improving educational standards and conditions for Lake County's black youths. In 1954, Harrison Academy's name was changed to Cromartie Elementary School to honor Cromartie's service to education. (Courtesy of the Tavares Historical Society.)

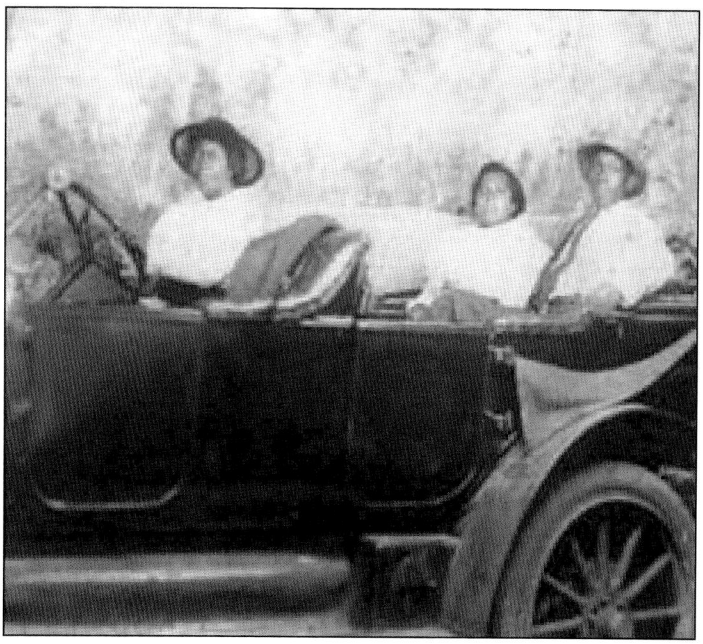

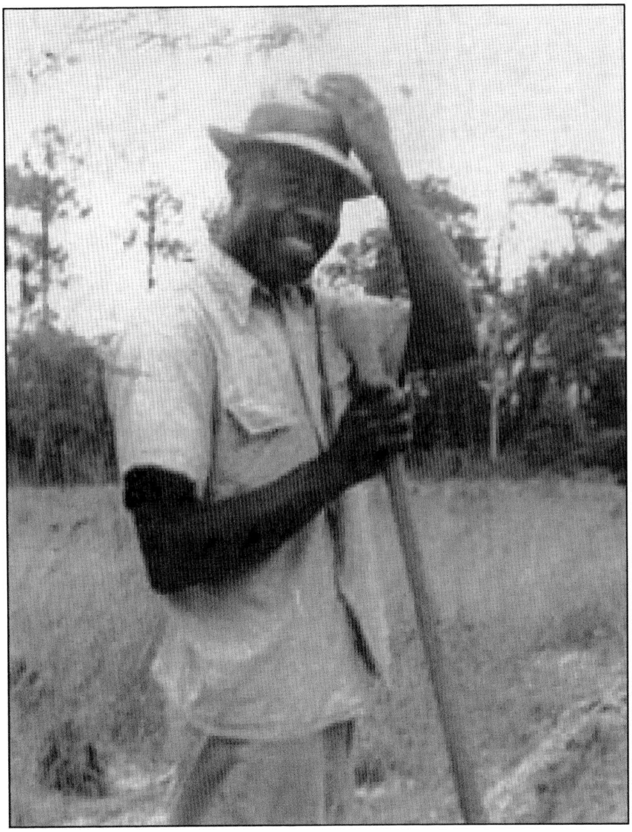

In the late 1920s and 1930s, James "Buddy" Jenkins Sr. (pictured) with his wife, Willie Lee, lived in one of four houses that were grouped together near the intersection of Lane Park Cutoff and County Road 561. These houses were known as Shorts Quarters, named for the Shorts family, who also lived there. Jenkins worked in the turpentine industry and also picked oranges and did yard maintenance. The Jenkins moved into Tavares near the intersection of Alfred Street and Bloxham Avenue, where they raised 11 children. Their home was among a group of houses that were painted red, called the Red Quarters. Five of the Jenkins children (below) are, from left to right, Isaiah, James Jr., John Edward, Frances, and Alma. (Both, courtesy of the Tavares Historical Society.)

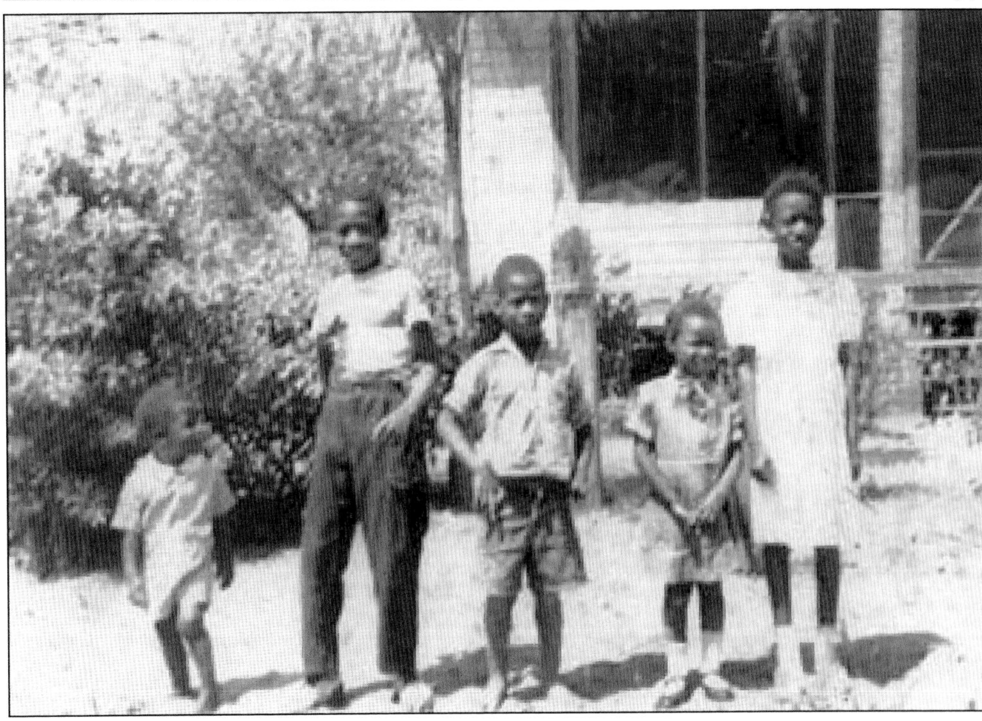

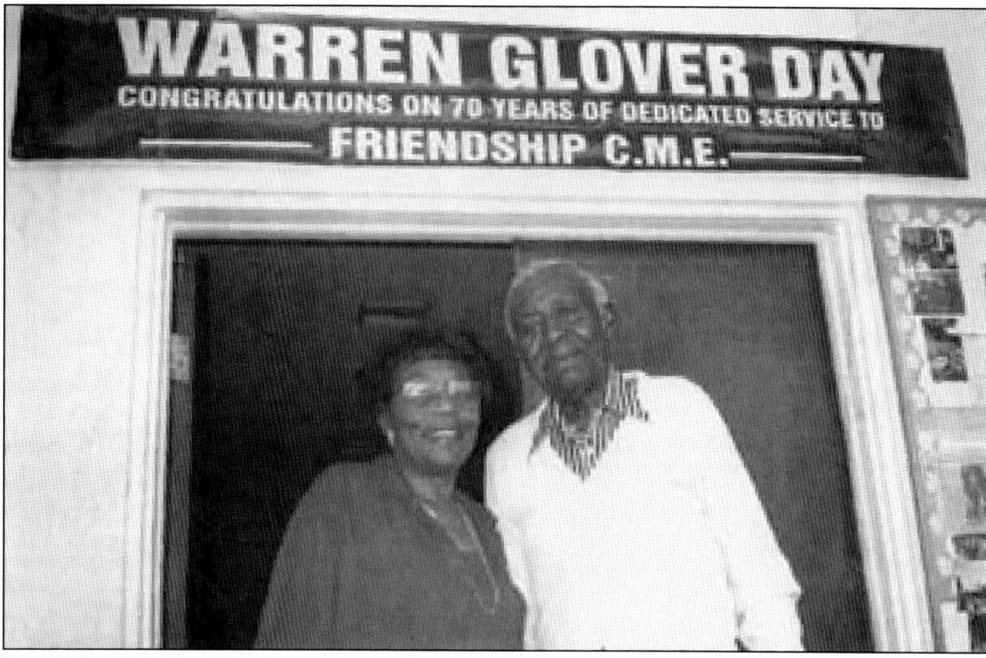

Friendship C.M.E. Church in Lane Park was organized in 1896 under the leadership of presiding elder Alfred Hall. The church received the name "Friendship" because the local people were so friendly. Warren Glover, pictured above with his eldest daughter, Juanita, moved to Lane Park in 1925. Glover met his wife, Zola, while attending Friendship C.M.E. Church and married there in 1929. In 1994, Glover was honored for his 70 years of service to Friendship. He died in 2000. Glover's son, Edward, (below) was married at the old Friendship Church building that preceded the church used today. The wedding party is, from left to right, Pauline Glover, Mabel Murphy, Margaret Hicks, Patricia Glover, bride LeVerk Youman, groom Edward Glover, Christopher Walker, Howard Short, and Arthur Lee Davis. The flower girl is Sharon Walker, and the ring bearer is Horace Orr. (Both, courtesy of Mary Glover.)

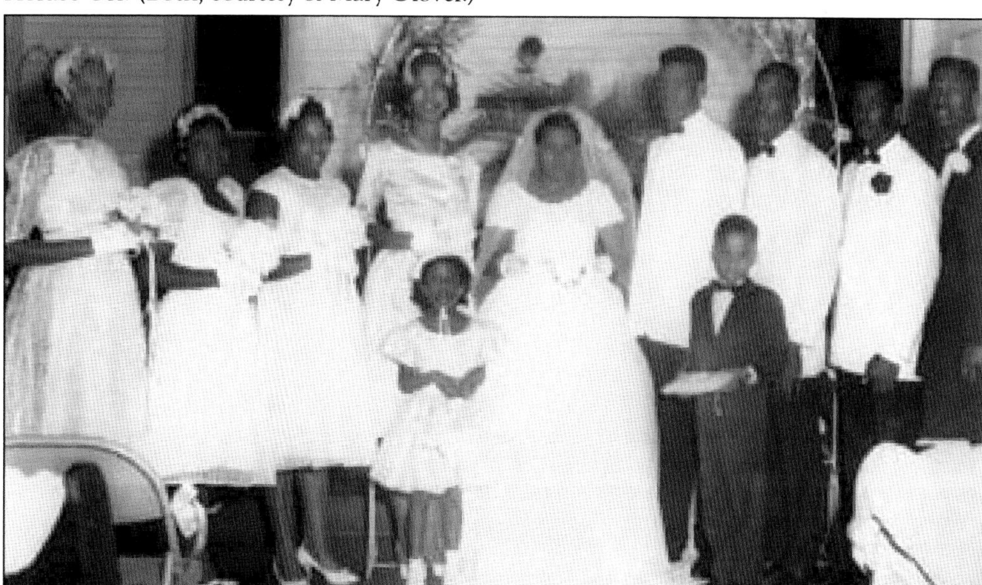

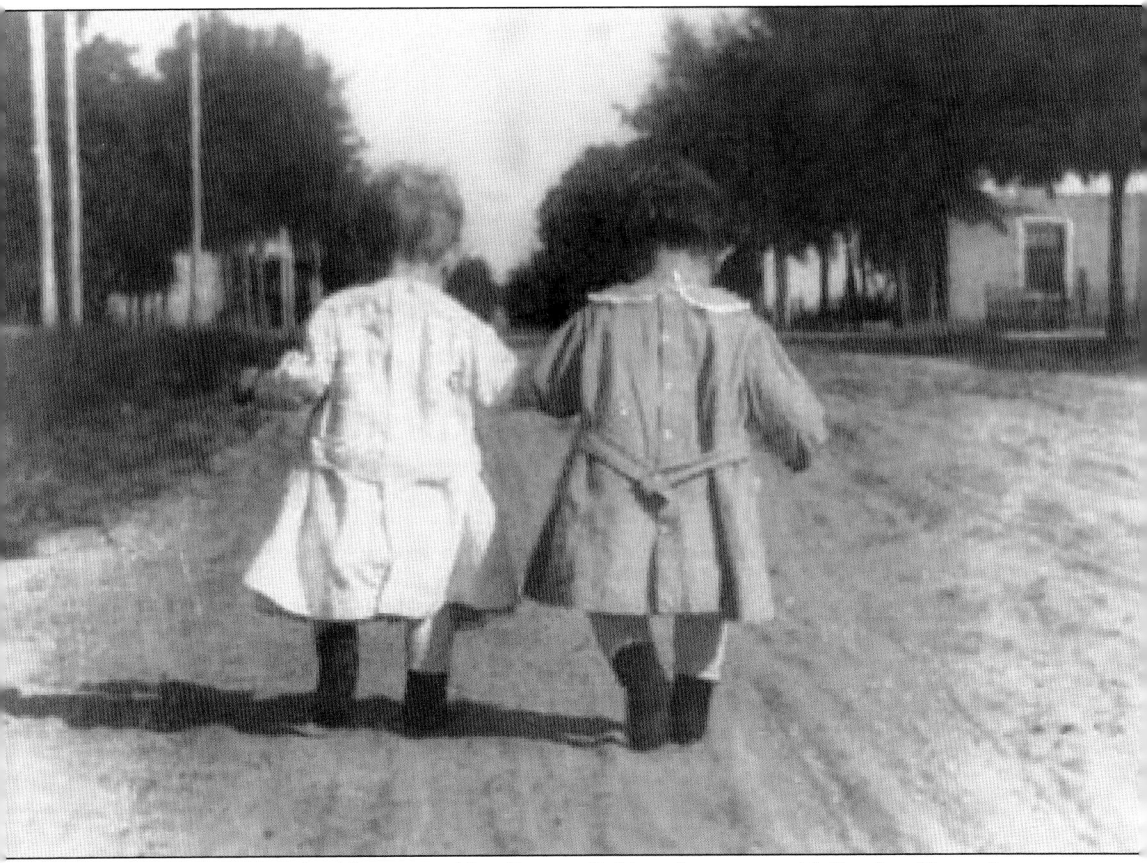

In 1917, nine-month-old Marian Alice Rogers (left) and one-year-old Carolyn Kennedy venture east on Irma Street (now Main Street). Marian Alice was the daughter of Dorothy "Dolly" and William "Bill" Rogers Sr. Rogers was the cashier at the Bank of Tavares. Marian was named for her grandmother Marian Duncan. Marian's grandfather was Henry H. Duncan, the Lake County clerk of the court. Marian Alice would grow up and marry Bill Haywood. Carolyn was the daughter of Christine and Walker "Red" Kennedy, who was an attorney. Carolyn's grandfather was Prof. William T. Kennedy, who wrote the book *History of Lake County Florida* in 1929. Carolyn would grow up and marry Army officer Lemuel Downs of Mount Dora, who served in the South Pacific during World War II. The law office of Harry Johnson is on the left, and the law office of Duncan, Hamlin, and Duncan is on the right. The Pioneer Building is to the right. (Courtesy of the Tavares Historical Society.)

Three

Seaboards, Seascapes, and Seaplanes

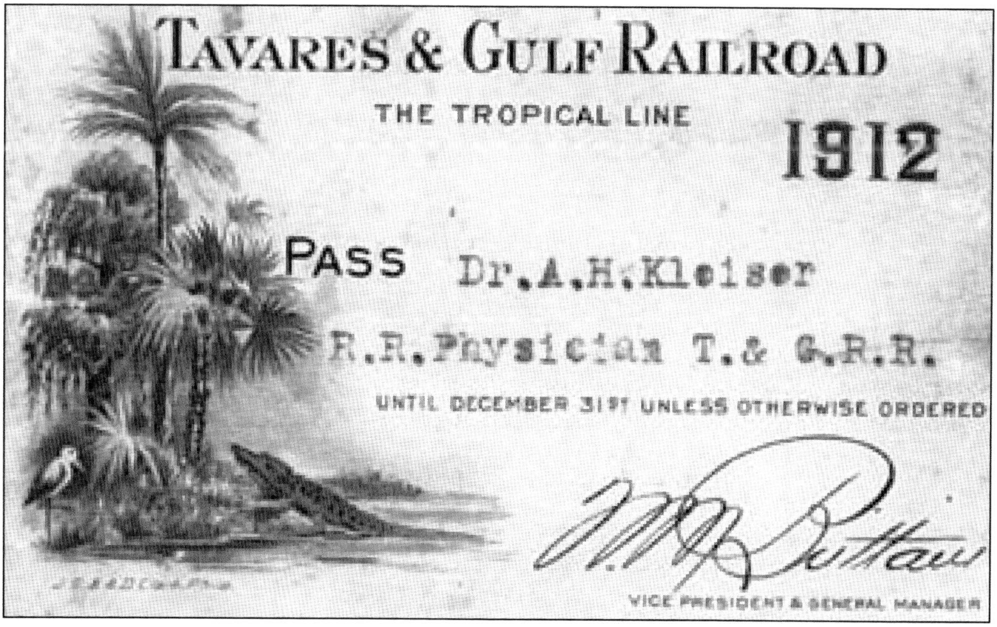

Major St. Clair Abrams chose the land for Tavares because of its strategic position in the center of the state. His emphasis on location was based on rail and water travel routes. Tavares was located in between Lakes Dora, Eustis, and Harris, which were all connected by the Dora Canal and Dead River. Physicians were scarce and made house calls, so it was necessary for them to get around quickly and conveniently. Pictured is Dr. Albert Kleiser's railroad pass. (Courtesy of Jane Kleiser Whaley.)

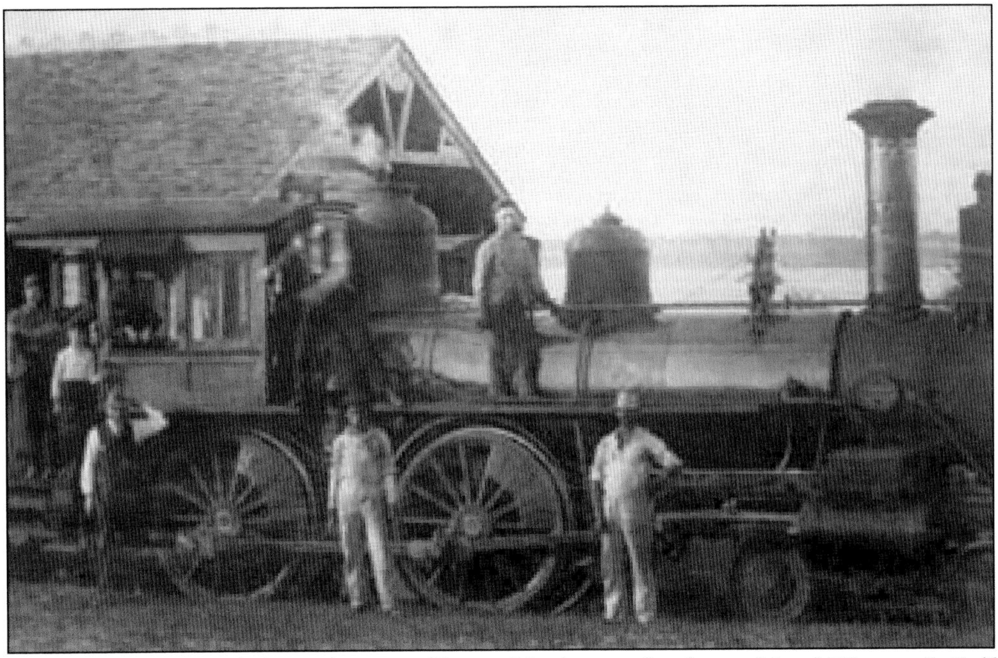

This c. 1900 photograph shows the crew of Engine No. 1 stopped in front of the old Tavares & Gulf depot. The Tavares & Gulf Railroad was originally incorporated as the Tavares, Apopka, & Gulf Railroad Company in 1885. The crew's first project was to lay 400 miles of track from Tavares south to Punta Rassa, but they made it only as far as Clermont in 1887. (Courtesy of Clayton Bishop.)

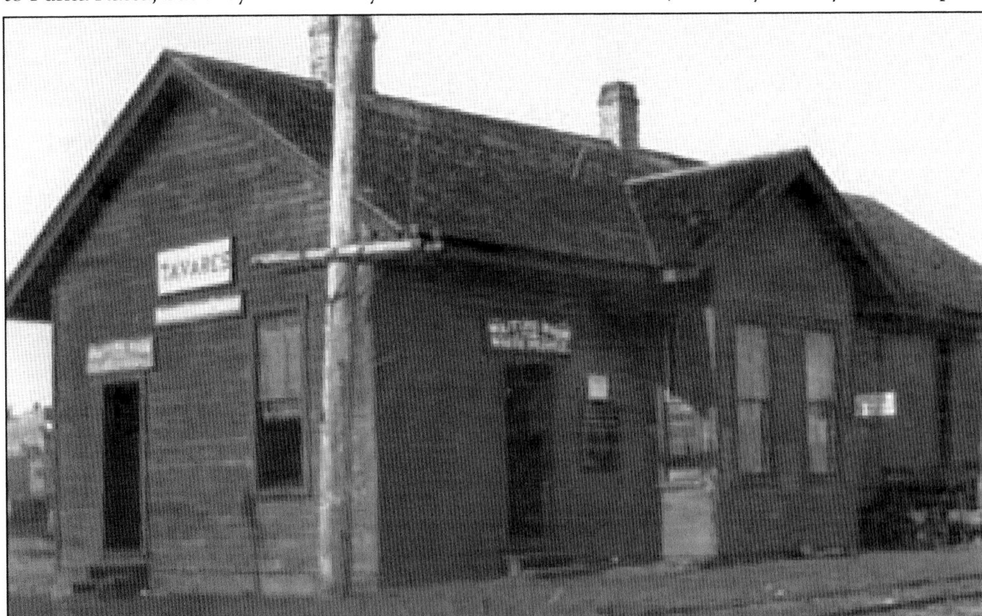

This Seaboard Air Line depot, seen here in the early 1900s, was located on the west end of town. The term "Air Line" in the name was a marketing enticement to suggest that Seaboard's rail service routes were shorter than their competition, enabling travelers and goods to arrive at their destination quicker. The Southern Express Company, located inside the depot, specialized in the delivery of valuable packages such as gold and silver. (Courtesy of Clayton Bishop.)

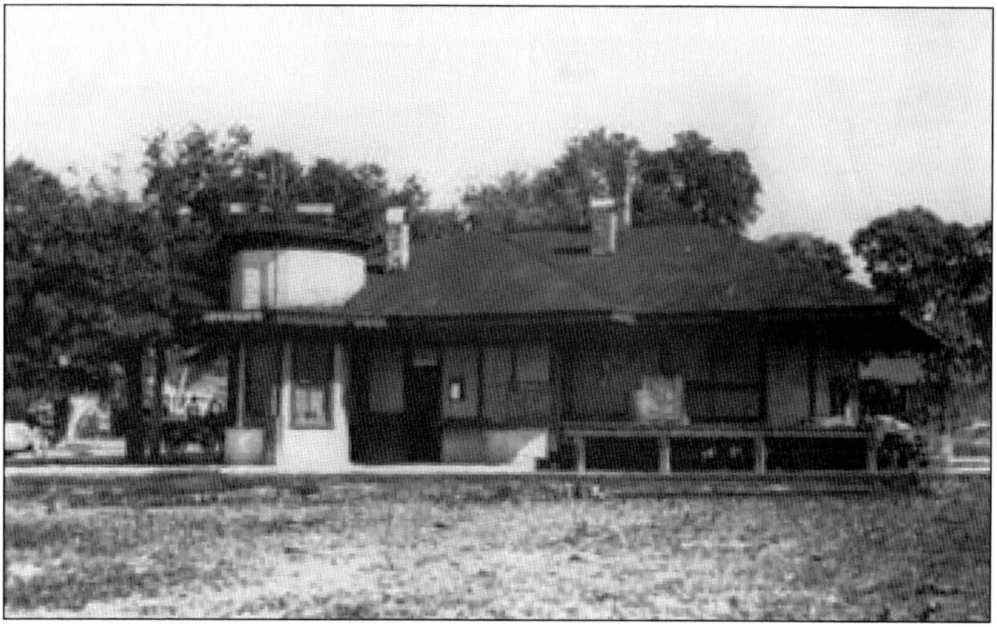

This Atlantic Coastline Railroad depot was built in the late 1880s. It was located at the east end of Main Street next to the Opera House facing Lake Dora. Trips were made from here to many metropolitan cities along the East Coast. This 1926 photograph shows the depot's distinctive cone-shaped roof of the turret removed. The depot burned down on July 24, 1988. (Courtesy of Clayton Bishop.)

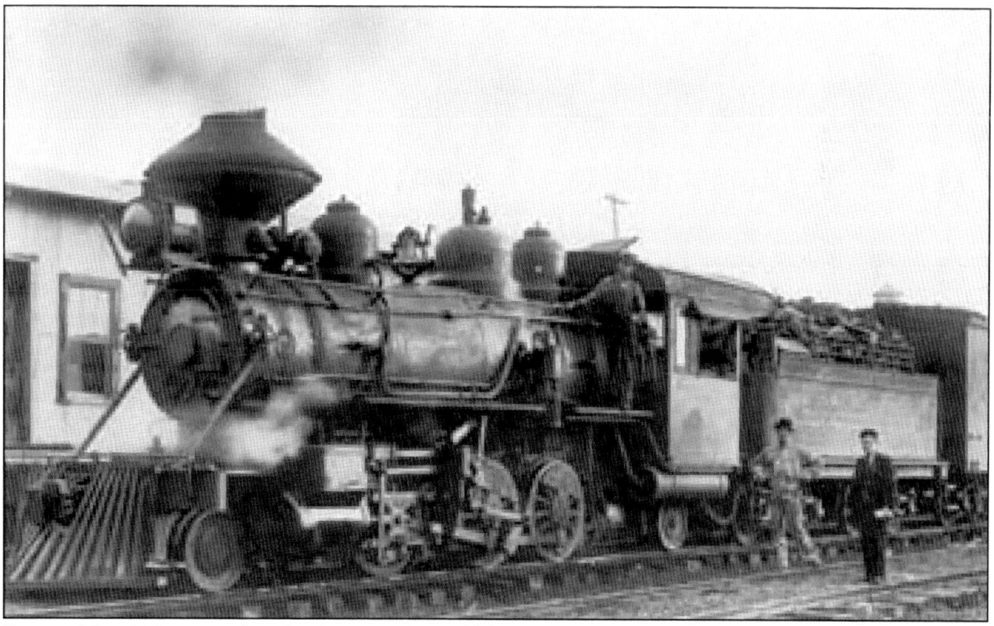

Engine No. 100 stopped at the Tavares & Gulf depot in Tavares in 1916, shortly after the Tavares & Gulf Railroad purchased it from Baldwin Locomotive Works of Philadelphia for $10,000. The engine was converted from wood to coal in 1922. The Tavares & Gulf suffered through many nicknames in its history, including the Tug & Grunt, Taters & Grits, and the Try & Go. (Courtesy of Clayton Bishop.)

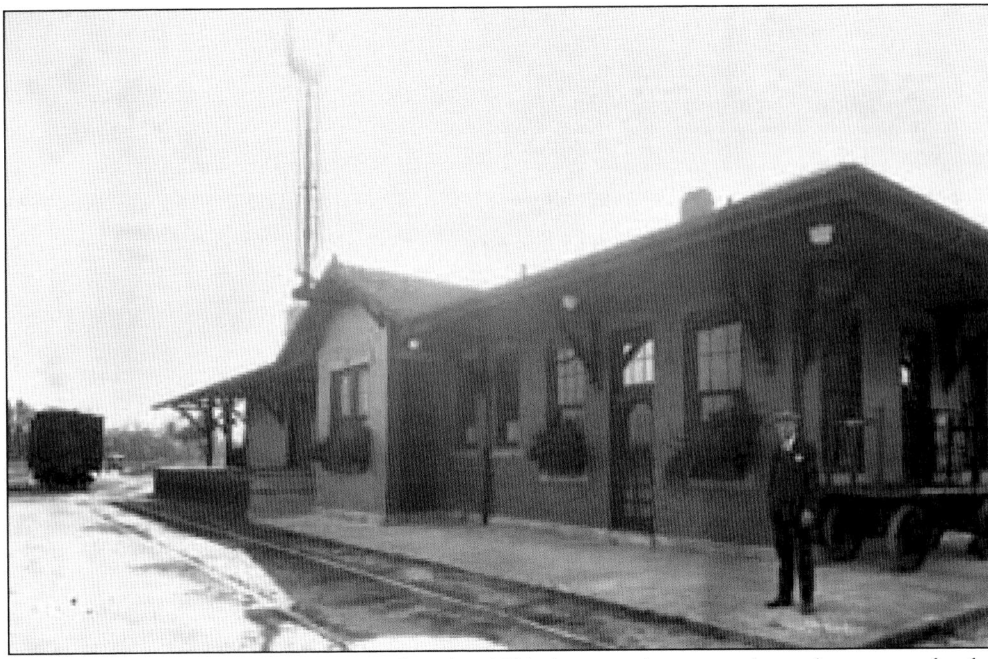

Tennessee-born Jack W. King, pictured in this 1931 photograph, was a telegraph operator for the Atlantic Coastline (ACL) Railroad. King is standing on the platform of the ACL depot located on Alfred Street in Tavares. This 100-by-36-foot depot was built in 1925 at a cost of $40,000. (Courtesy of Charlene Nichols King.)

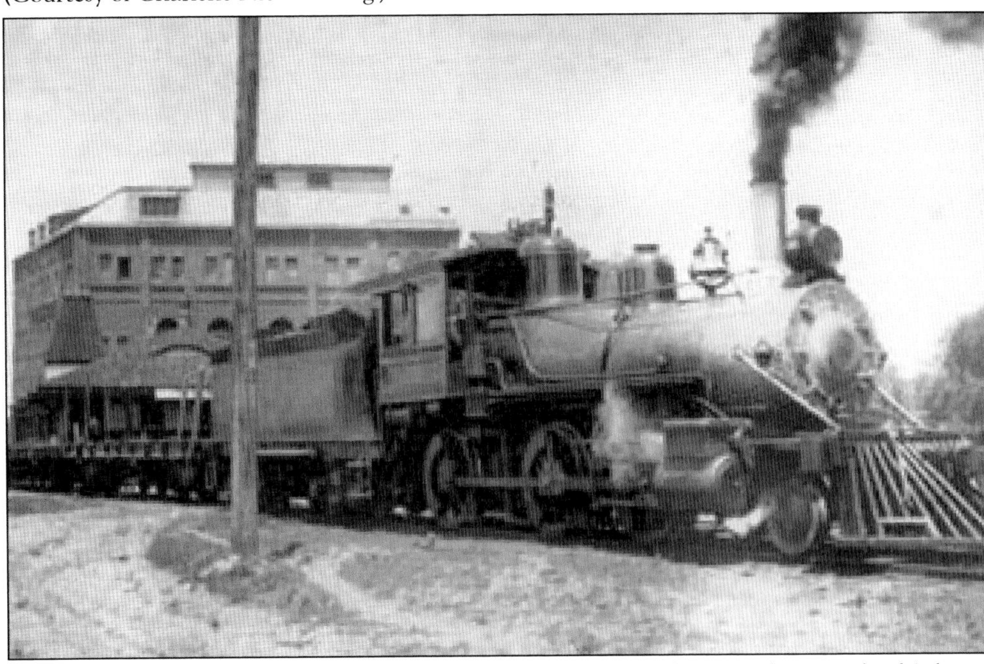

Major St. Clair Abrams's Opera House provides the backdrop for this 1914 photograph of Atlantic Coastline Engine No. 233 pulling out of the ACL depot. This engine is a 2-6-0 (two pony wheels in front, six drivers, and no rear wheels). This engine was used from Eustis to Astor and on to Tavares, Mount Dora, Sorrento, and Sanford. (Courtesy of Clayton Bishop.)

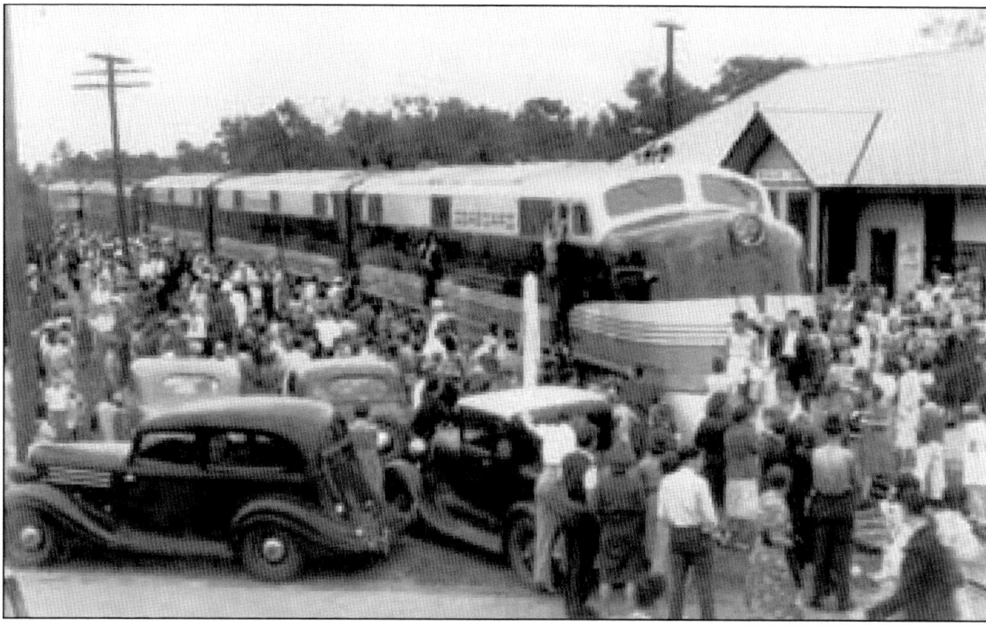

The famous *Orange Blossom Special*, which inspired the popular bluegrass song of the same name, made a visit to Tavares in 1938. In the early 1920s, Solomon Davies Warfield, the president of Seaboard Air Line Railroad, wished to take advantage of the Florida land boom. With a fast and extravagant train, Warfield could lure influential people to Florida. On November 21, 1925, the *Orange Blossom Special* was christened with much fanfare. Though service of the luxury train was temporarily suspended during World War II, the popular train ran through Florida until 1953. These 1938 photographs were taken at the Seaboard depot on West Main Street. (Both, courtesy of Charlene Nichols King.)

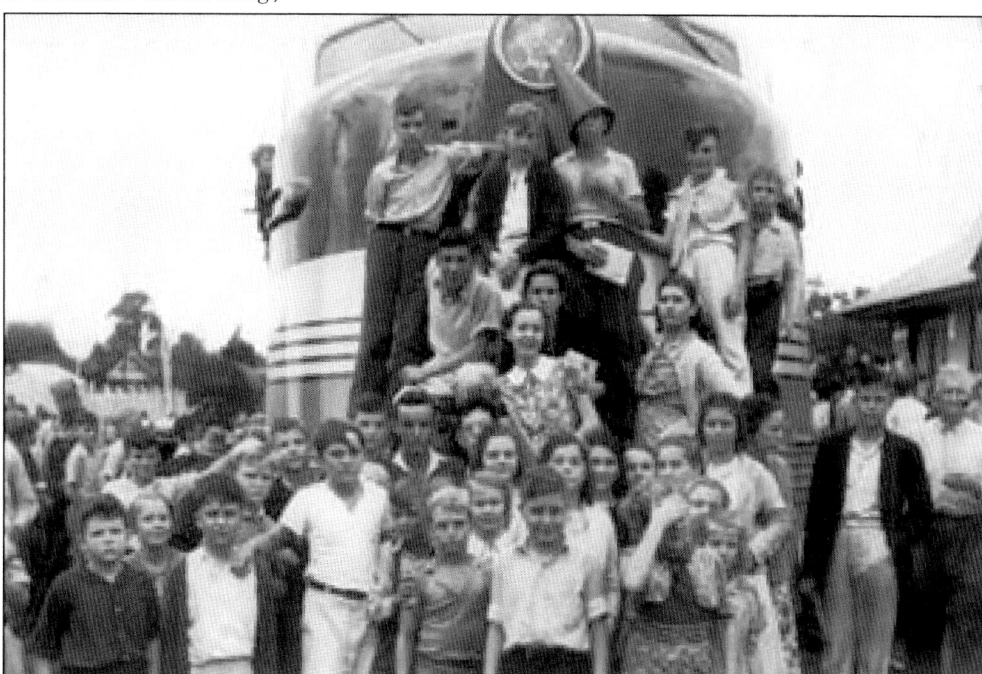

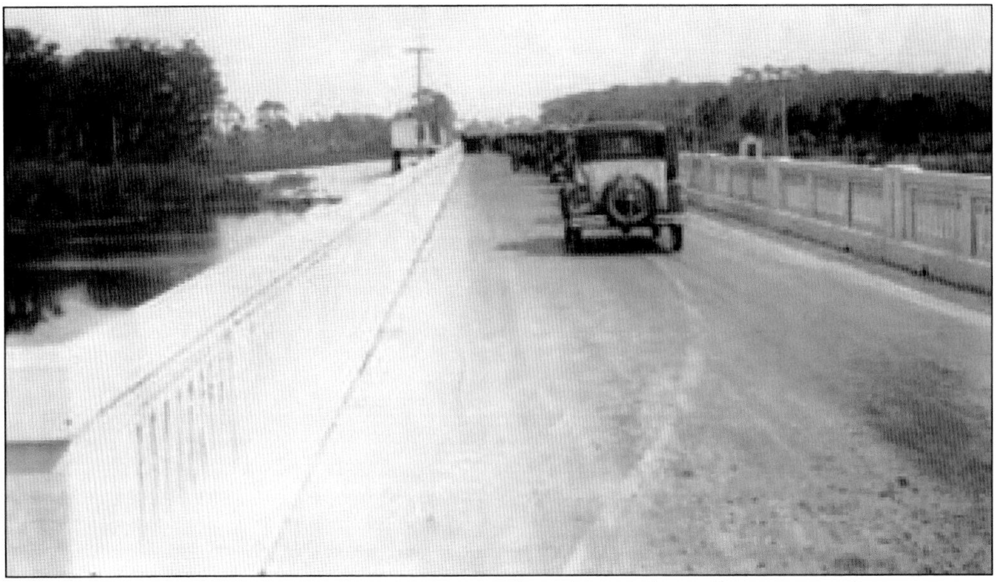

On March 19, 1929, public officials and citizens gathered to celebrate the opening of a continuous two-lane paved road and bridge across the Dead River, connecting Tavares with Leesburg (above). This bridge was a man-powered "swing-bridge." The bridge tender walked the circle to open and close the bridge. The small house on the outside of the bridge at right is the freight house for the Seaboard Airline Railroad at Eustis Transfer, where freight and oranges from Lake Eustis and other lake landings were loaded and unloaded for shipment north via Leesburg to Wildwood. Prior to the new road and bridge's completion, wagon, automobile, and foot travel across the Dead River was on an old wooden bridge, shown in this 1910 photograph. The wooden bridge, with its giant moss-draped cypress on the Tavares side, was located where Dead River Road ends now. (Courtesy of Clayton Bishop.)

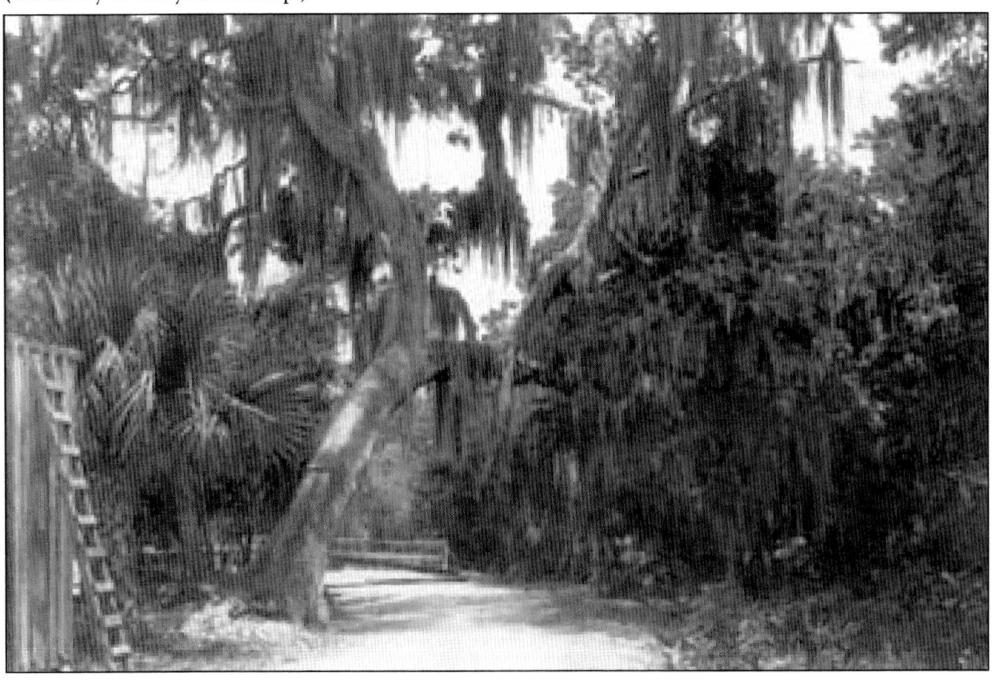

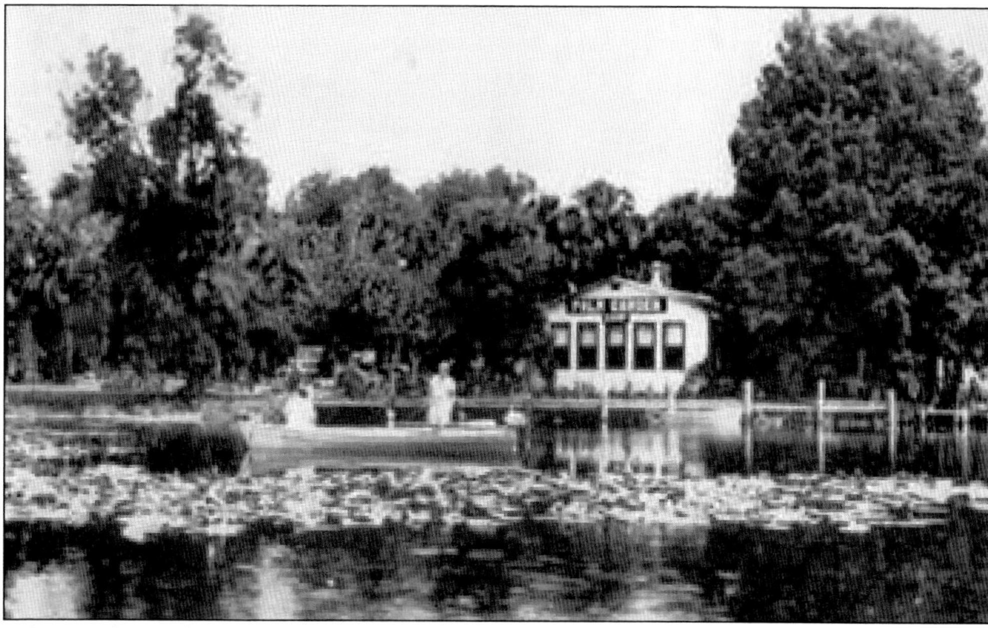

Palm Gardens Fish Camp was opened in 1934 by Albert E. Buse. Buse developed the camp with his priority to preserve the natural landscape. Palm Gardens is located on the Dead River between Lake Eustis and Lake Harris. Today, Palm Gardens, which is still owned by the Buse family, has a public boat ramp, restaurant, cabin rentals, and a full-service marina. (Courtesy of Clayton Bishop and the Buse family.)

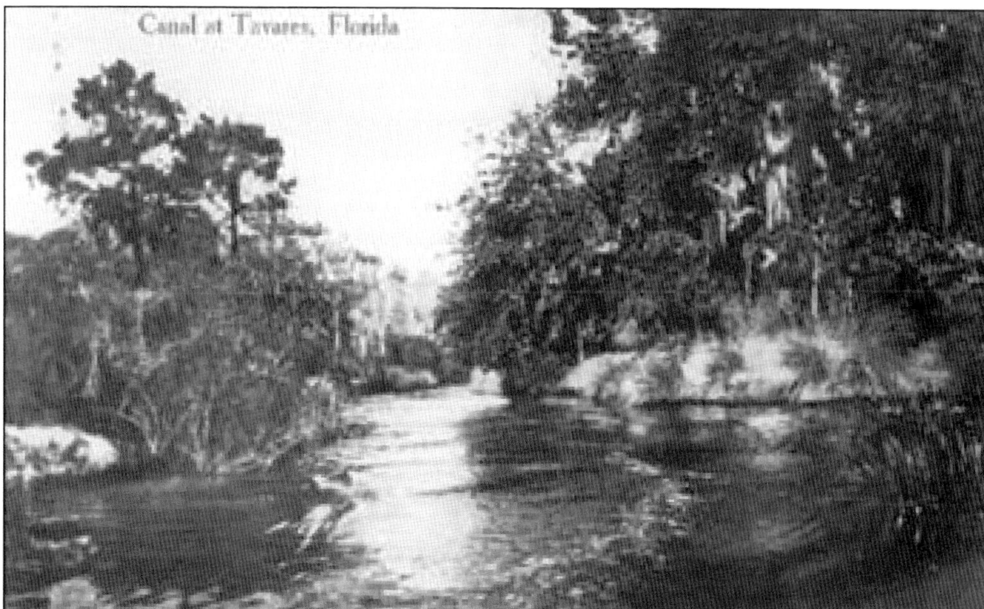

This 1911 postcard features the famous Dora Canal, the "most beautiful mile of waterway in the world." Though classified as a canal because of dredging by Capt. T.R. Boyd in 1879 and St. Clair Abrams in 1880, the Dora Canal is a natural geographic feature once known as the Elfin River or the Little Ocklawaha. The Dora Canal runs solely and entirely through Tavares, connecting Lake Dora with Lake Eustis. (Courtesy of Clayton Bishop.)

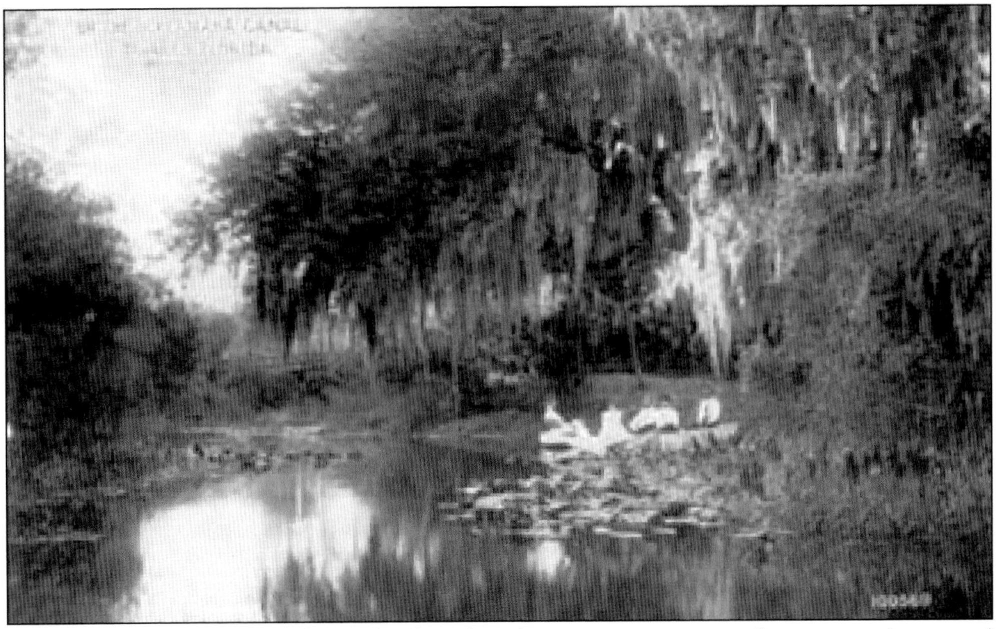

The cypress-lined Dora Canal provides these friends a picturesque setting for enjoying the natural beauty of Florida's waterways. The old wooden bridge is seen in the background. Notice the caption at the top of this 1911 postcard, which says, "On the Ocklawaha Canal." *Ocklawaha*, a word from the language of the Creek Indian Nation, means "muddy." (Courtesy of Clayton Bishop.)

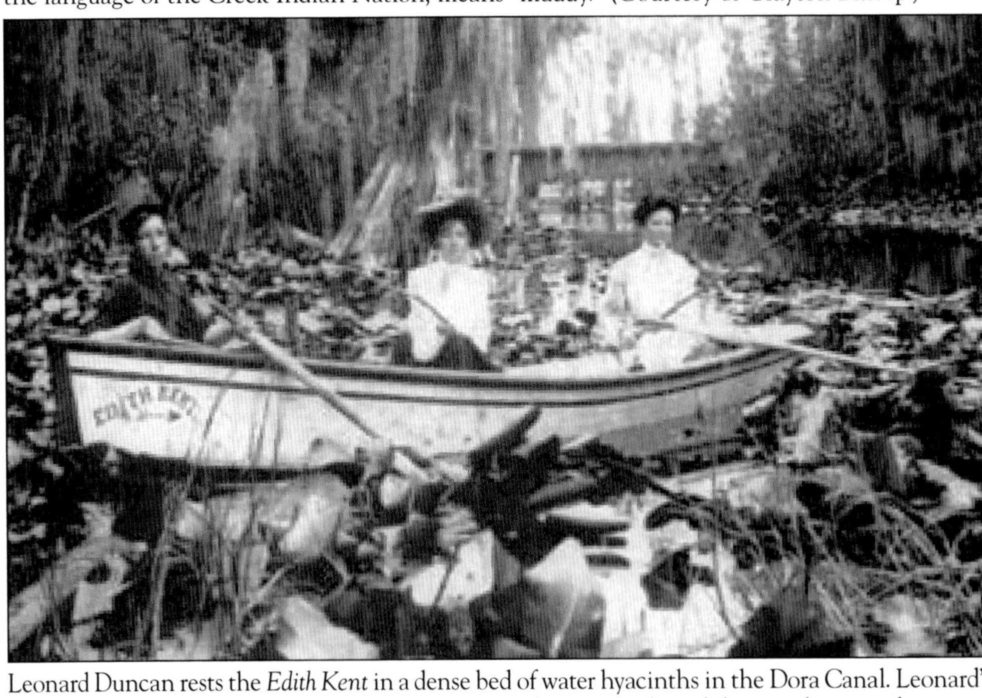

Leonard Duncan rests the *Edith Kent* in a dense bed of water hyacinths in the Dora Canal. Leonard's sister Marian (center) and friend Edith Hutchings have cast their fishing poles into the water. Sitting in a thick growth of water hyacinths, Marian and Edith most likely received more bites from mosquitoes than from fish. The photographer of this scenic 1904 picture captured a beautiful reflection of Marian in the still water. (Courtesy of the Lake County Historical Society.)

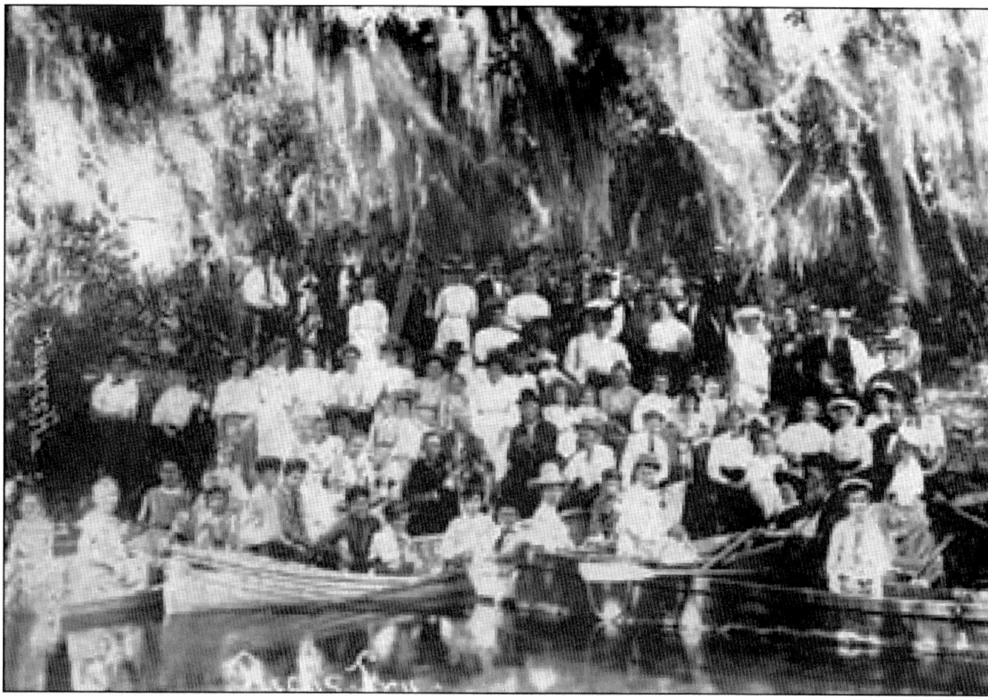

In March 1908, the entire population of Tavares (above) gathered for a picnic along the Dora Canal. Legend has it that the "Dora" in Dora Canal and Lake Dora are named in honor of Dora Drawdy. In 1882, a group of US surveyors were camped near the Drawdy home, where Dora served them meals and did their laundry. When they sent their survey report to Tallahassee, they called the large lake on the Tavares shore Lake Dora. However, the deputy surveyor's field notes of May 1849 also list the lake as Lake Dora. In the c. 1910 photograph below, the Duncan family, along with some friends, takes a cruise on the Dora Canal in Harry C. Duncan's boat, *Geneva*, which was named for his wife. (Both, courtesy of the Lake County Historical Society.)

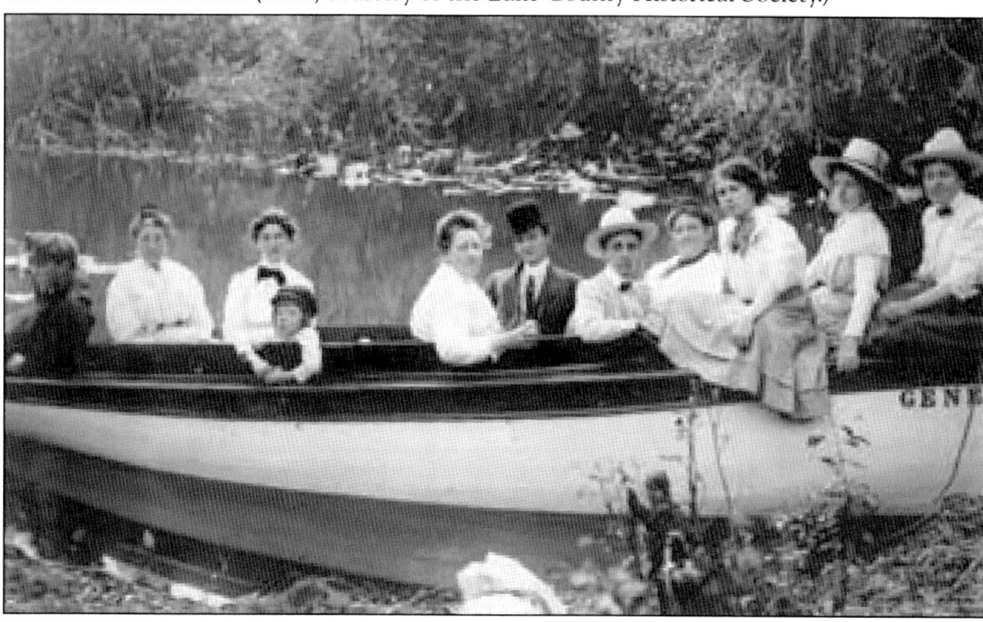

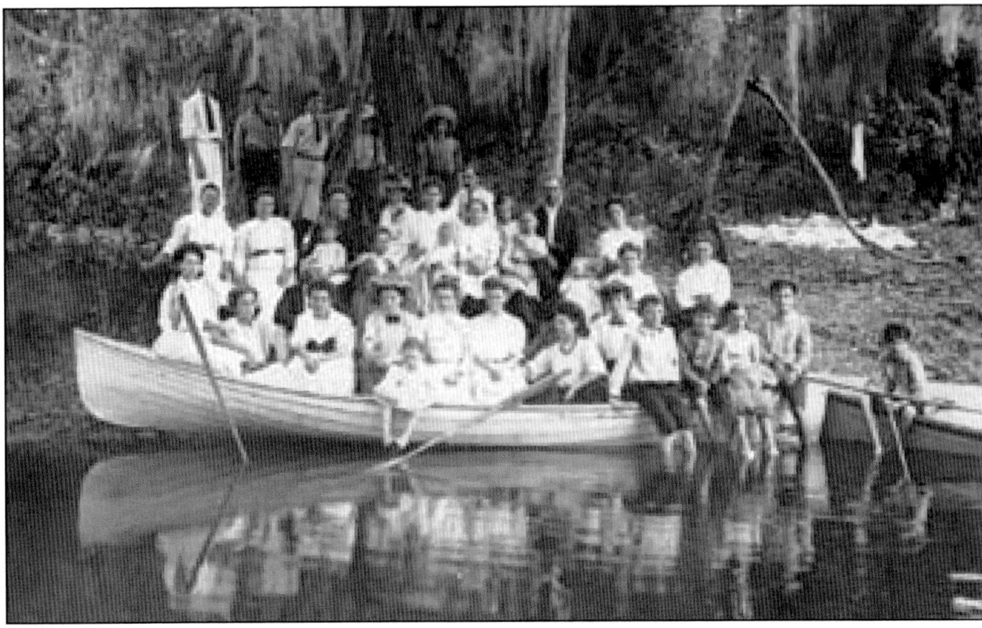

In the spring of 1906, newlyweds Maud and Guilford Wakelin enjoy a Sunday picnic with the Burleigh family and other friends at the Dora Canal. Guilford is pictured in the center of the photograph in front of the boy with the wide-brim straw hat. Maud is to Guilford's right wearing a hat and corsage. After graduating from Williams College in 1901, Guilford moved to Lane Park to manage his father's Woodlea orange groves. (Courtesy of the Tavares Historical Society.)

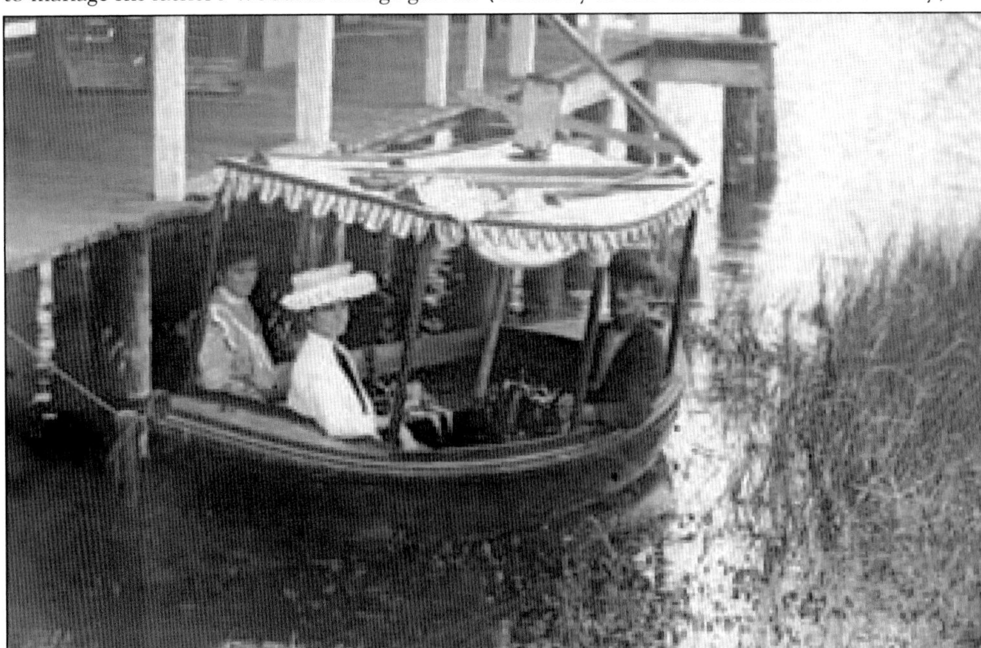

In this c. 1898 photograph, G.H. Barclay is seated at the engine of this early inboard motorboat. Alice Cottrell and Minnie Paubley are Barclay's passengers for a cruise on the Dora Canal. (Courtesy of the Lake County Historical Society.)

In 1953, eighteen-year-old Lila Lee LeVar hauls in the "big catch" on Lake Eustis near the mouth of the Dora Canal. This photograph appeared with a feature article in the *Tavares Citizen* newspaper about recreational activities in Tavares. The "big catch" in this photograph is actually a stuffed fish from the taxidermist. (Courtesy of Lila Lee LeVar Buckbee.)

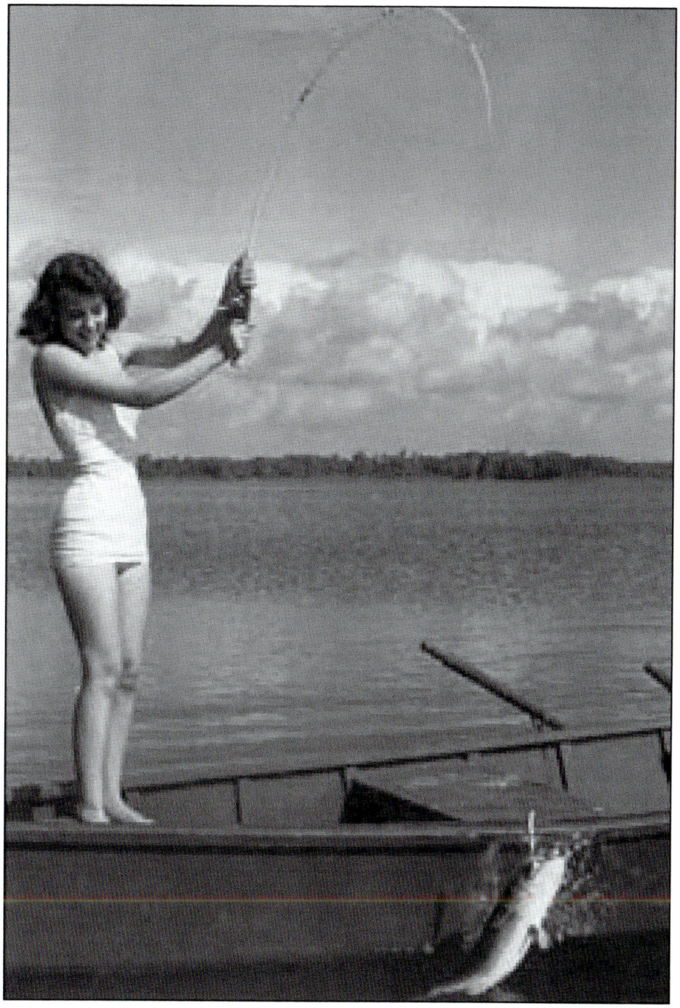

Until the 1970s, swimming in Florida's lakes was a common recreational activity. These swimmers in Lake Eustis were not concerned about gators, snakes, or snapping turtles. Clayton Bishop, a Lake County native, recollects that in the 1930s through the 1950s, the water was so clear that he could see his toes when he stood in knee-deep water. Later, pollution from many sources ruined the swimming in the local lakes. (Courtesy of Clayton Bishop.)

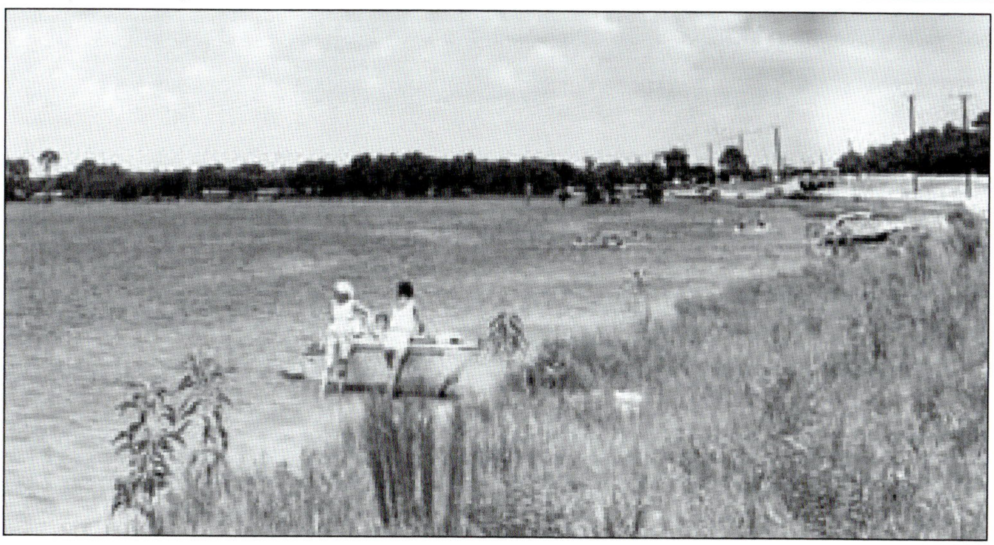

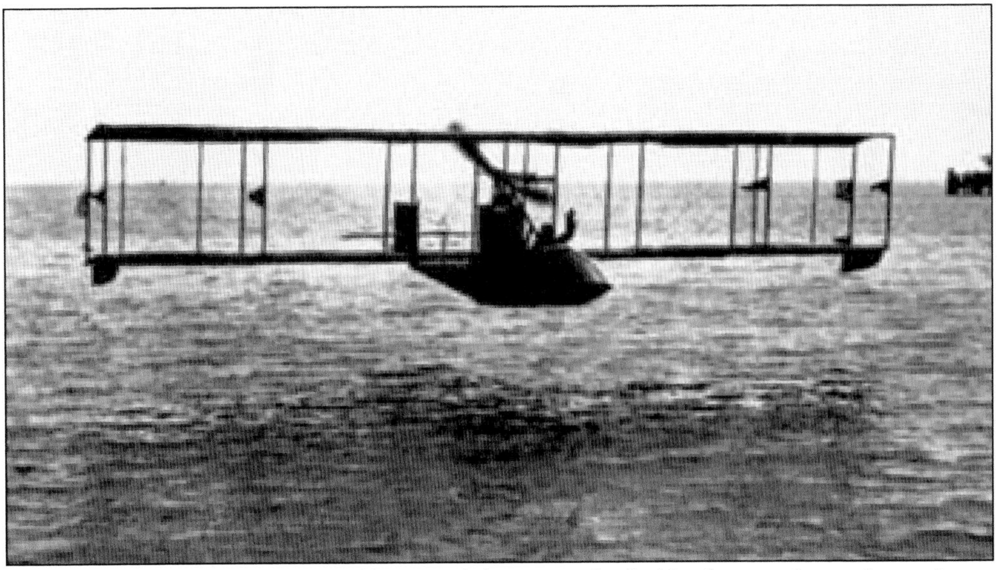

In the dawn of aviation, Florida's wild terrain did not provide ideal landing conditions for airplanes. With Lake County's 1,400 placid lakes providing a natural runway, seaplanes could easily land and take off. In 1914, three years after Glenn Curtiss made the first American seaplane flight, Tony Jannus (the first licensed airline pilot in the United States) landed his Benoist XIV in Lake County waters. (Courtesy of the Florida Photographic Collection.)

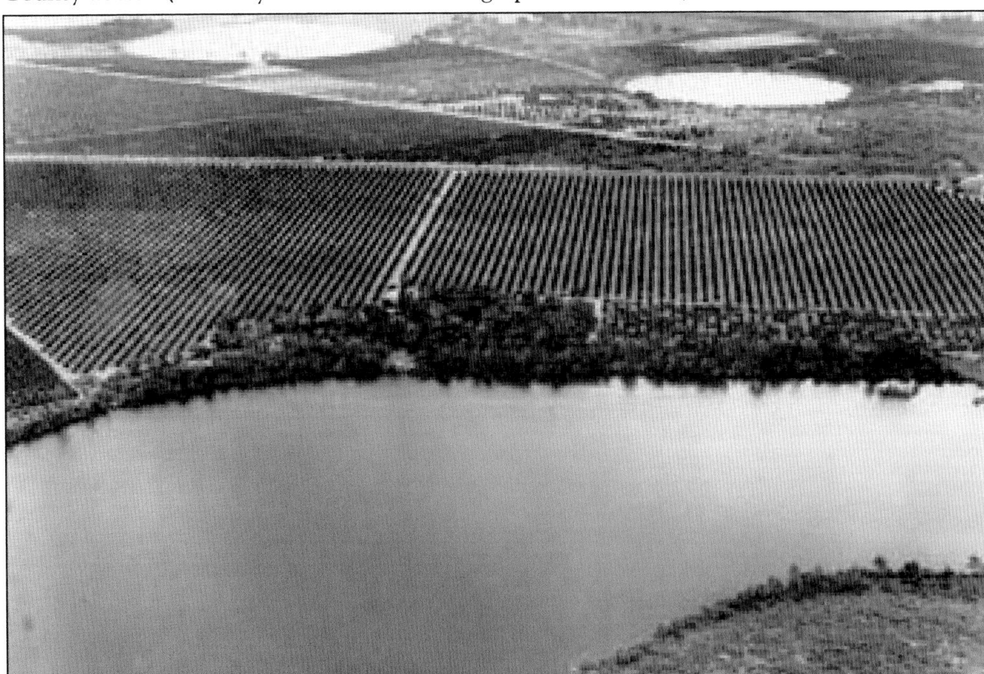

Seen from this 1954 seaplane aerial are the Tavares orange groves of William and Vera Baker from Bucks County, Pennsylvania. The Bakers purchased the groves from James Cooper in 1953. In 1957, the Bakers sold some of their land to the state for the construction of Highway 441. Today, Highway 441 crosses right through the heart of Lake Junietta. (Courtesy of Lura Hall and Dot Dean.)

Four

For Our School, Tavares Bulldogs, We Will Ever Stand

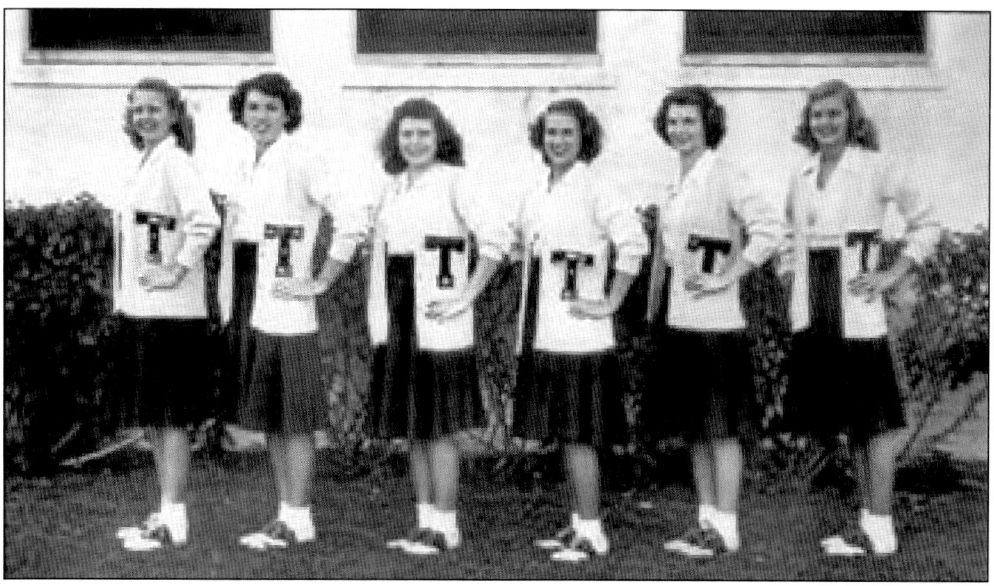

Stand up and cheer! "On the shores of old Lake Dora proudly lies our land; For our school, Tavares Bulldogs, we will ever stand; For our dear old Alma Mater we will sing her praise; And we'll fight for greater glory for our future days!" The words were written by Gwen Pace Hastings and Jean Sperry Higgenbottom, with music by Annie Lisle. These 1949 cheerleaders are, from left to right, Charlene Nichols, Mary Pat Wells, Jackie Floray, Betty Dykes, Juanita Johns, and Eleanor Nichols. (Courtesy of Charlene Nichols King.)

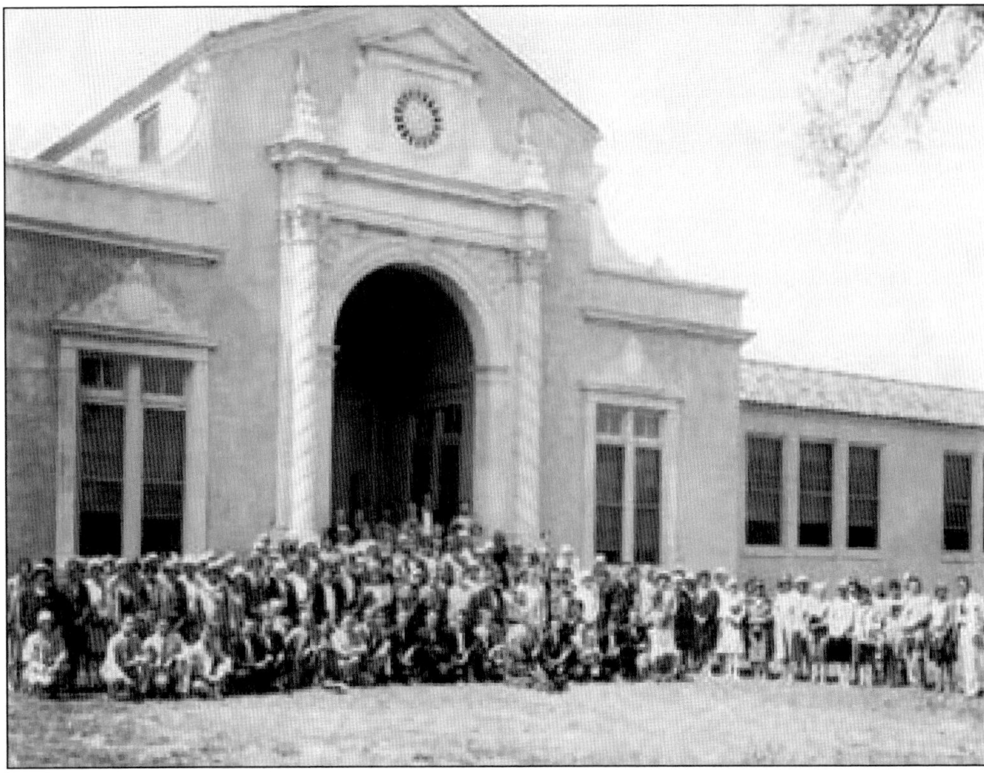

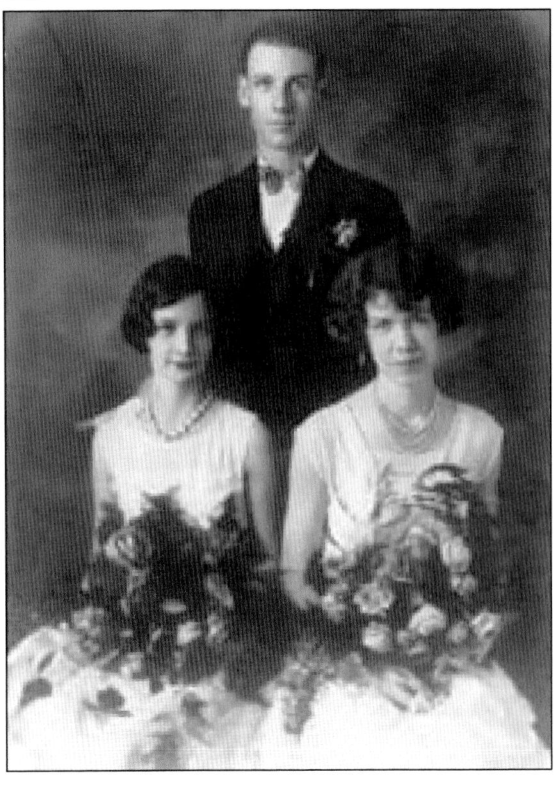

In 1926, Tavares held a dedication for its brand-new and very first high school, located on New Hampshire Avenue. Tavares High School was built in the Spanish Colonial Revival style of architecture, which was popular in the 1920s, especially in Florida. Early principals of Tavares High School were John Miller, Paul Colbert, and Jennings Rou. Rou served as supervising principal of Tavares schools for 25 years. (Courtesy of the Tavares Historical Society.)

Prior to the 1927–1928 school year, junior and senior students were traveling to Eustis High School. With the opening of Tavares High School in 1927, Tavares students had an accredited school that could grant graduates a high school diploma. The first Tavares High School graduating class is, from left to right, (first row) Ruth Fuller Crowder and Dottie Mae Barksdale; (second row) Russell Coven. (Courtesy of Bettye Coven Wilcox.)

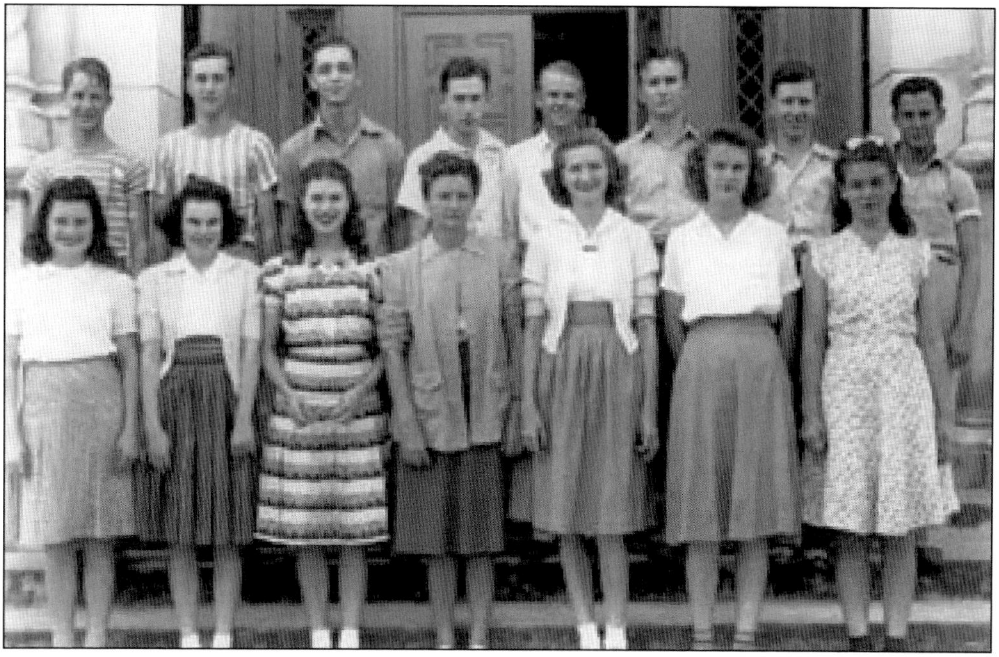

The students here are members of the Tavares High School class of 1941. From left to right are (first row) Dorothy Edmunds, Beulah Wilkerson, Margaret Treadway, teacher MaryJo Key, Lilian Hooten, Jane Breckenridge, and ? Gause; (second row) Cary Peeples, Edward Doss, Lloyd Knight, Myrix Crouch, James Jackson, Travis Messer, Leod "Babe" Coven, and Willie Kemp. (Courtesy of Lura Messer Hall.)

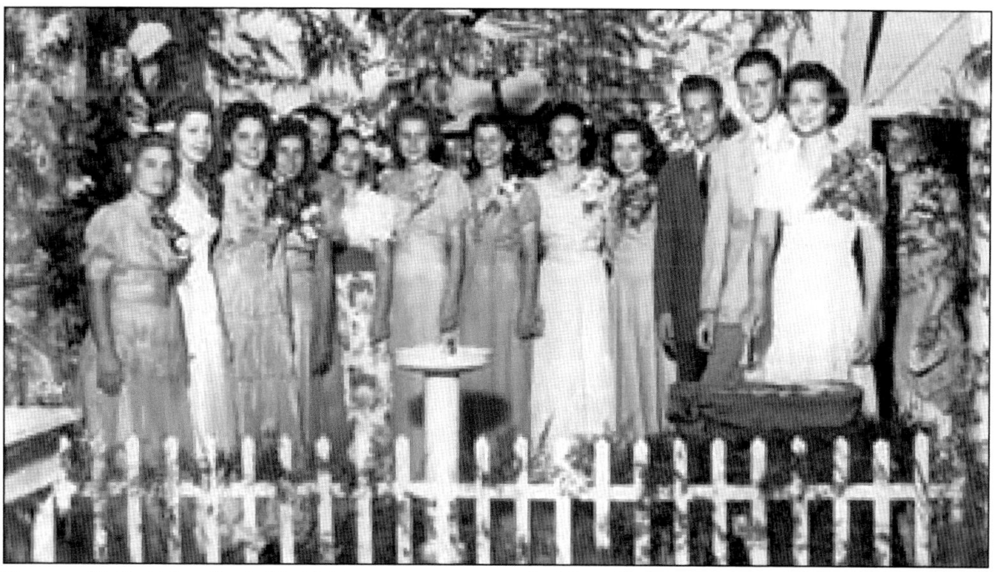

Tavares High School's 1943–1944 junior prom was held at the Pavilion on Lake Dora. From left to right are Frances Gause, Mary Etta Holly, Louise Gay, Lucy Gause, Blanche Daniels, Yvette Averitt, Susan Moorhead, Imogene Messer, Marian Rhea, teacher Ruth McLain, George Revels, Ogden Breckenridge, Frances Nichols, and homeroom mother Henrietta Arrington. Note that George and Ogden were the only two boys because many of the young men were serving in World War II. (Courtesy of Lura Messer Hall.)

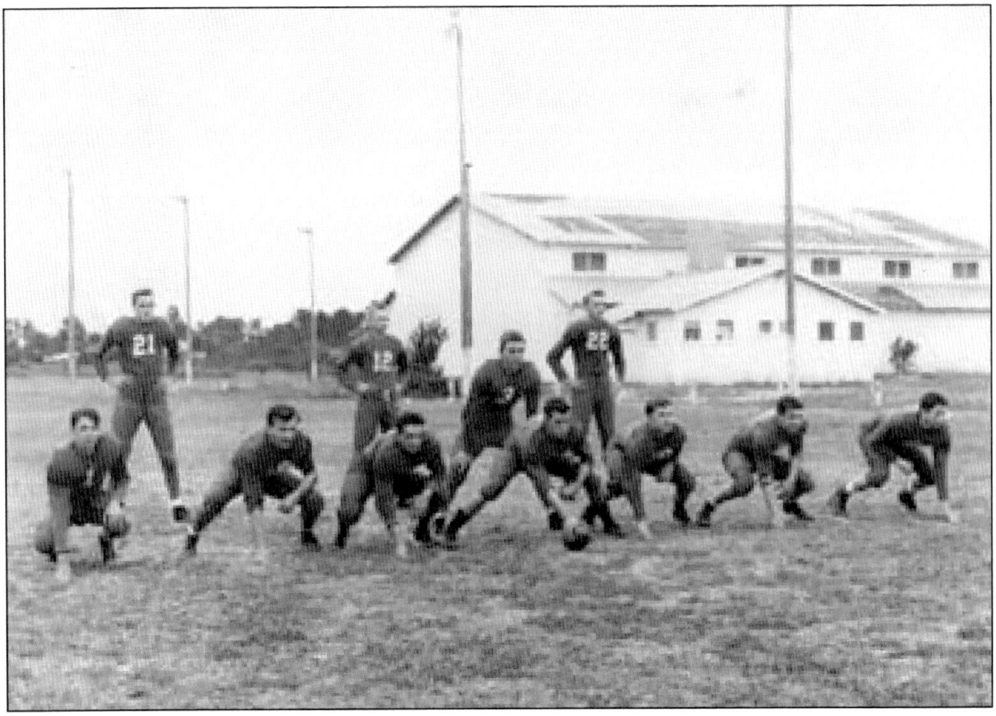

The 1945 Tavares High School football team (above) went undefeated, untied, and unscored upon in one of the best seasons ever recorded in Florida history. The coach was Joe Jenkins. Jack King, who played on both sides of the football as a center and linebacker, says Coach Jenkins was ahead of his time, using flankers and sleepers in his game plan. From left to right are (first row) Harold Holland, James Maddox, John Edmunds, center Jack King, Bernard Dykes, Alvin Nichols, and Bob Hall; (second row) Edward Sirmons, Jack Sperry, Marvin Fretwell, and Dick Pace. The 1930 Tavares football team is pictured below. (Both, courtesy of Charlene Nichols King.)

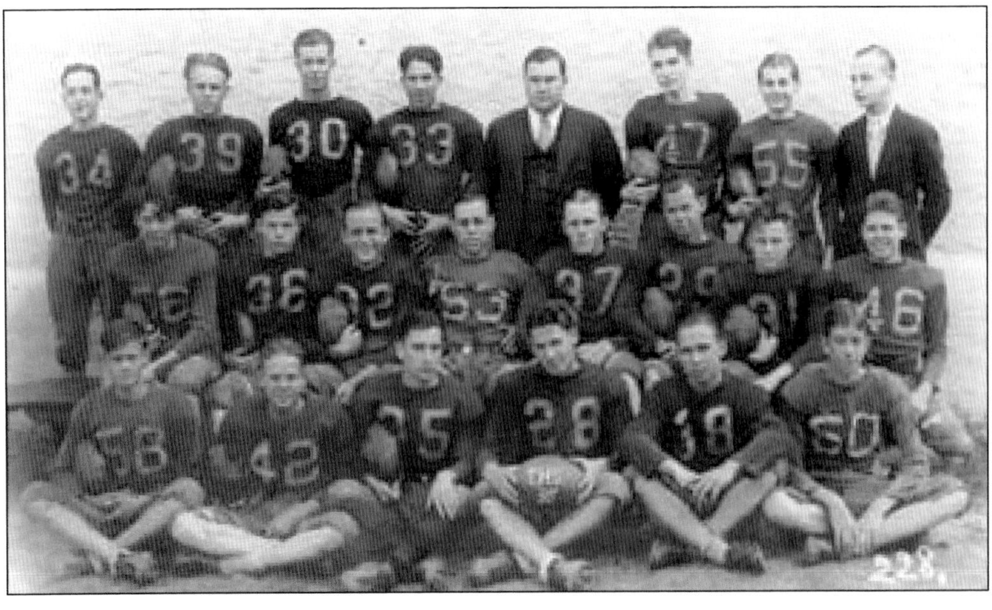

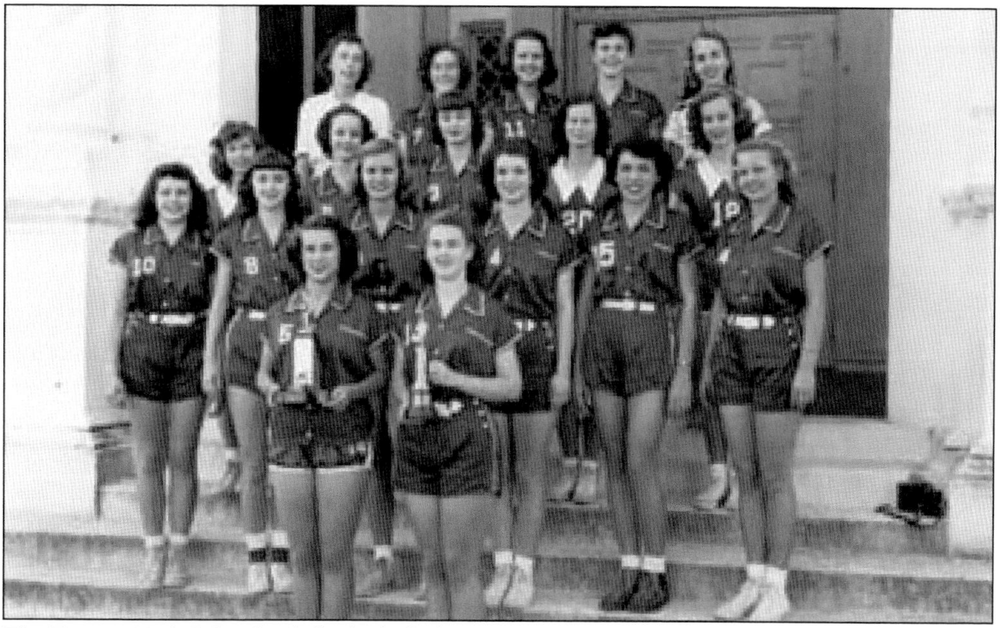

The Tavares High School girls' basketball champions of 1949 are, from left to right, (first row) Betty Dykes and Ellyne Strickland; (second row) Jackie Floray, Dot Wilson, Eleanor Nichols, Juanita Johns, Mary Pat Wells, and Charlene Nichols; (third row) Evelyn Beasly; Barbara Banning, Peg Wilson, Ina Ruth Reaves, and Ruth Marie Notz; (fourth row) coach Mary Whipple, Elva Sears, Beverly Boulware, Joanne Griffin, and Shirley Bassett. (Courtesy of Charlene Nichols King.)

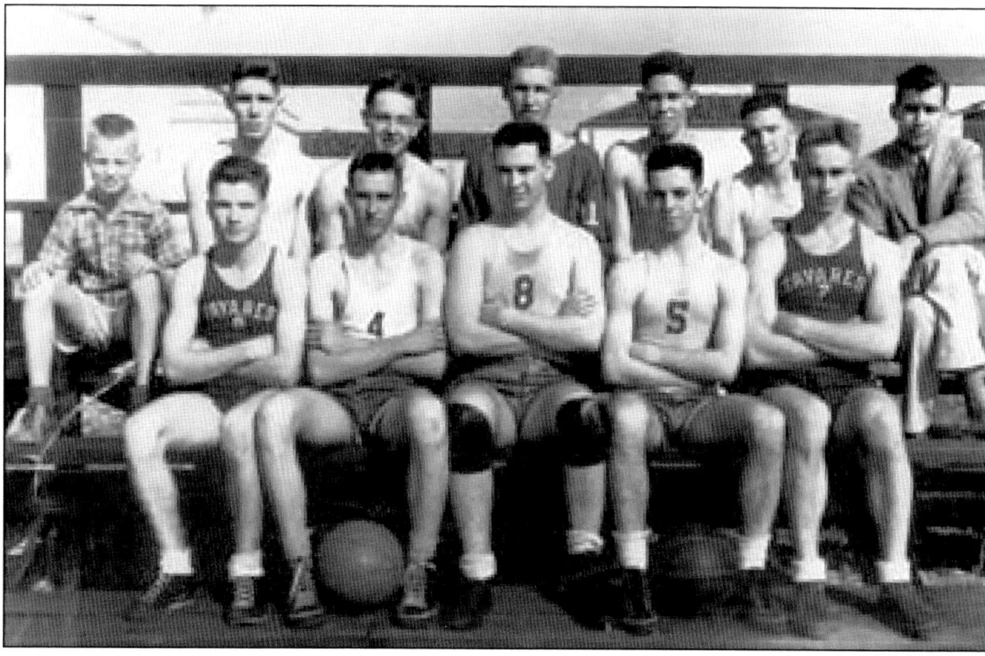

The 1940 Tavares High School men's basketball conference champions from left to right are (first row) Wendall Watson, Edward Doss, Art Hastings, Bill Rogers, and Franklin Johnson; (second row) manager Dick Pace, Joe Duncan, Bob Mulholland, Jack Hooten, Charles Blocker, Bernard Newman, and coach John Davis. (Courtesy of Bettye Coven Wilcox.)

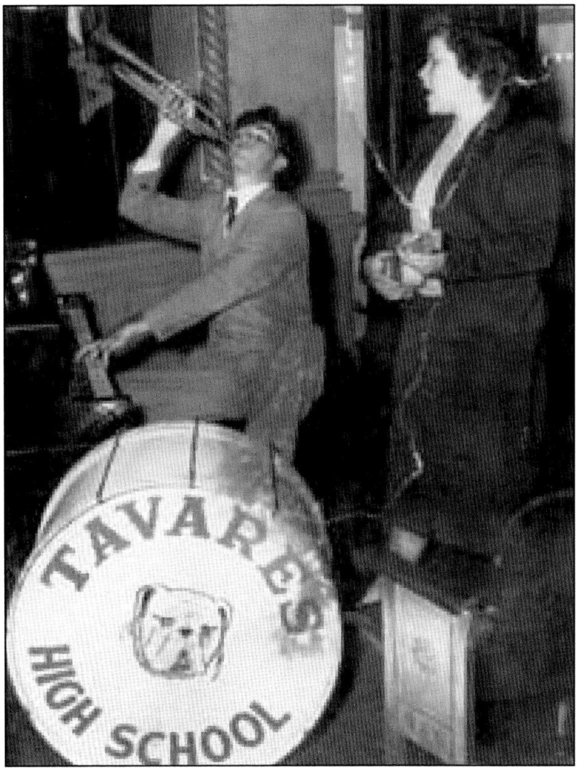

The 1951 Tavares High School yearbook, *Bulldog Tracks*, pictures Herbert Junior Adkison and Lura Messer jamming in the school auditorium. Adkison (playing the trumpet, piano, and drum simultaneously) and Messer were chosen as the 1951 Senior Superlatives "most talented." Adkison, though, actually could not play any of these instruments. Because of his nature to talk nonstop, under his yearbook picture is the quote, "Have I said enough, or shall I go on?" (Courtesy of Lura Messer Hall.)

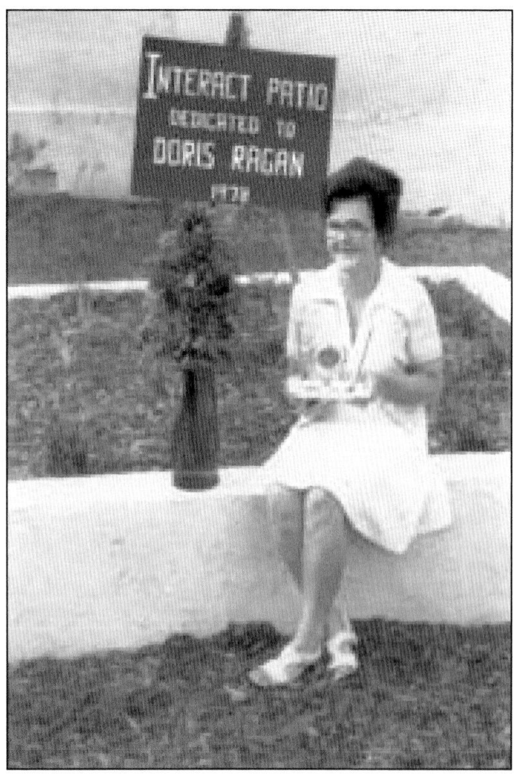

A random drop of a nickel on the Florida map brought educator Doris McCall Ragan from her teaching job in Kentucky to Tavares. Arriving in 1946, Doris was hired by Tavares High School principal Jennings Rou. Doris spent the majority of her teaching career at the high school, retiring from full-time teaching in 1981. Doris is an accredited master gardener. In 1981 and 2002, Doris Ragan Day was proclaimed by the mayor. (Courtesy of Doris McCall Ragan.)

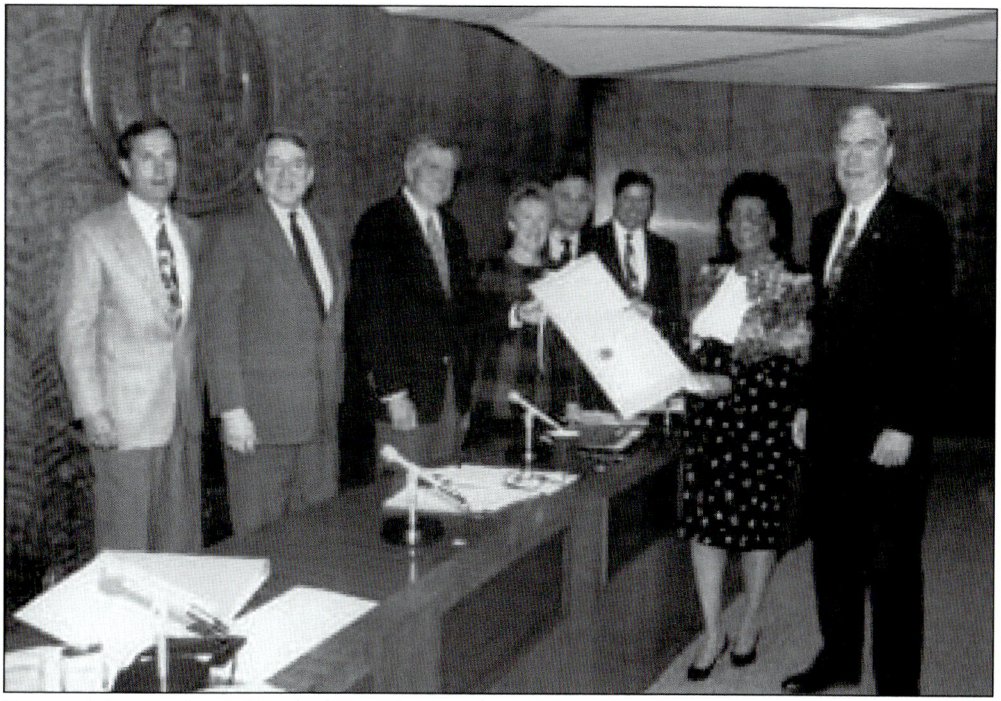

Bennye Montine Jones-Kinsler began her teaching career in Lake County, Florida, in 1932, with the majority of her teaching career being spent in Tavares. She retired from teaching in 1992 after nearly 60 years. Upon her retirement, Bennye Kinsler was recognized and honored by Florida governor Lawton Chiles (above, third from left) and the Florida legislature with a resolution as having taught school longer than any other individual in Florida school history. She spent 35 years as principal and teacher at Harrison Academy, renamed Cromartie Elementary School. Bennye, who passed away in 1999, has received many honors throughout her life. In 2002, she was elected to the Lake County Women's Hall of Fame and a wing at Tavares Elementary School was named in her honor. Bennye Kinsler is pictured below with her 1973–1974 Tavares Elementary School second-grade class. (Both, courtesy of Jackie Kinsler.)

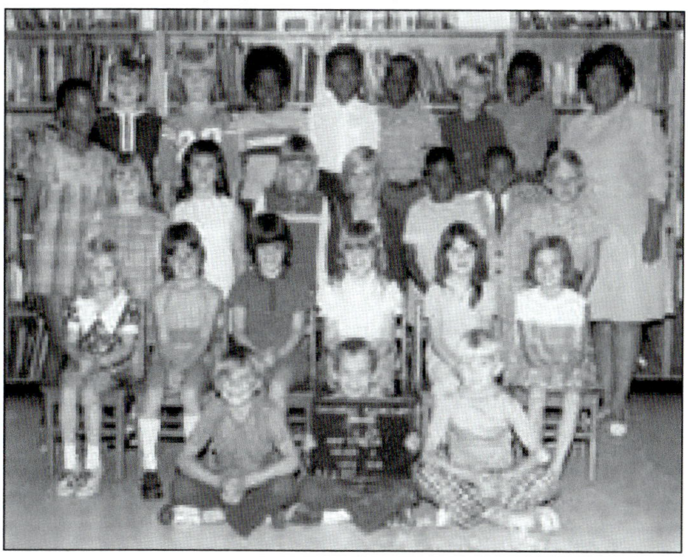

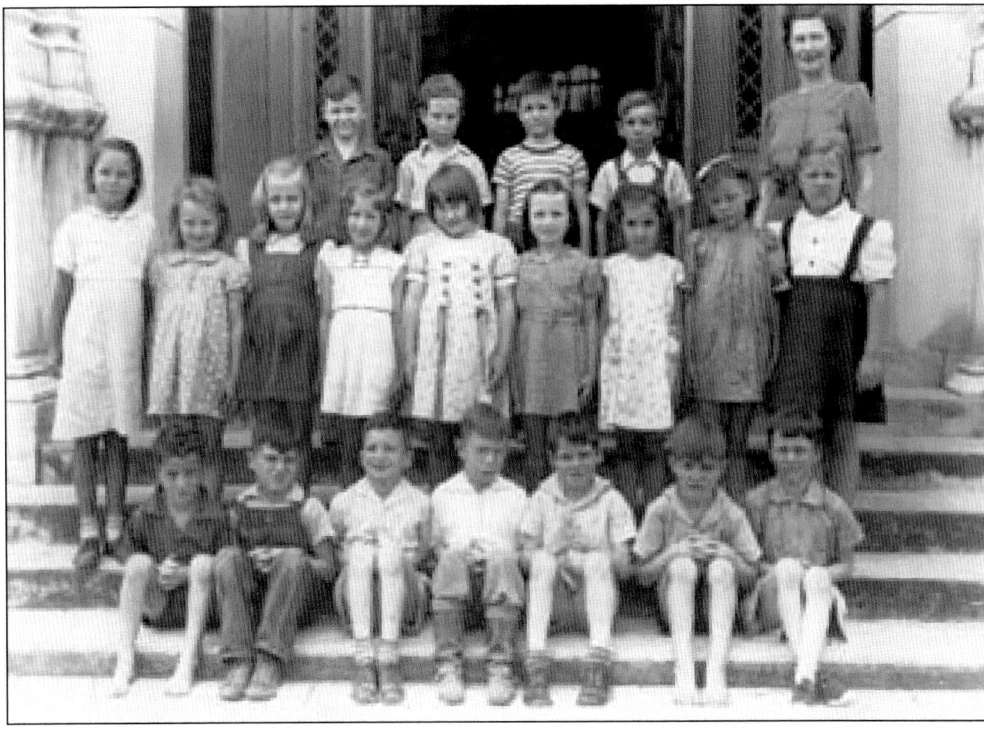

The 1940–1941 second-grade glass and its teacher, from left to right, are (first row) Dale Breedlove, Allen Keller, David McGee, Dave Treadway, Gene Paul, Dan English, and Franklin Holley; (second row) Daisy Watson, Virginia Barnhill, Shirley Bassett, unidentified, Lura Messer, Alice Coven, Margie ?, Anna Lee Holley, and Rosemary ?; (third row) Bill Burleigh, Fred Conner, two unidentified, and teacher Montine Roberts. (Courtesy of Lura Messer Hall.)

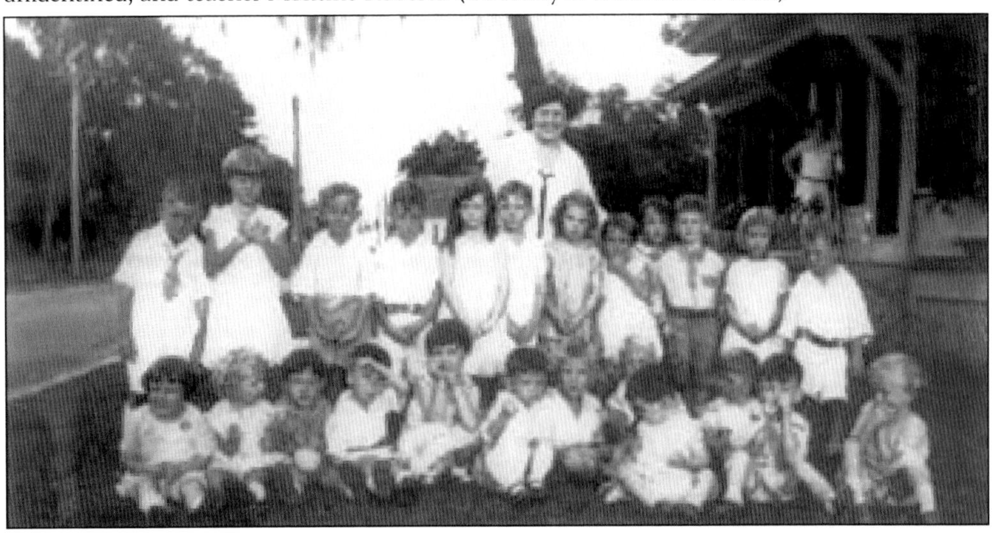

Mrs. DeWeese's 1928 kindergarten class members had not yet eaten any birthday cake prior to having their picture taken. Bettye Coven (first row, fourth from right) is preoccupied trying to catch a critter crawling in the grass. Today, when Bettye drives around Tavares, she reminisces about her father, builder Leo Coven. She says, "Seeing all the buildings my dad built, which are still standing, is like seeing a monument to him." (Courtesy of Bettye Coven Wilcox.)

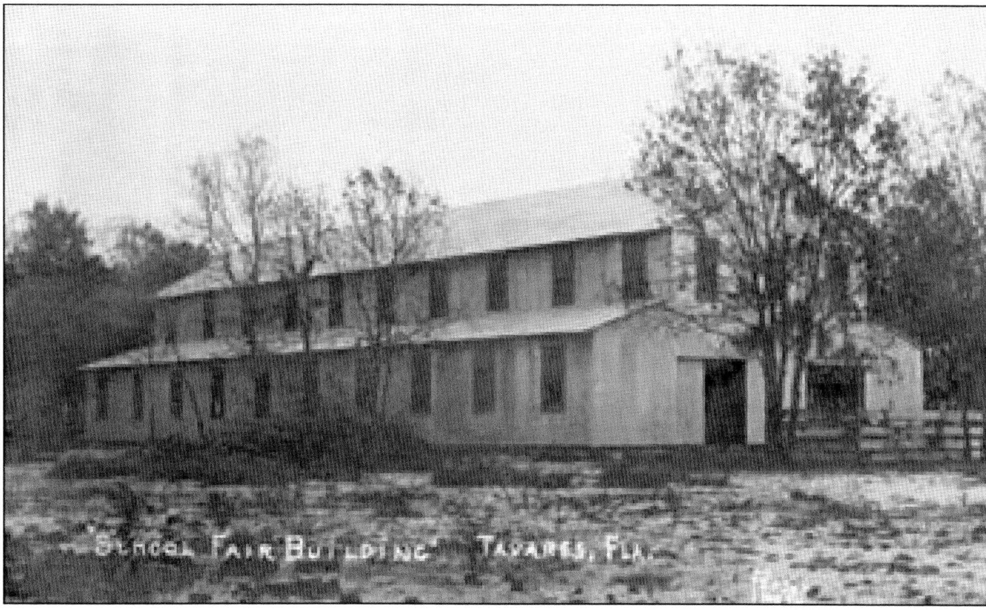

In 1913, the first school fair in Lake County was held in Tavares. This structure was the only school fair building in the United States. It was built through the influence and efforts of the first traveling teacher, Flora H. Brown. In 1915, the Tavares & Gulf Railroad ran a train from Groveland and Mascotte to Tavares so the children could go to the fair. They rode in the boxcars. (Courtesy of the Tavares Historical Society.)

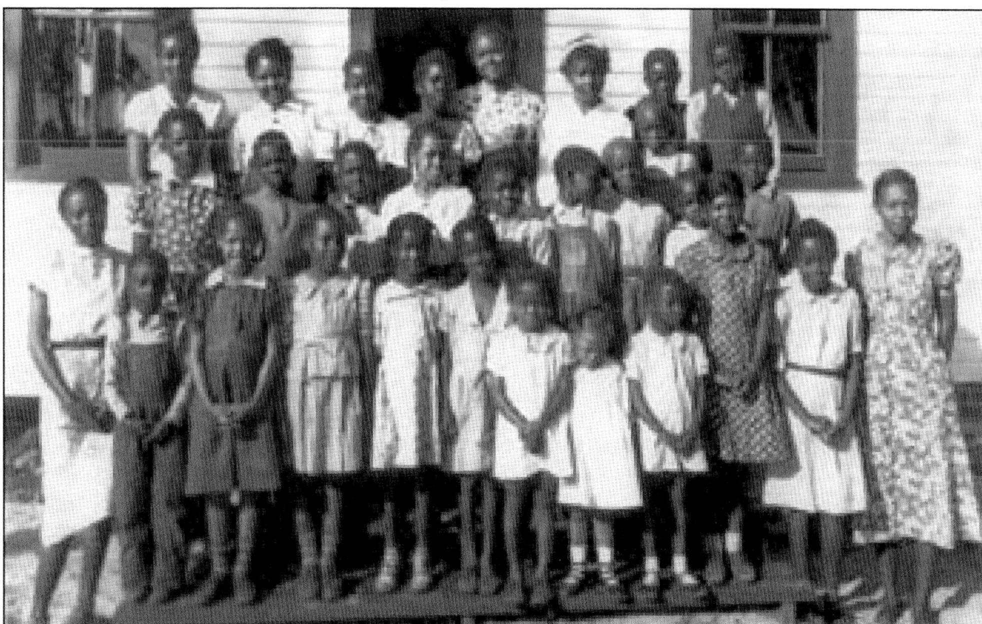

A school for black children was established in Tavares on March 14, 1887. At that time, the children had been attending school at Mount Moriah Church in Lane Park. In about 1937, this school was built and was originally known as the Tavares Colored School. Later it was called Harrison Academy and then was changed to Cromartie Elementary, in honor of Reed Cromartie. (Courtesy of the Tavares Historical Society.)

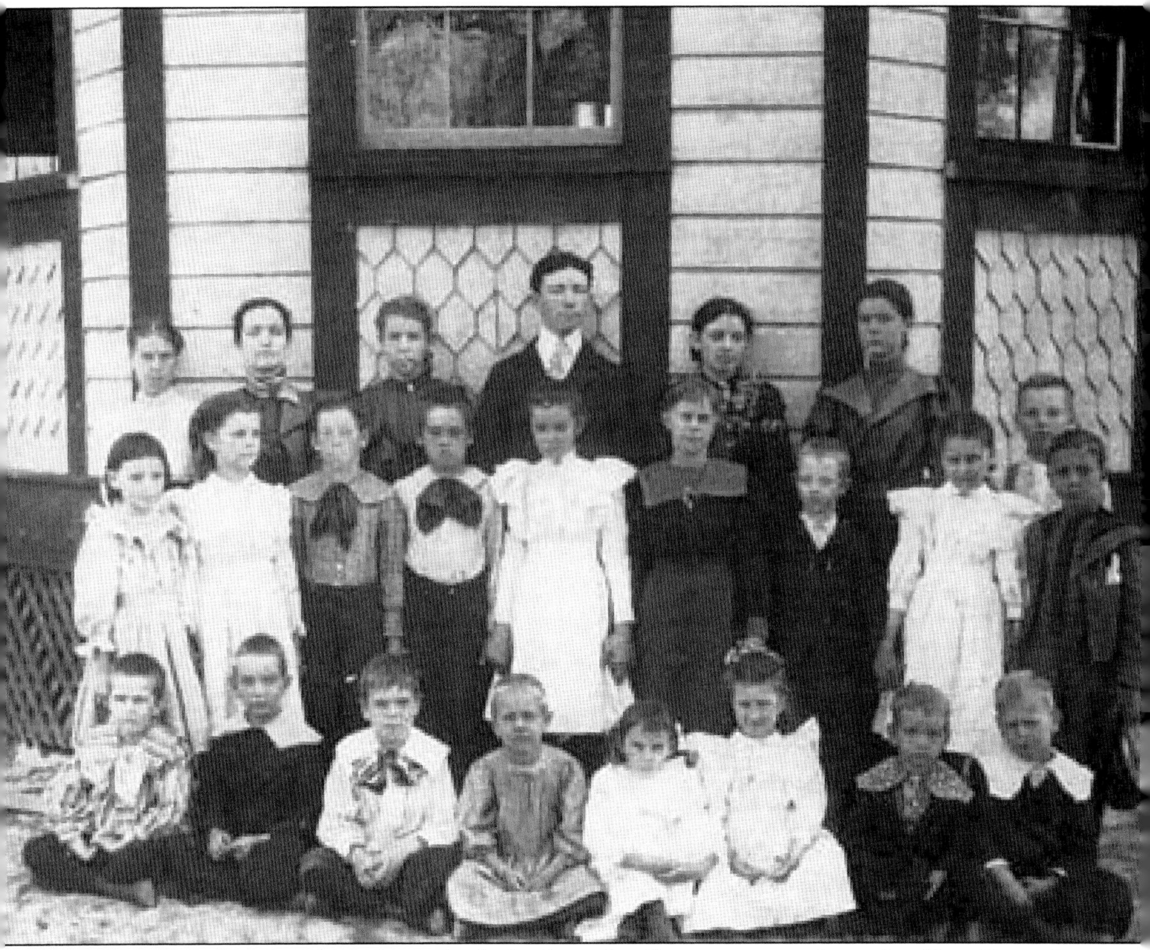

In 1886, Major St. Clair Abrams built the first schoolhouse in town, located at New Hampshire Avenue and Ianthe Street. The school was a two-story, wood-frame building with a belfry. There was an auditorium on the second floor and two classrooms on the first floor. The auditorium was used for town meetings and club and lodge meetings. The first floor was also used as a Sunday school. Students from all grade levels attended this school. Gertrude "Miss Gertie" Gates was the teacher for many years. Kate Lacey, Maud Wakelin, and Lucille Tally were some of the teachers who taught at this first school. Tavares's original schoolhouse was used until 1916, when a new elementary school was built. The entire school body is shown in this 1897 photograph. From left to right are (first row) Wilbur Northrup, Walter Northrup, Ethel Lanier, and five unidentified; (second row) Dolly Duncan, Ruth Newell, Leonard Duncan, unidentified, Lena Nutt, Franca Burleigh, Albert Donaldson, Bonnie Bell, and unidentified; (third row) Irma Lanier, teacher Gertrude Gates, Margaret Burleigh, Harry Duncan, Marian Duncan, Beth Burleigh, and Fred Donaldson. (Courtesy of the Tavares Historical Society.)

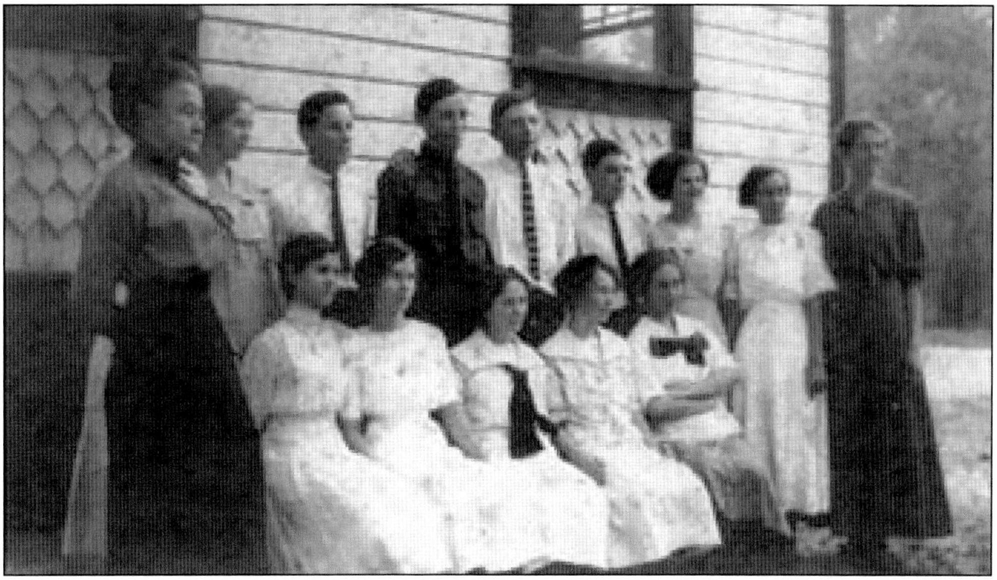

Mrs. Stivender's 1911–1912 junior high class members are, from left to right, (first row) Hazel Entz, Annabel Scott, Mary Cassady, Hattie Miller, and Clara Nutt; (second row) Mrs. Stivender, Margie Entz (obstructed), Lena Nutt, Carl Duncan, Wyeth Duncan, Raleigh Belknap, Allen Coven, Evelyn Shaffer, Nellie Hux, and teacher Essie Long. This class photograph was taken at the original 1887 schoolhouse. (Courtesy of the Tavares Historical Society.)

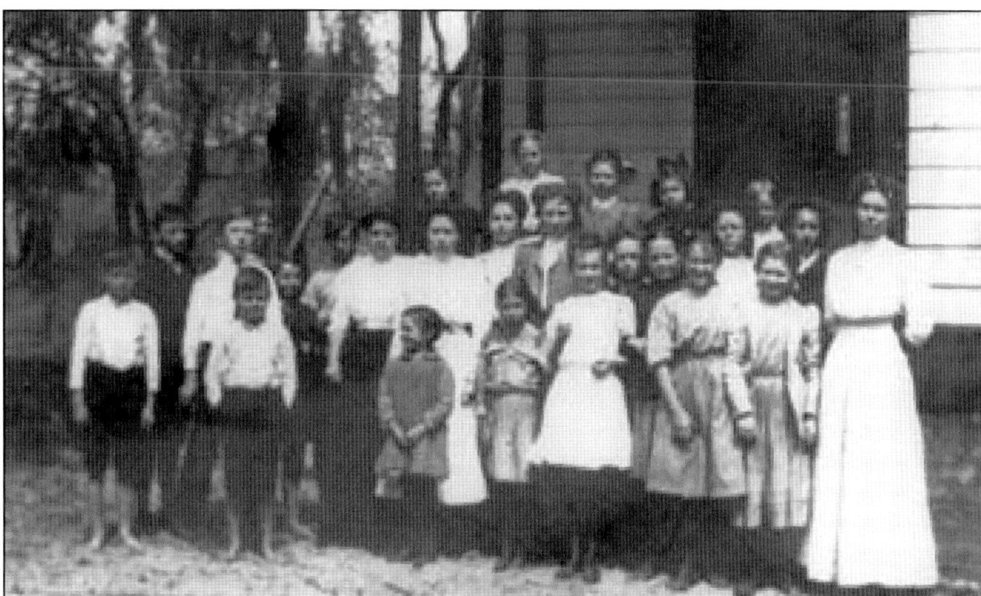

Essie Long (right) was born in Lake County and came to Tavares in 1907. For 15 years, she served as a teacher in Tavares. Long graduated from Florida State College for Women, where she majored in Greek and Latin. She was a skilled musician at the organ and piano. In 1913, Long married Leonard Duncan. (Courtesy of Harryette Anne Duncan.)

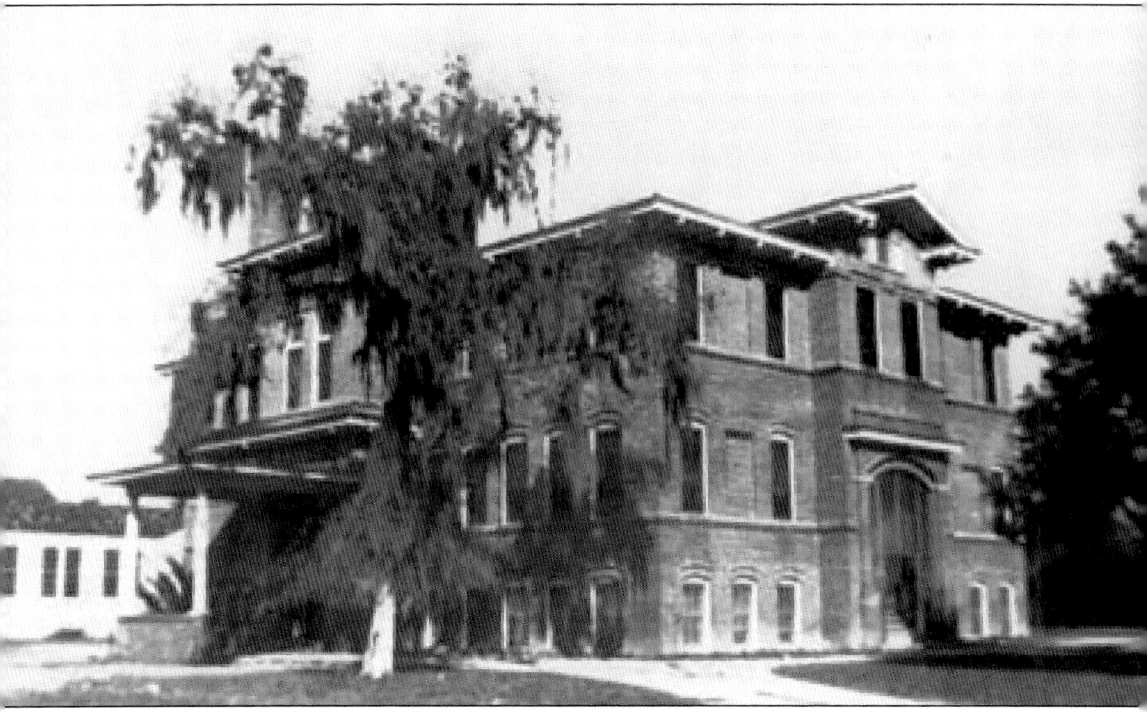

In 1916, the old wooden schoolhouse on Ianthe Street was replaced by a new, three-story, redbrick building on the southeast corner of the campus facing New Hampshire Avenue. The first floor was a half basement where the lunchroom was located. The second floor had four classrooms, and the third floor had two classrooms and an auditorium. During renovations, sometime after the new high school was built in 1926, the principal's office and library were added to the second floor. The auditorium was divided into two classrooms, and a new lunchroom was built. During World War II, the third floor was blocked off for reasons unknown to the students. After the war, the third floor was refurbished and reopened. After the new elementary school was built, this school was used for a library and storage area for the school district before it was razed in 1982 after a fire damaged the second floor. (Courtesy of Lura Messer Hall.)

Five

The Friendly Circle of Tavares

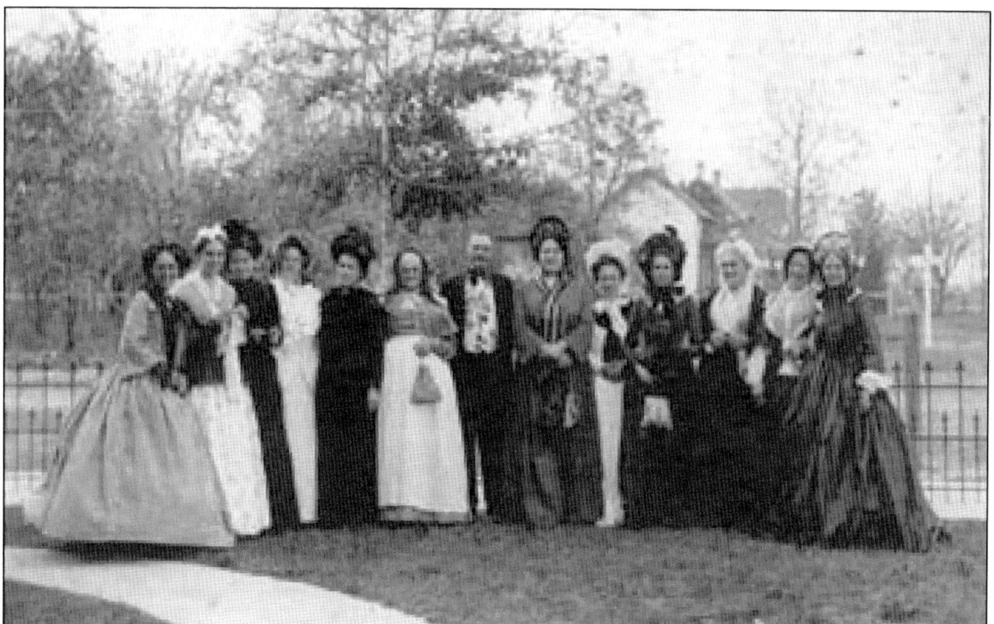

From the time Tavares was established, the citizens were a close-knit community. Picnics, parades, celebrations, and festivals were frequent. Clubs and organizations were formed. The Back Numbers, in this 1911 photograph, were a Tavares theatrical group of the early 1900s that performed at the Opera House on Irma Street. (Courtesy of the Tavares Historical Society.)

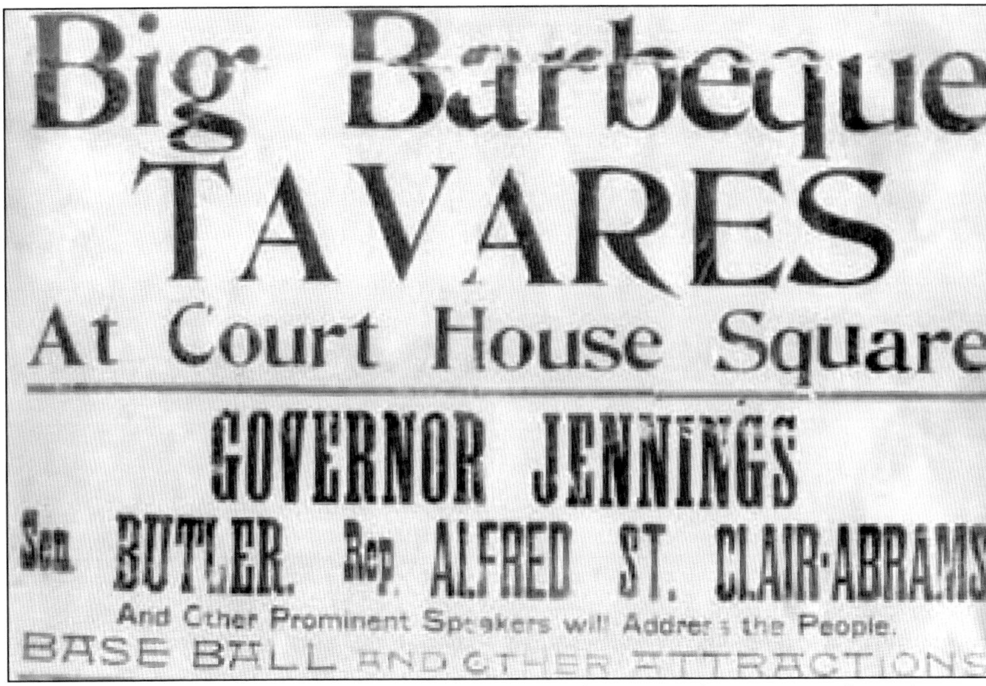

The "Glorious Fourth" was first staged on July 4, 1893, and it remained a Tavares tradition for many years. In 1893, Tavareans invited the whole county to celebrate the Fourth of July with them. Huge posters were placed throughout the county inviting people to bring their picnic baskets and attend a big barbecue at the Courthouse Square. A band was brought in from Orlando. A special flag was ordered for the occasion, which arrived on July 3. The flag was "no larger than a handkerchief," so four ladies—the Misses Northrup, Duncan, Peet, and Hammond—worked diligently through the night to make a suitable flag. Almost 3,000 people attended. In 1903, Gov. William Sherman Jennings, Sen. P.W. Butler, and Rep. Alfred St. Clair Abrams were the featured speakers at the "Glorious Fourth" celebration. (Both, courtesy of the Tavares Historical Society.)

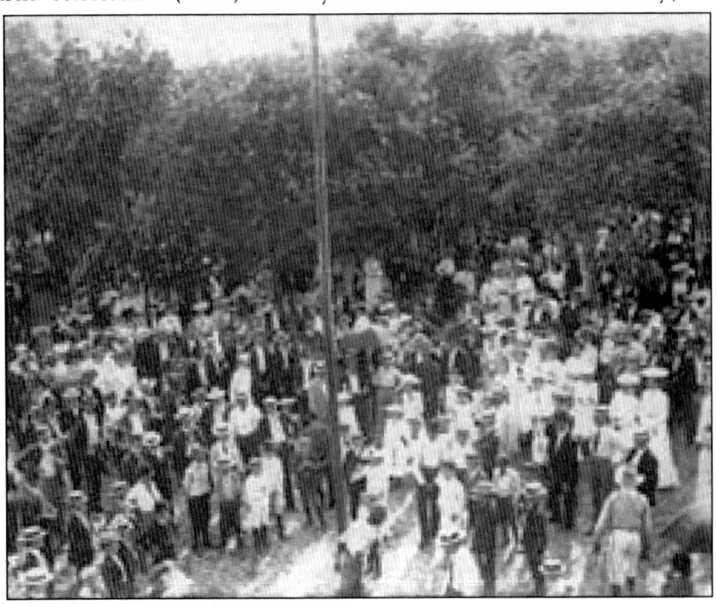

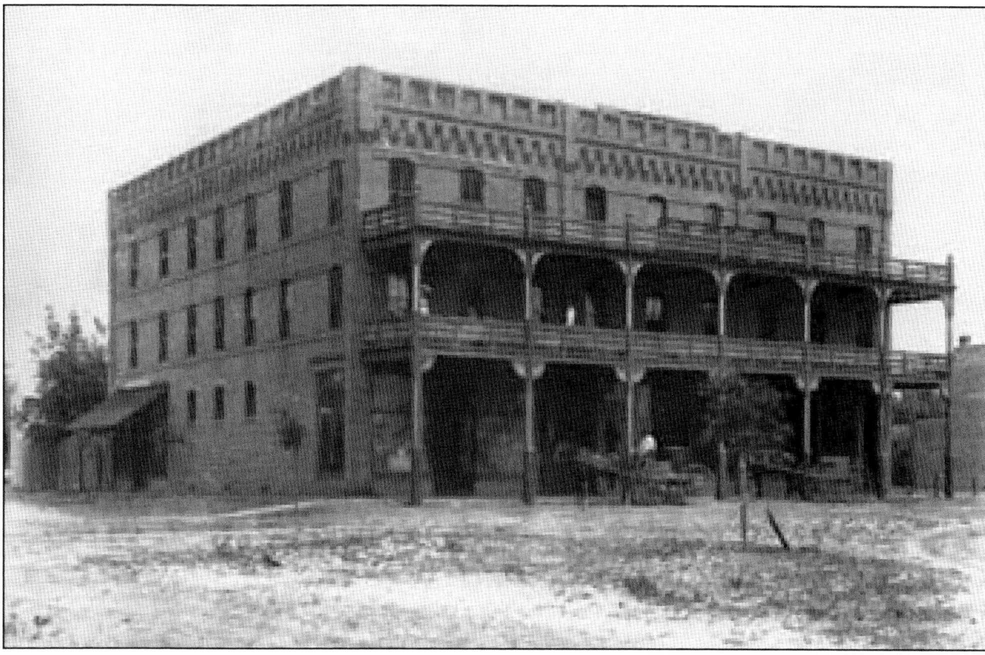

With the loss of the Peninsular Hotel, the Tavares House, and two boardinghouses in the 1888 fire, a brick office building under construction on Main Street became the Osceola Hotel. The hotel, which featured a popular restaurant, was built by Charles Sinclair. The building changed hands many times over the years, including ownership by Frank Jones and Robert Lee Nutt. Nutt was the vice president of the Bank of Tavares, located at the hotel. In 1927, the Osceola Hotel became the Biltavern. The hotel closed in 1929 after the stock market crash and the collapse of the Florida land boom. Later, the building was remodeled into stores and apartments. From 1980 through 1992, the building was used as Tavares City Hall and then razed for the new city hall, which opened in December 1993. (Both, courtesy of the Tavares Historical Society.)

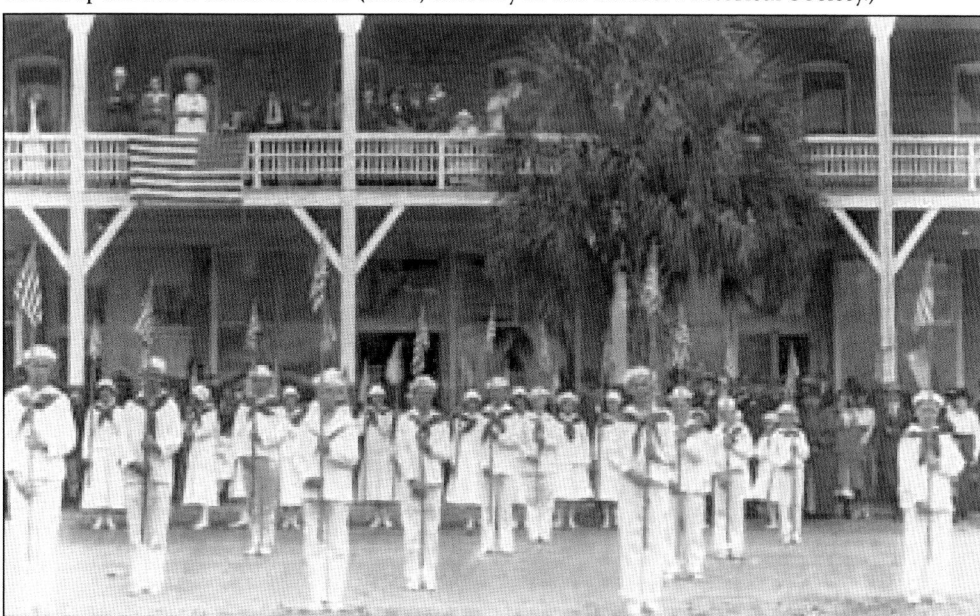

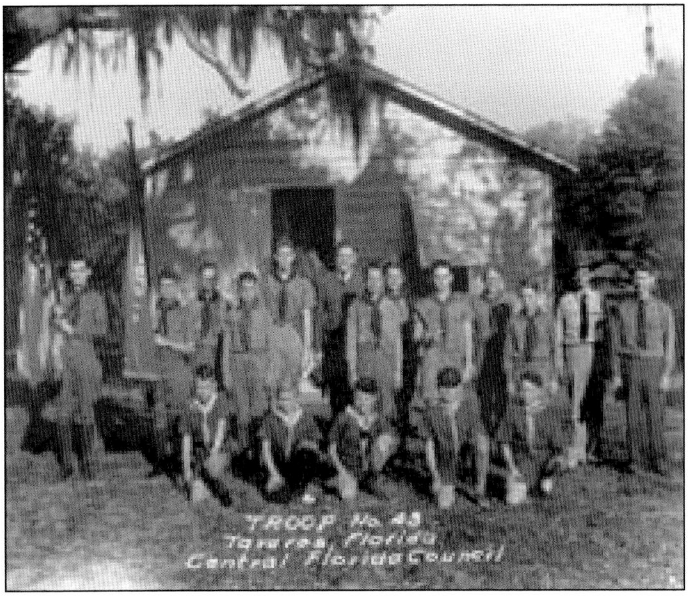

In 1912, Guilford Wakelin established the Tavares Boy Scouts, the first troop in Florida. Pictured is Tavares Troop 43 around 1935. From left to right are (first row) Alvin Nichols, Marvin Fratwell, Dick Pace, Ed Sirmons, and Jack Sperry; (second row) Tommy Robertson, J.N. Clark, Earl Griggs, Robert Jackson, Joe Duncan, unidentified, Carey Peeples, Babe Coven, Bill Rogers, James Jackson, Ed Gay, Truman Moorhead, and Johnathan Smith. (Courtesy of the Tavares Historical Society.)

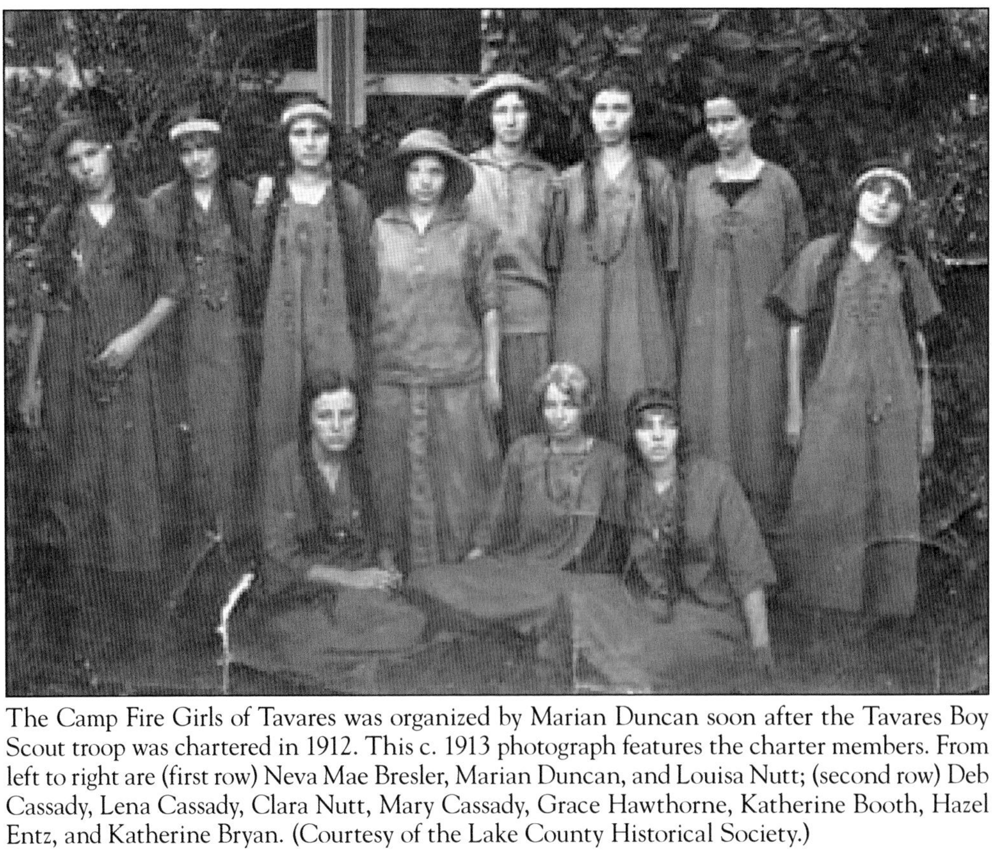

The Camp Fire Girls of Tavares was organized by Marian Duncan soon after the Tavares Boy Scout troop was chartered in 1912. This c. 1913 photograph features the charter members. From left to right are (first row) Neva Mae Bresler, Marian Duncan, and Louisa Nutt; (second row) Deb Cassady, Lena Cassady, Clara Nutt, Mary Cassady, Grace Hawthorne, Katherine Booth, Hazel Entz, and Katherine Bryan. (Courtesy of the Lake County Historical Society.)

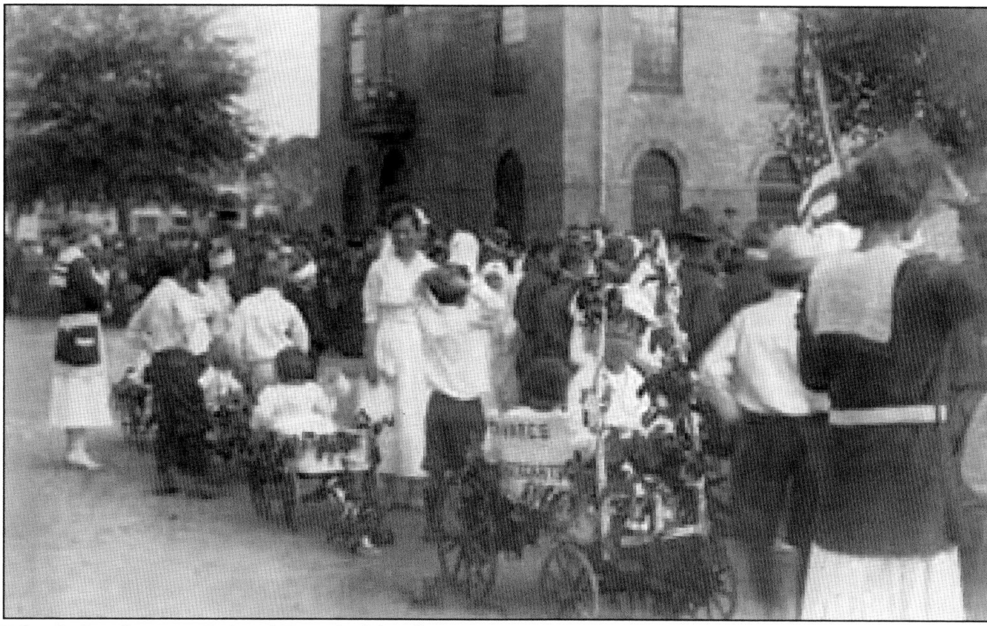

The Lake County School Fair, held February 26–28, 1919, was billed as the "War-Time Fair." This photograph depicts the great "Get-Together" by the Pioneer Building. The fair committee paid close attention to the needs overseas and planned for Red Cross work wherever it could be done. The various prizes given at the fair appealed to the children's patriotism. (Courtesy of the Lake County Historical Society.)

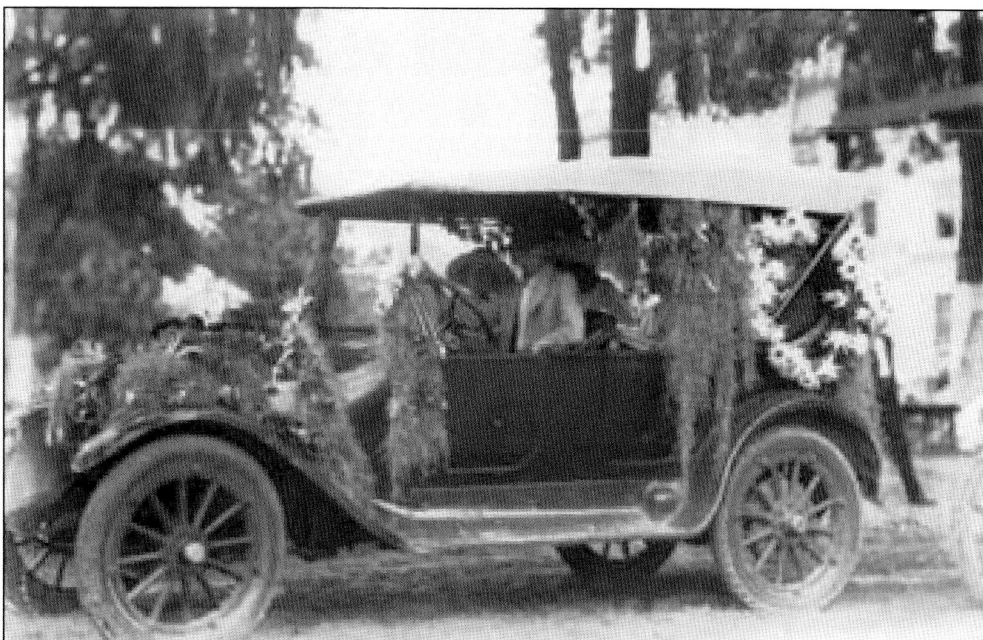

This decorated Dodge touring car is driving in the 1926 4-H Club grand march and parade. 4-H clubs met in the schools, where agricultural agents taught the boys about livestock and farming. Home demonstration agents taught the girls economics and projects associated with the home and family. (Courtesy of Charlene Nichols King.)

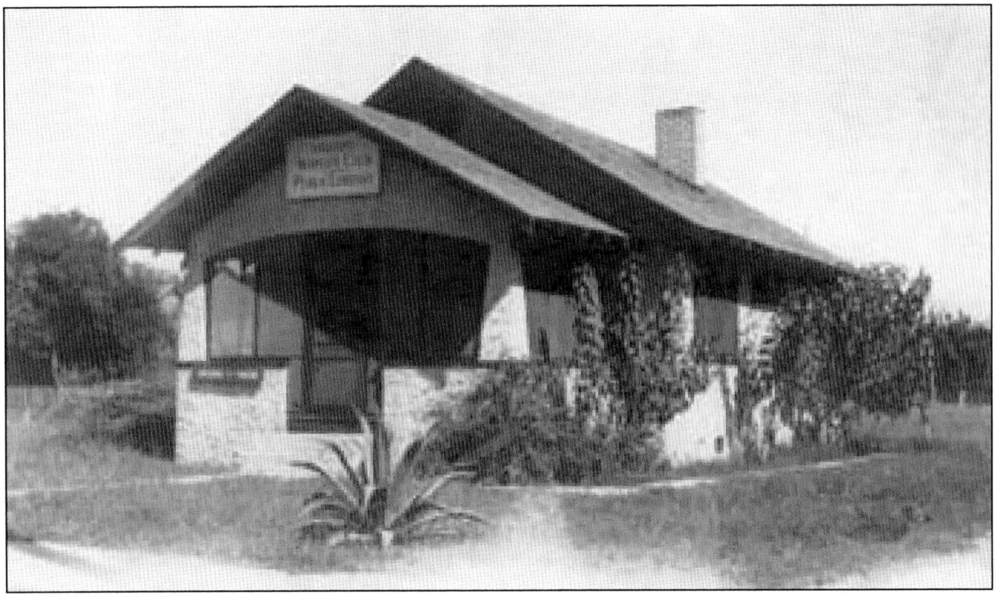

The Tavares Woman's Club was organized in 1915. The club established the city's first public library at the corner of Maud Street and St. Clair Abrams Avenue. The woman's club was influential in the protection of the cypress trees along the Dora Canal, which were being logged. In May 2011, after 96 years, the Tavares Woman's Club held their last meeting. (Courtesy of Charlene Nichols King.)

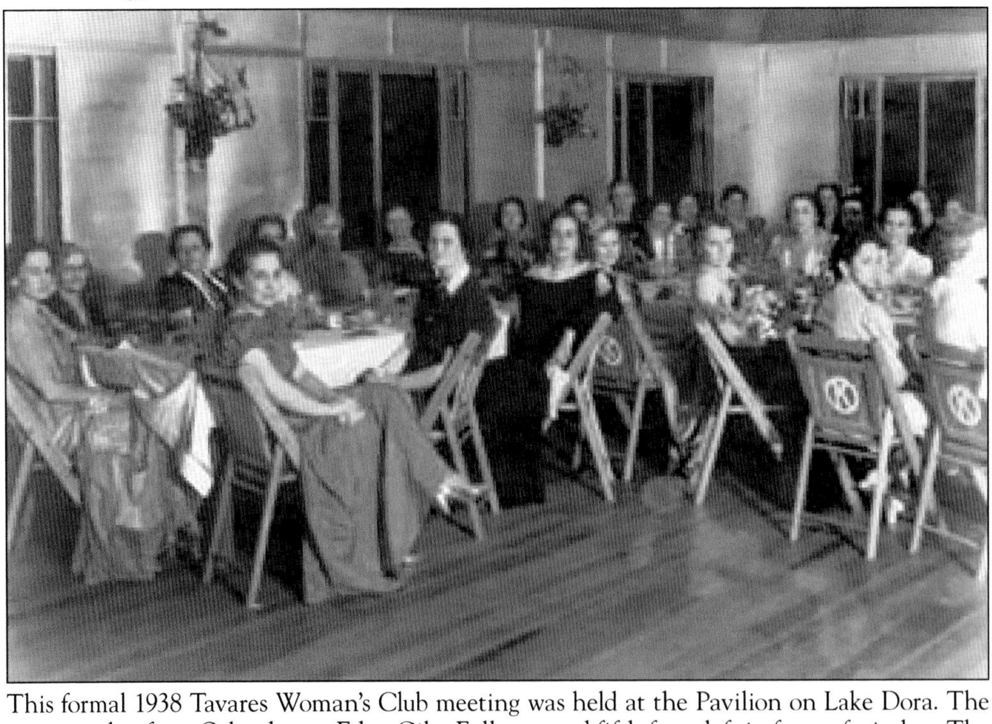

This formal 1938 Tavares Woman's Club meeting was held at the Pavilion on Lake Dora. The guest speaker from Orlando was Edna Giles Fuller, seated fifth from left in front of window. The Tavares Woman's Club had 44 different presidents. Effie Treadway, seated to Fuller's right, served as president five times. (Courtesy of Harryette Anne Duncan.)

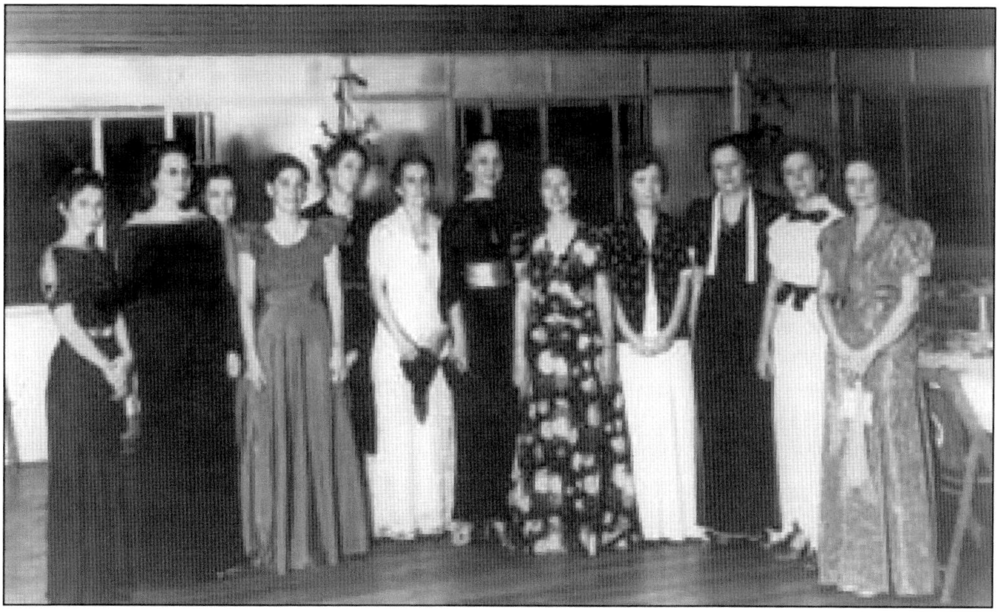

The 1938 officers of the Tavares Woman's Club are, from left to right, Kathryn Chester, Lilly Leary, Dora Hunter, Mrs. Magie, Marie King, Lucille Tally, Leola Pace, Peggy Duncan, Elizabeth Booth, Dolly Rogers, Bena Wells, and Ann Lee Duncan. (Courtesy of Harryette Anne Duncan.)

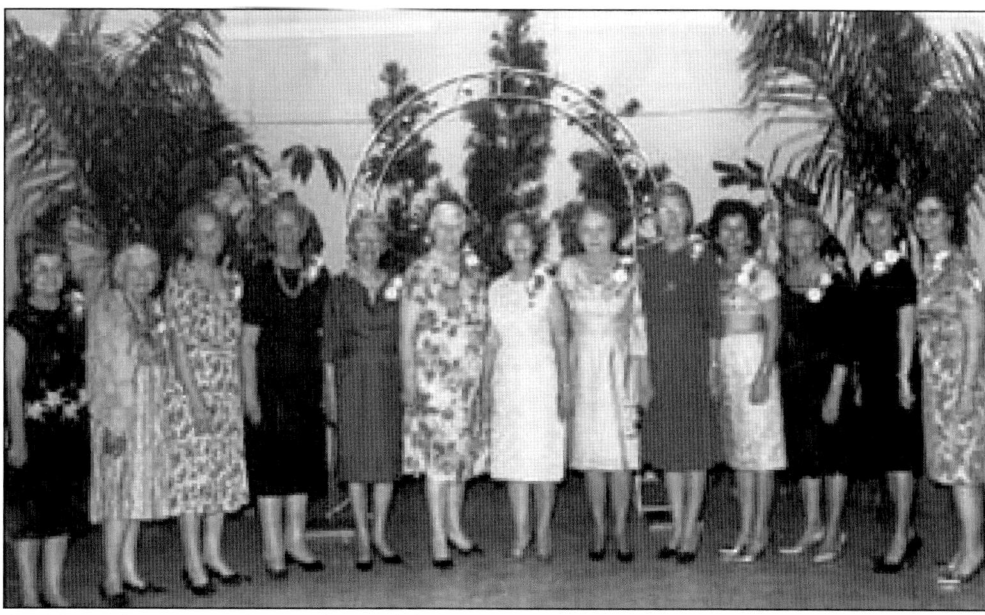

On November 12, 1965, presidents of the Tavares Woman's Club have their picture taken on the occasion of the club's 50th anniversary. From left to right are Mrs. Don Peabody of Miami, Marian Duncan, Beth Burleigh, Pearl Cullens, Lucille Tally, Effie Treadway, Peggy Roth, Dolly Rogers, Marie King, Catherine Chester, Bena Wells, Peggy Mathias, and Harriet Sims. (Courtesy of Charlene Nichols King.)

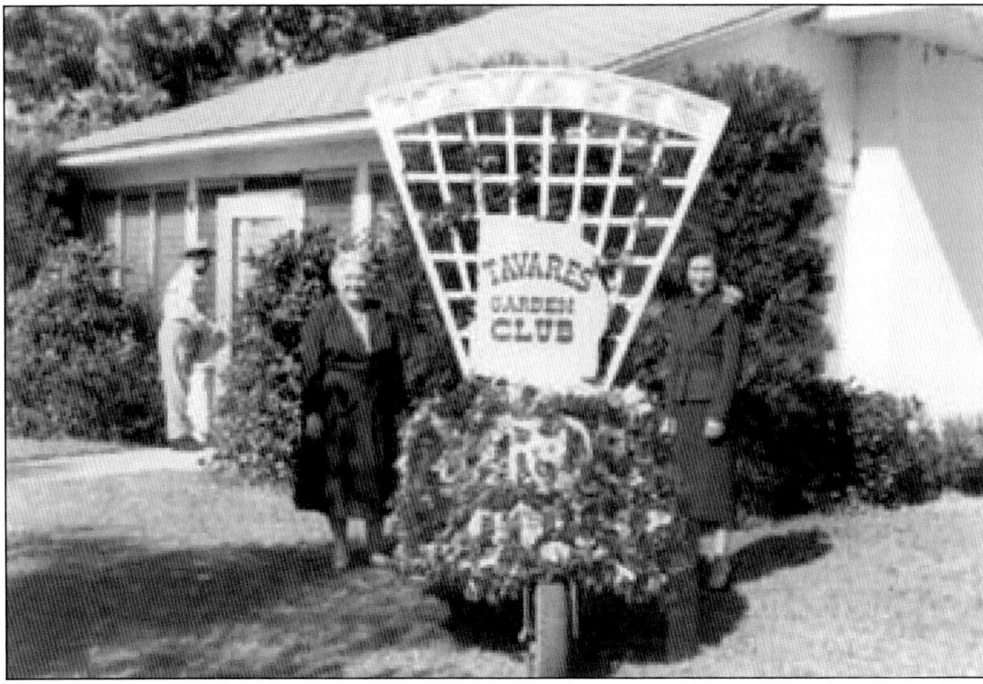

The Tavares Garden Club was organized on January 22, 1947, with 40 charter members. Bena Wells served as the club's first president. In her president's report for 1954–1956, Elizabeth Austin says the greatest achievement of that period was the fulfillment of a dream: a clubhouse of their own. (Courtesy of the Tavares Historical Society.)

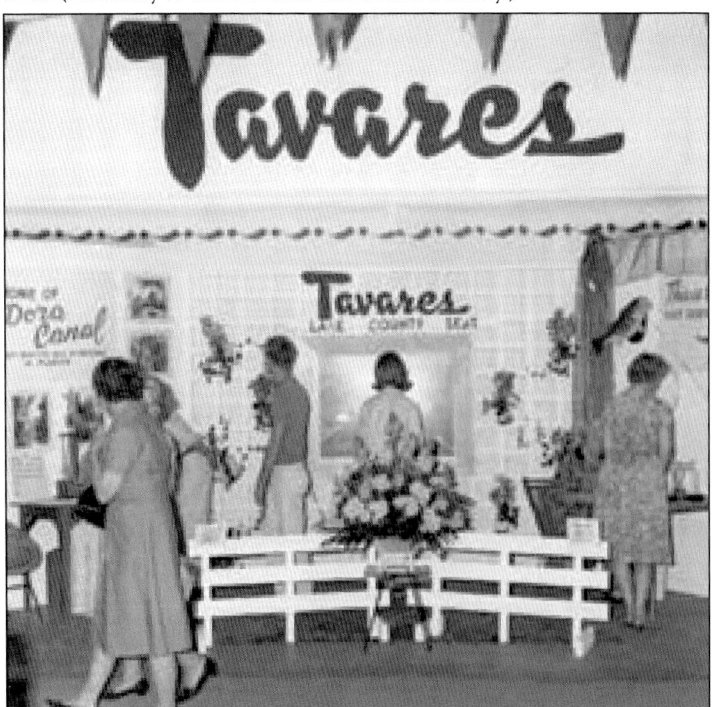

The Lake County Fair evolved from the Florida Sportsmen Exposition, which began in 1921. This exhibit at the March 1965 fair highlights Tavares as the county seat and home to the Dora Canal. The exhibit also features Tavares as an outdoor sportsman's destination. Today, Tavares hosts several major national bass and crappie tournaments. (Courtesy of the Lake County Historical Society.)

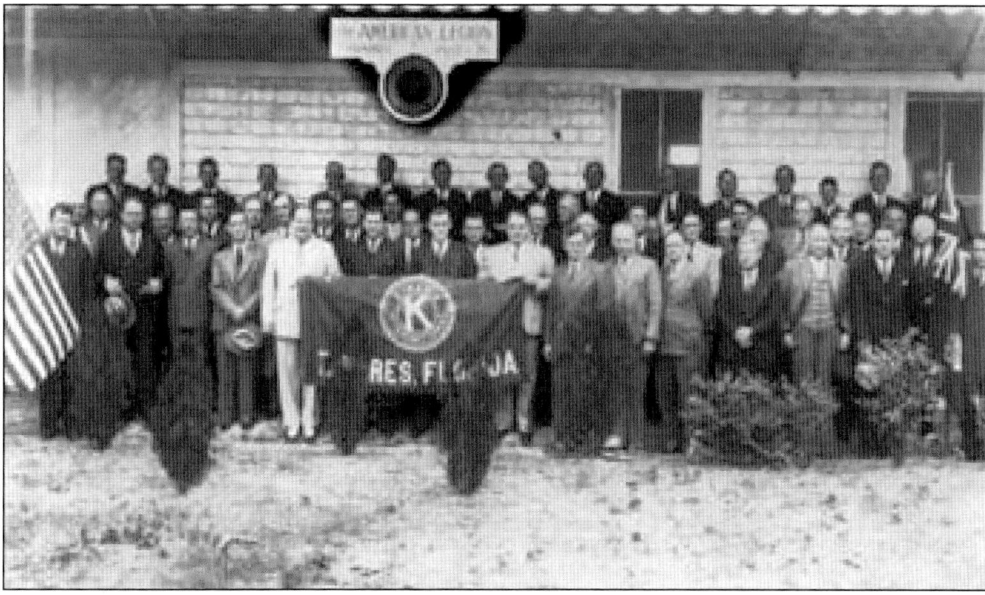

The Tavares Kiwanis Club was chartered in 1925. This club photograph was taken in 1940 on the occasion of the club's 15th anniversary. The focus of Kiwanis is serving the children of the world. One of the major fundraising events the Tavares Kiwanis held each year was the "white-elephant" sale. (Courtesy of the Lake County Historical Society.)

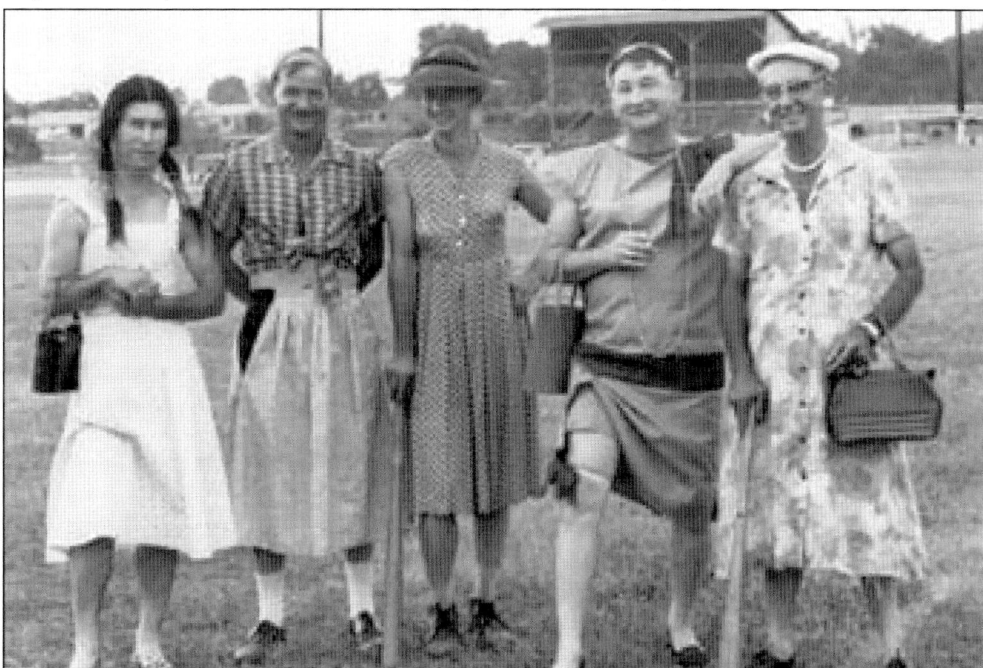

The Tavares Lions Club was chartered in 1955. Its many fundraisers support the local community and assist worldwide. Fighting blindness and children's needs are its top priority. Participating in this 1958 Lions Club fundraiser are, from left to right, Horace Kilgore, Harvey Smith, Gene Smith, Charlie Holder, and Truman Moorhead. (Courtesy of the Tavares Historical Society.)

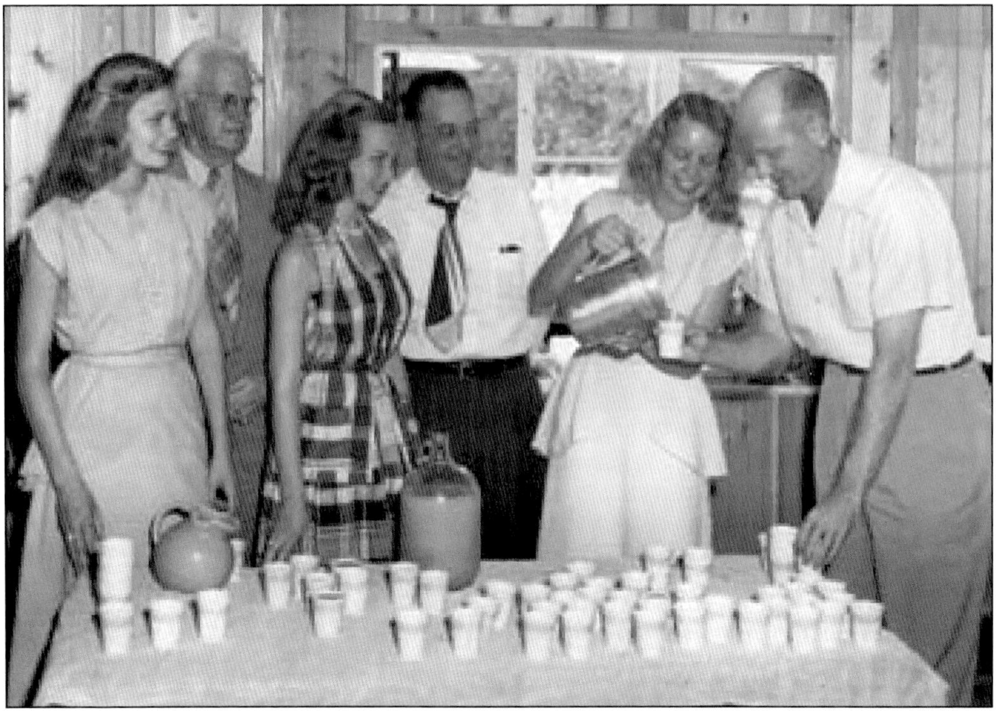

The Watermelon Festival originated around 1930 in Leesburg and was scheduled around harvest time, usually in June. There were no festivals held during World War II, but it resumed in 1946. Activities included a parade, celebrity guest speakers, the largest watermelon contest, melon pageants, and a beauty contest to crown the watermelon queen. Young women from all over Florida participated. In the 1949 photograph above, Charlene Nichols (right), who was a contestant in the beauty pageant, pours juice for one of the festival officials at the kickoff reception at Venetian Gardens. Charlene's sister, Eleanor Nichols, is on the left, and Dolly Beard, who was crowned Watermelon Queen 1949, is in the center. Below, Sonye Holland (left) and Frances Austin ride on a float during the 1956 Watermelon Festival. (Both, courtesy of Charlene Nichols King.)

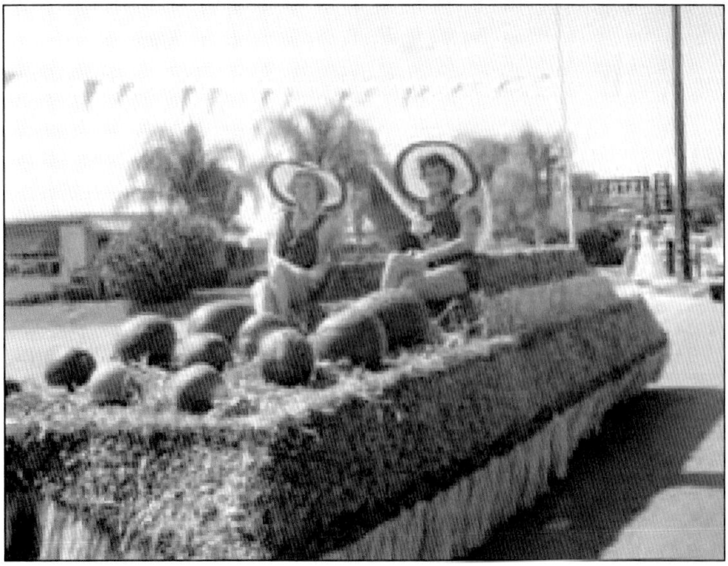

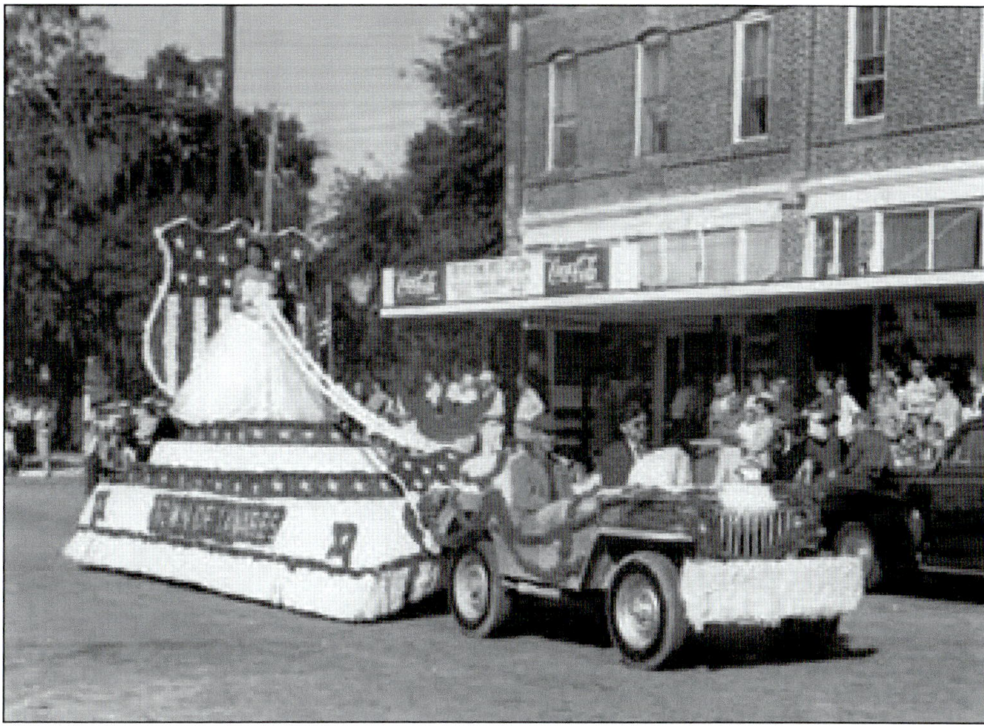

On Friday, November 11, 1955, Frances Austin (above) stands atop the "Town of Tavares" float in the annual Veterans Day parade. The parade was held in Tavares each year since 1919 to commemorate Armistice Day, which was the day the armistice was signed calling for a cessation of hostilities during World War I (November 11, 1918). In 1954, Armistice Day was officially changed to Veterans Day to honor soldiers from all wars. The annual parade down Main Street continued under the new holiday name. Jeanette Nolan (below) stands on top of the "Welcome to Tavares" float in the 1956 Veterans Day parade accompanied by Mary Lee Palmer (left) and Sylvia Briggs. (Both, courtesy of the Lake County Historical Society.)

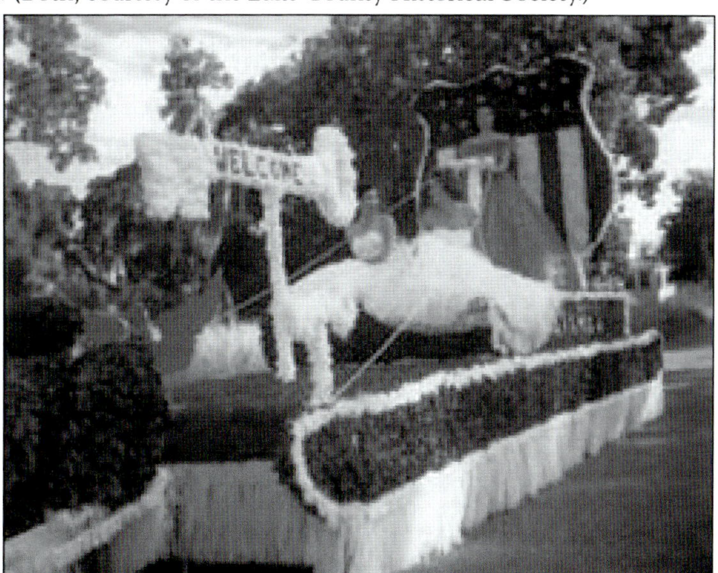

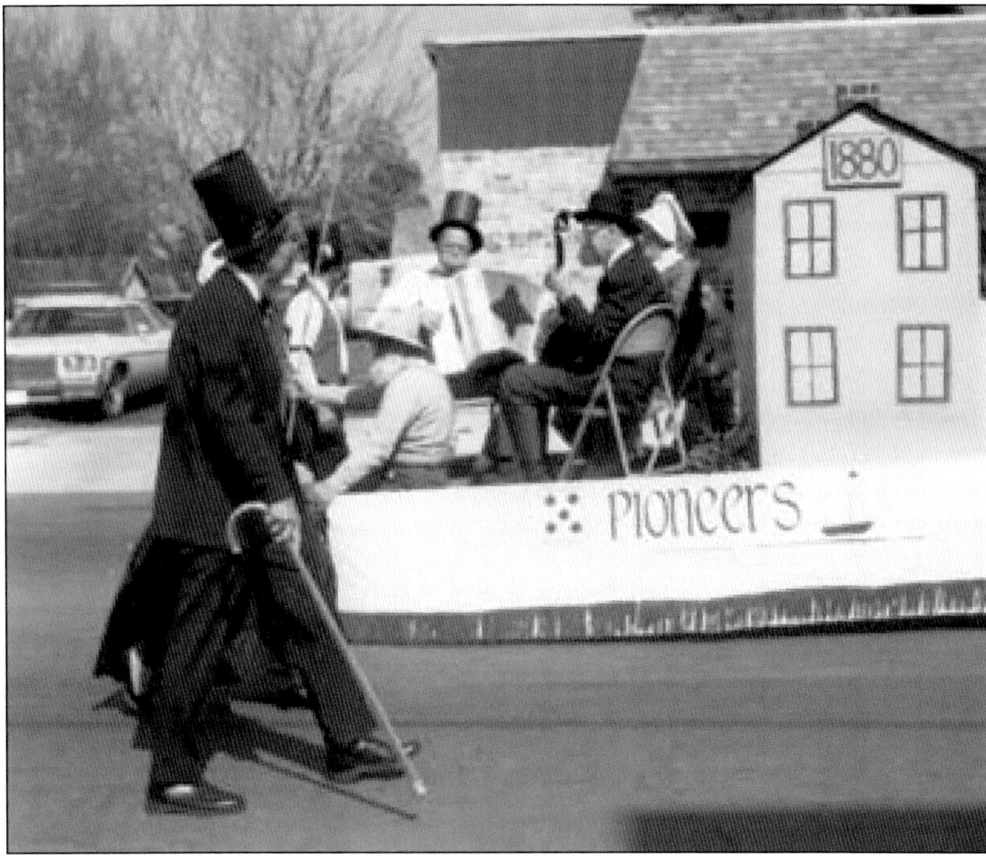

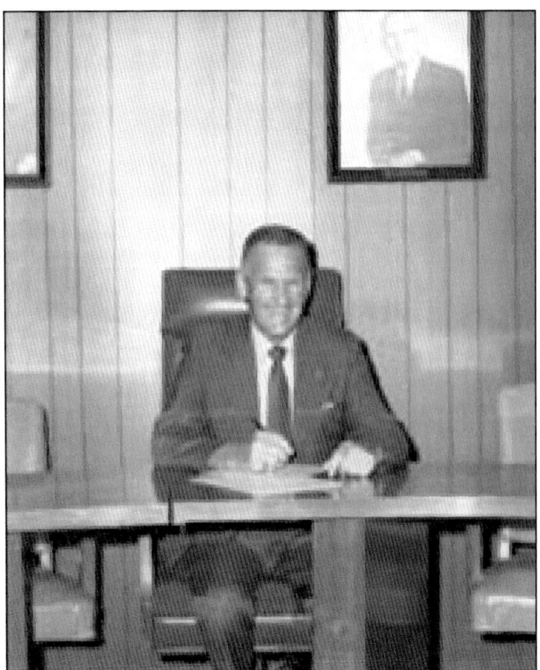

The Pioneer Days parade is one of several patriotic parades that were held annually in Tavares. The festival was highlighted by many attractions, which included choosing a longtime resident to be the Pioneer Days king and queen. Major St. Clair Abrams purchased the land for building Tavares in 1880, marking its founding. (Courtesy of the Lake County Historical Society.)

Fred Stover, with his wife, Dorothy, moved to Tavares in 1958. Stover served as a city councilman and was elected mayor in 1968. He was interested in providing modern sports equipment for Tavares schools and instrumental in building new athletic fields. The baseball complex on Disston Avenue is named for Stover. He died in 1973 while still mayor. (Courtesy of the Tavares Historical Society.)

Robert Lee Nutt, born in 1865, was the Lake County tax assessor, a position he held for 32 years until his death in 1927. Nutt was the first Worshipful Master of Tavares Masonic Lodge 234, which was chartered on February 4, 1916, with 13 members. William Garrett Long was the senior warden, and Emmett Murchison Tally was the junior warden. (Courtesy of the Lake County Historical Society.)

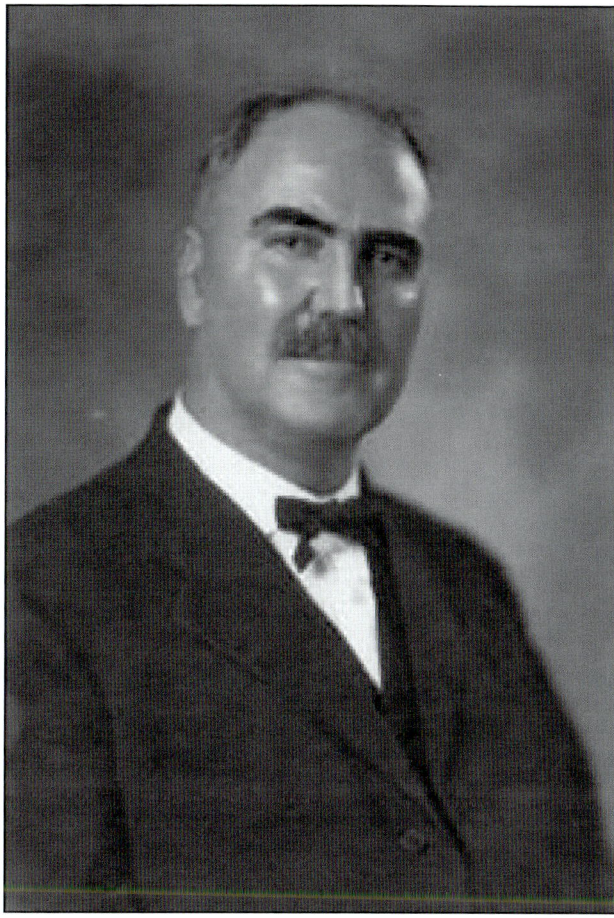

This bronze statue of the World War I doughboy "going over the top" was located at Summerall Park in Tavares. The inscription reads, "Erected by the People of Lake County in Memory of Her Soldiers and Sailors November 11, A.D. 1924." General Summerall was the keynote speaker at the unveiling of the statue in 1924. In 1997, the doughboy statue was moved to the old courthouse. (Courtesy of Clayton Bishop.)

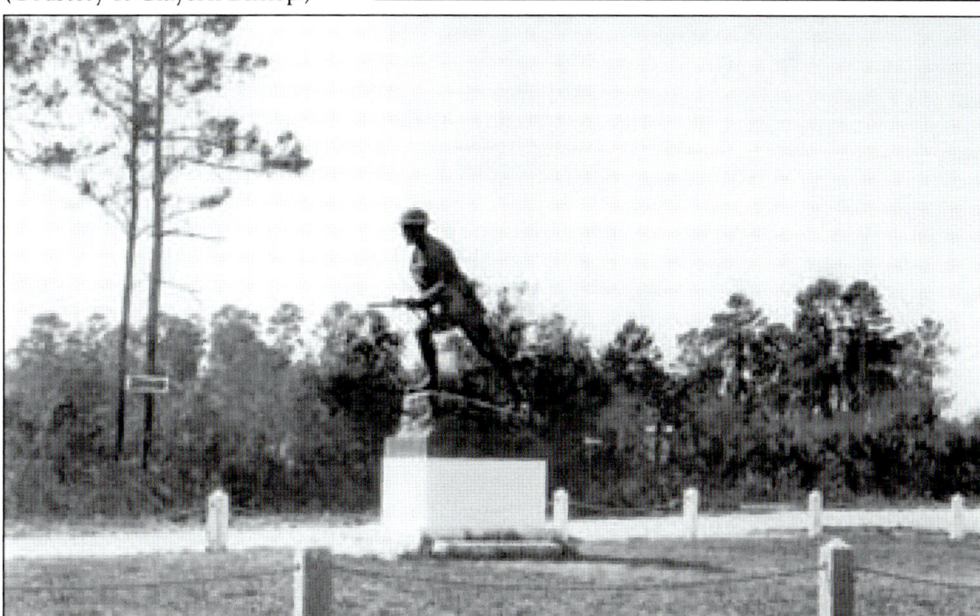

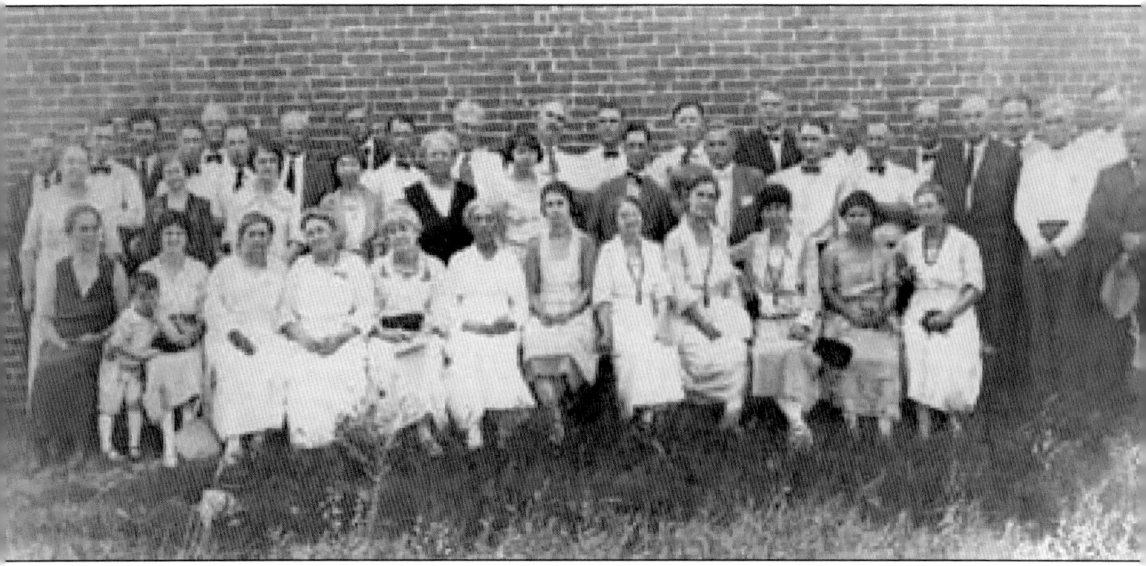

Members of the Friendly Circle of Tavares in the 1920s are, from left to right, (first row) Kate Lacey, Eleanor Potter with son, Marian Peet Duncan, Matilda Conger, Mary MacDonald, Clara Nutt Rees, Mrs. C.H. Newell and sister, Ethel Anderson, ? Steverson, and Annie Burleigh; (second row) Lena Nutt, Jenny Thompson, Louise Stubbs, Elizabeth Booth, Cora Hammond, Violet Steverson, Bill Rogers, Bert Huntley, Red Kennedy, Emery Close, Al Huff, ? Steverson, and Robert Morrison; (third row) unidentified, D.H. Moore, Jeff Goss, Jerry Booth, Edward Burleigh, Irving Burleigh, Lee Conger, Judge Emmett Tally, Tuck Townsend, Joseph Hammond, Robert Lee Nutt, Dr. Stanford Carl Colley, Harry Duncan, Willis Powell, C.C. Chase, Donald Gardner, Lincoln Rees, and H.C. Hannah. (Courtesy of the Tavares Historical Society.)

Six

Blossoms, Bargains, and Biscuits

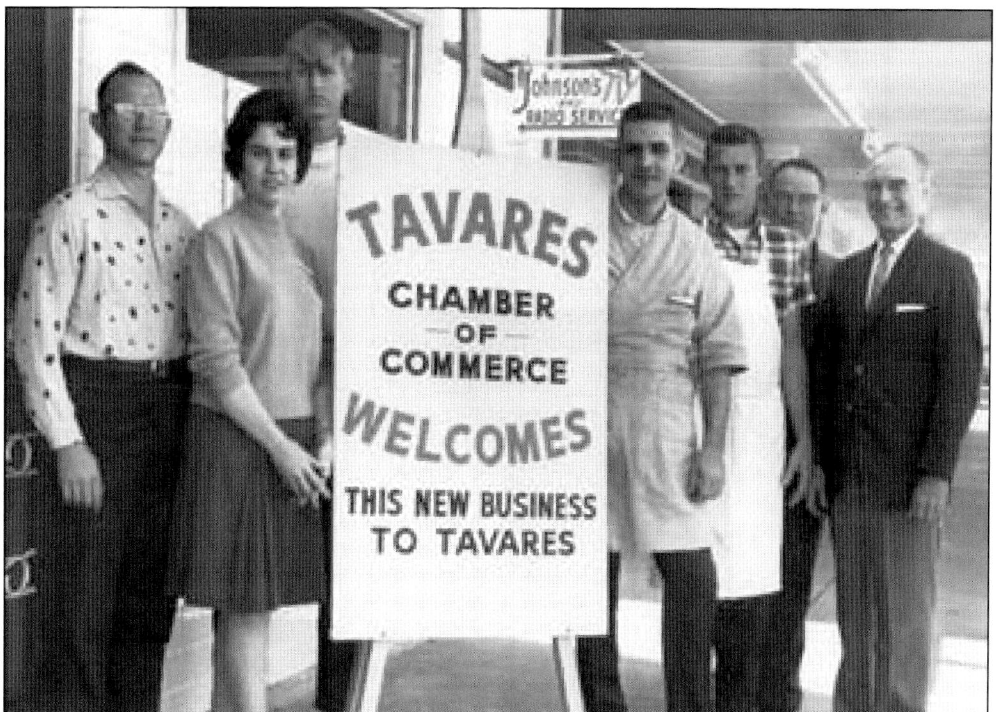

Since Tavares was the county seat, many people only thought of Tavares as the place you had to go for county business, such as paying taxes or going to court. But the people of Tavares believed the charm of their hometown went beyond the atmosphere of government, with restaurants, shops, and businesses within walking distance or a short carriage ride from their homes. (Courtesy of the Lake County Historical Society.)

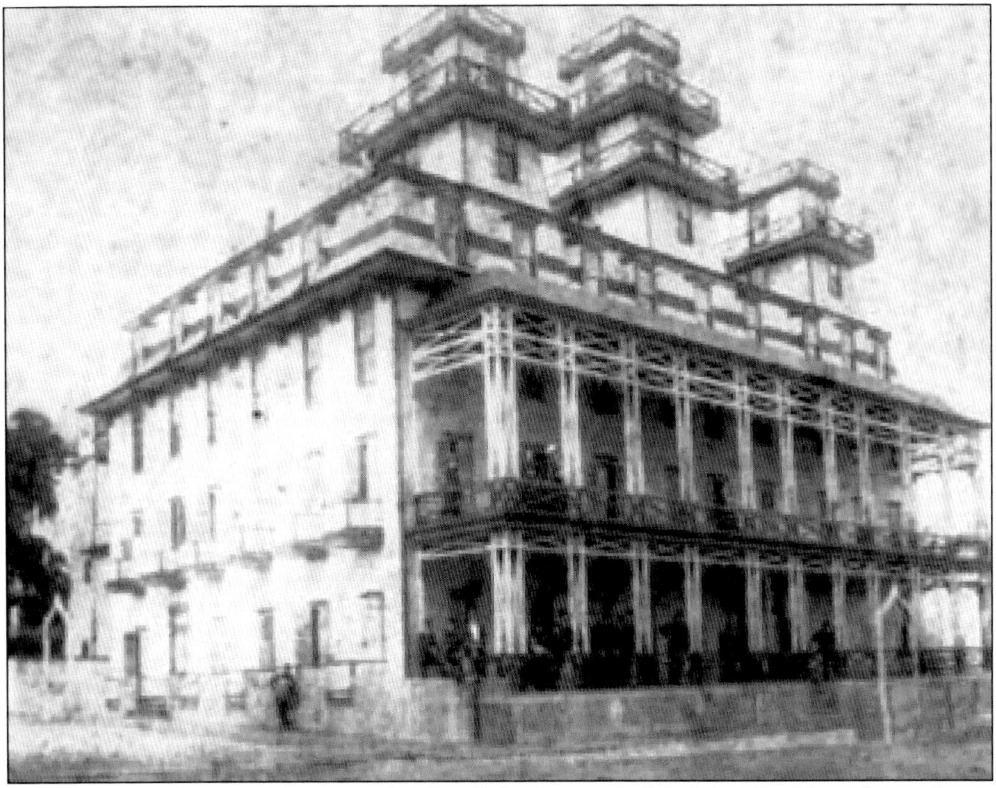

The Peninsular Hotel was a three-story hotel with three towers built by Major St. Clair Abrams shortly after laying out the town in 1882. The hotel was located along Lake Dora on the west end of town. A ball was held there in January 1885 celebrating the railroad coming into Tavares. The Peninsular Hotel was a victim of the Tavares fire of 1888. (Courtesy of the Tavares Historical Society.)

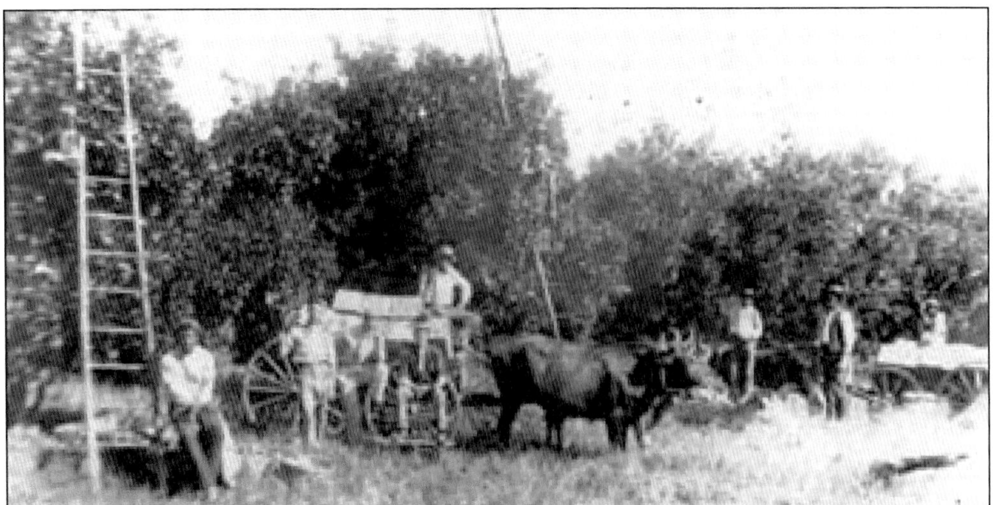

The citrus industry began in the lake region in 1845 when Melton and Bunberry Haynes planted a quarter acre of sweet oranges on the north side of Lake Harris. From these plantings, young orange trees were carried into various sections scattered about the great lake region and into adjoining counties. (Courtesy of Clayton Bishop.)

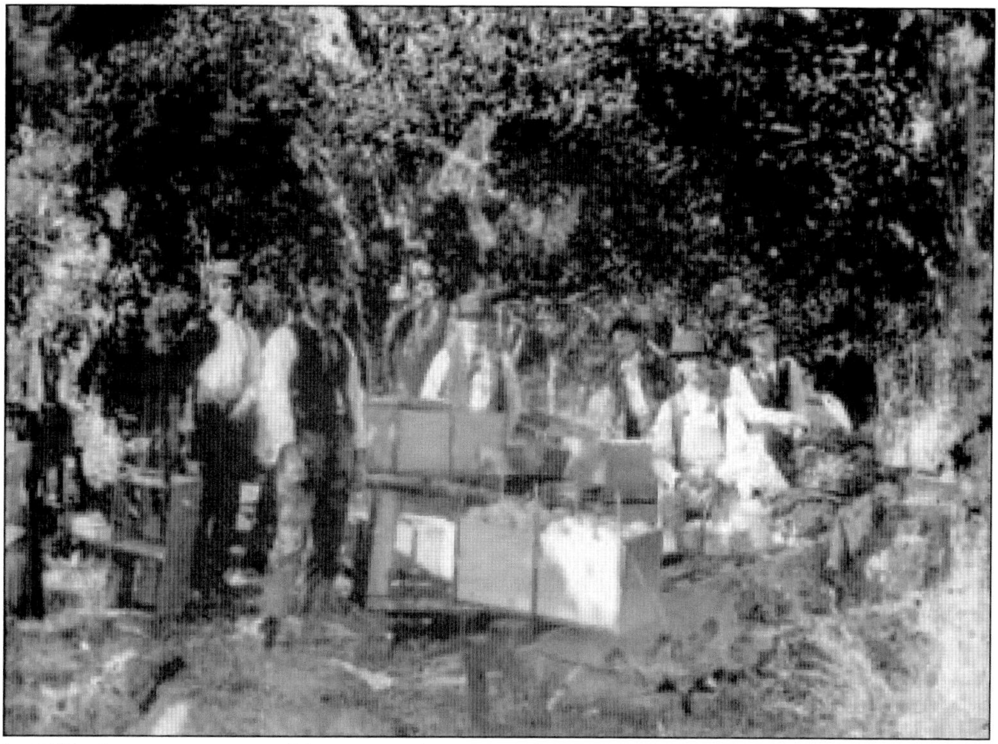

In 1850, the primary crops of farmers in the new settlements were sugarcane and cotton. Starting in 1851, the number of farmers planting citrus increased when Andrew Phares planted a large grove in Yalaha from trees he obtained from Melton Haynes. Pictured are orange pickers in Tavares in the early 1900s. (Courtesy of Clayton Bishop.)

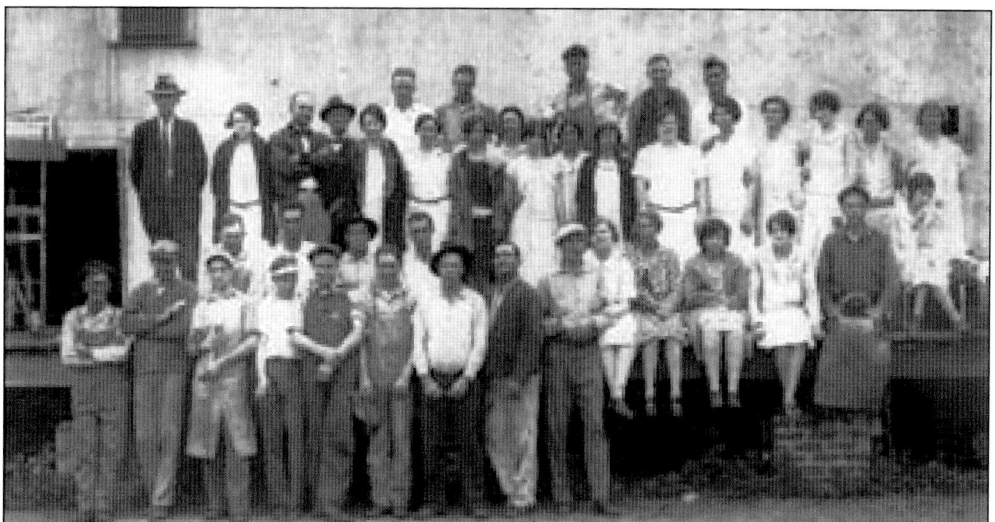

Following a severe freeze in 1895, citrus growers felt the need for grower cooperatives and central packinghouses. In 1909, an entourage of orange growers, including Tavareans Guilford Wakelin and Edward Burleigh, visited California to study their citrus operation. Upon their return, they established the Lake Region Packing Association in Tavares. The association prospered and employed many people. (Courtesy of the Tavares Historical Society.)

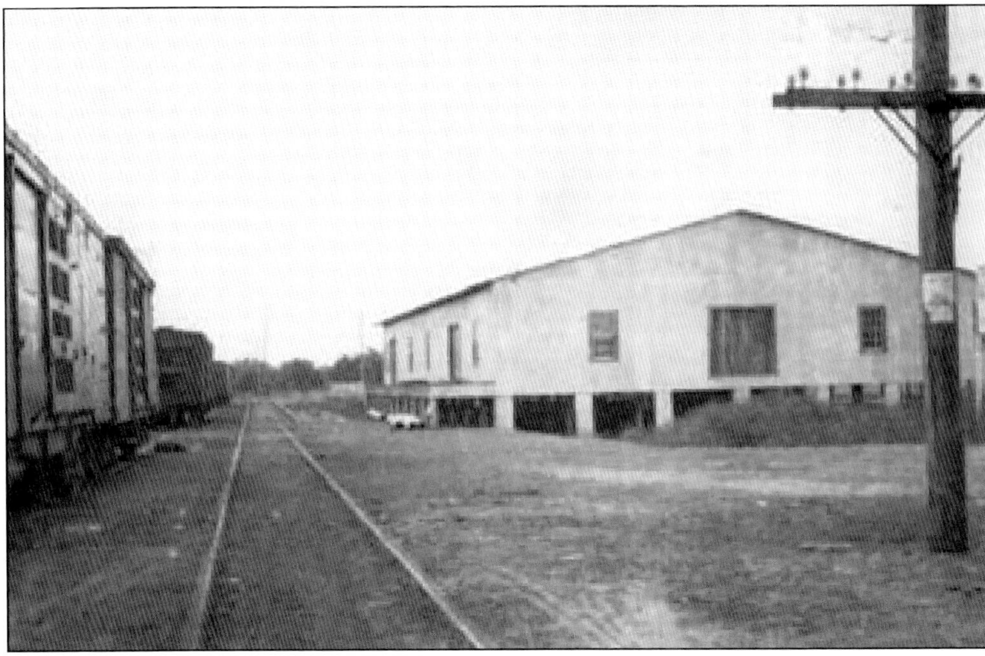

The Lake Region Packing Association plant was built on the shore of Lake Dora in Tavares. The railroad ran alongside the plant, providing convenient access to and from the plant by rail and water. The workforce consisted of locals and men from other regions of the country. Travelers who worked at the packinghouse found lodging at many of the homes around town. When the Lake Region Packing Association was established in 1909, the Florida Citrus Exchange was also created. The Florida Citrus Exchange was a statewide cooperative that assisted local growers in marketing their fruit. In 2005, after almost 100 years of operation in Tavares, the Lake Region Packing plant was closed and razed. (Both, courtesy of the Tavares Historical Society.)

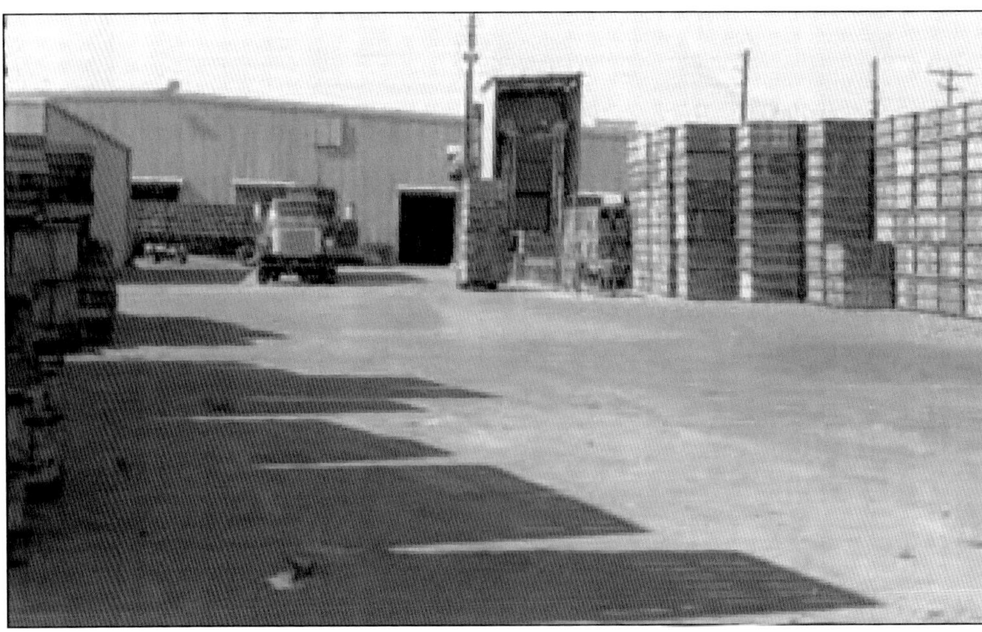

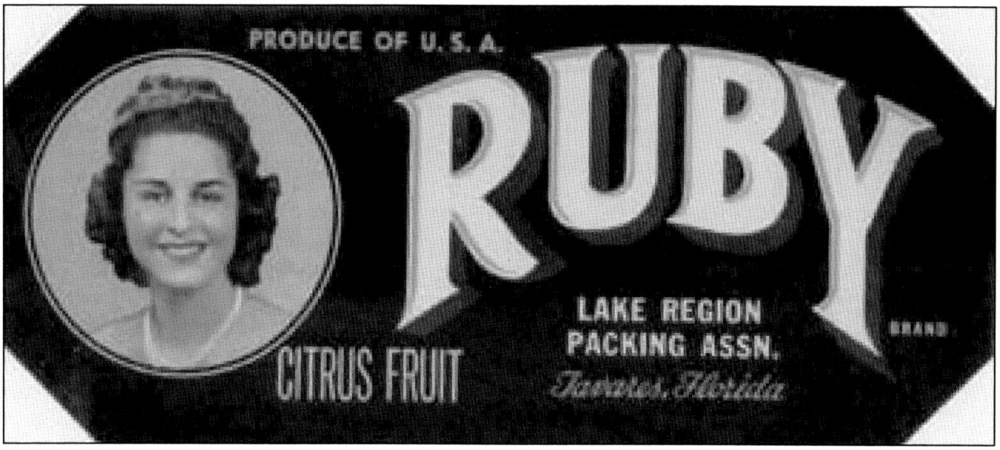

The Ruby-brand red grapefruit was introduced around 1938 and was named for Ruby Prevatt, pictured on this label. Ruby is the daughter of Jennings Bryant "Babe" Prevatt, who arrived in Tavares in 1925. Prevatt was a 45-year employee of the Lake Region Packing Association and served as its president. Prevatt was also mayor of Tavares. Ruby Street in Tavares is named for Ruby Prevatt. (Courtesy of Lura Messer Hall.)

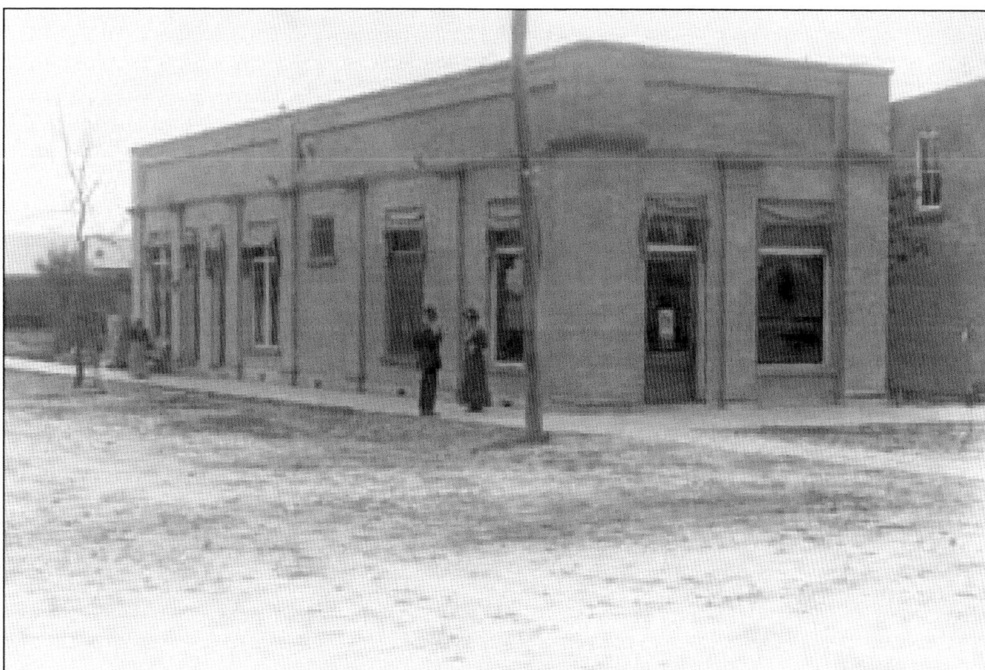

The Bank of Tavares was organized in 1913 in this building on the corner of Irma Street and New Hampshire Avenue. The Tavares Post Office is located at the side entrance in this 1914 photograph. The first bank president was G.W. Holmes, and the cashier was Charles Nutt. Dr. Sanford Colley also had an office in this building. (Courtesy of the Lake County Historical Society.)

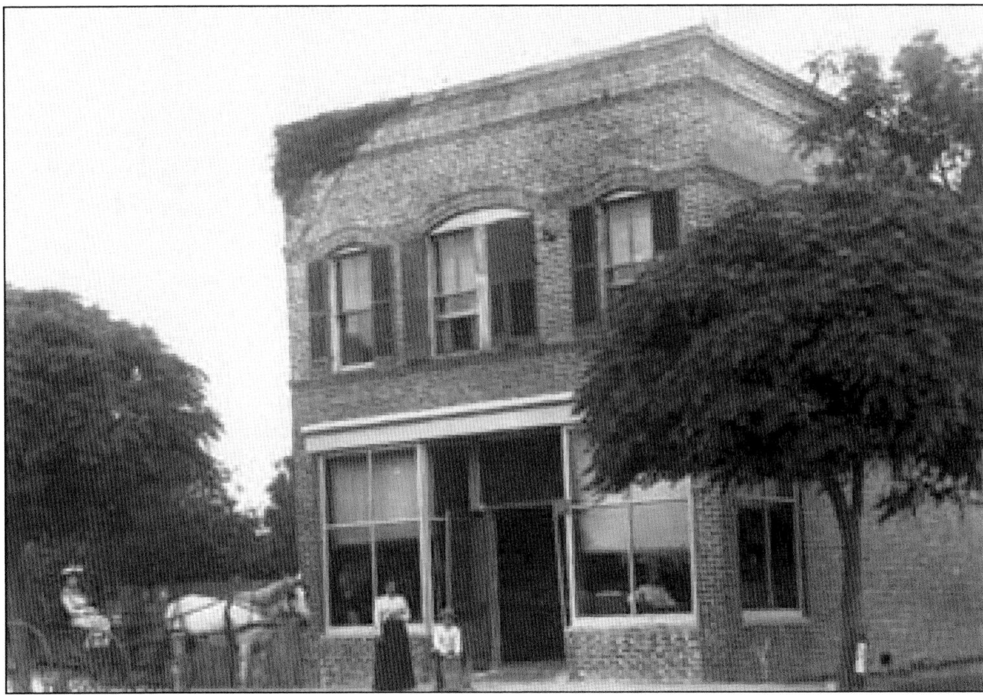

In April 1903, Grace Wakelin, the sister of Guilford Wakelin, struck this photograph (above) of the store and post office located on the corner of Irma Street and Joanna Avenue. Seated in the buggy drawn by Charlie the horse is Frances "Franca" Burleigh Fernald. Margaret Vanderhaven is standing on the sidewalk, and Irving Burleigh is the young boy sitting on the tree stump. Annie Burleigh is inside the building looking out the window. The sign mounted on the front entrance reads, "Agency for Chase and Sanborn Famous Boston Coffee." The photograph below shows the same building 13 years prior. (Both, courtesy of Clayton Bishop.)

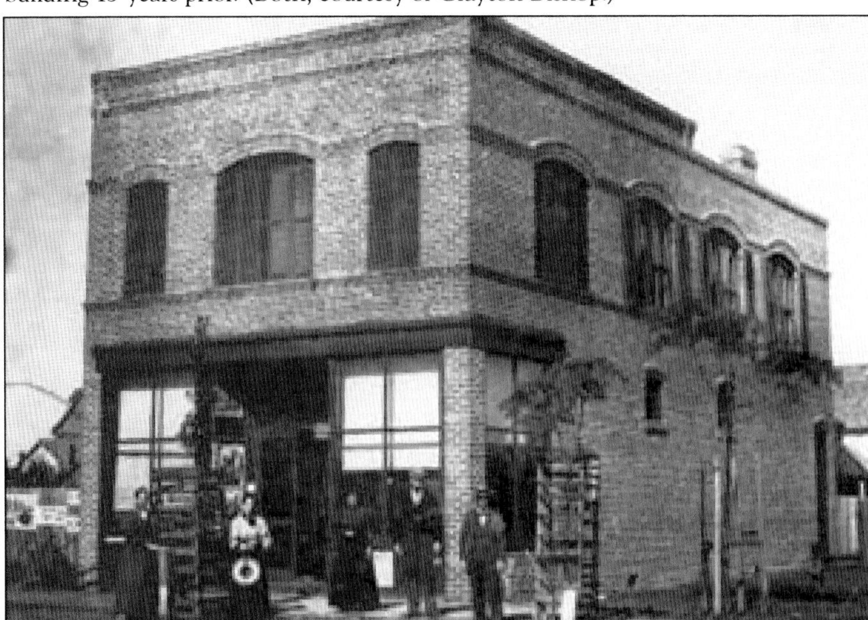

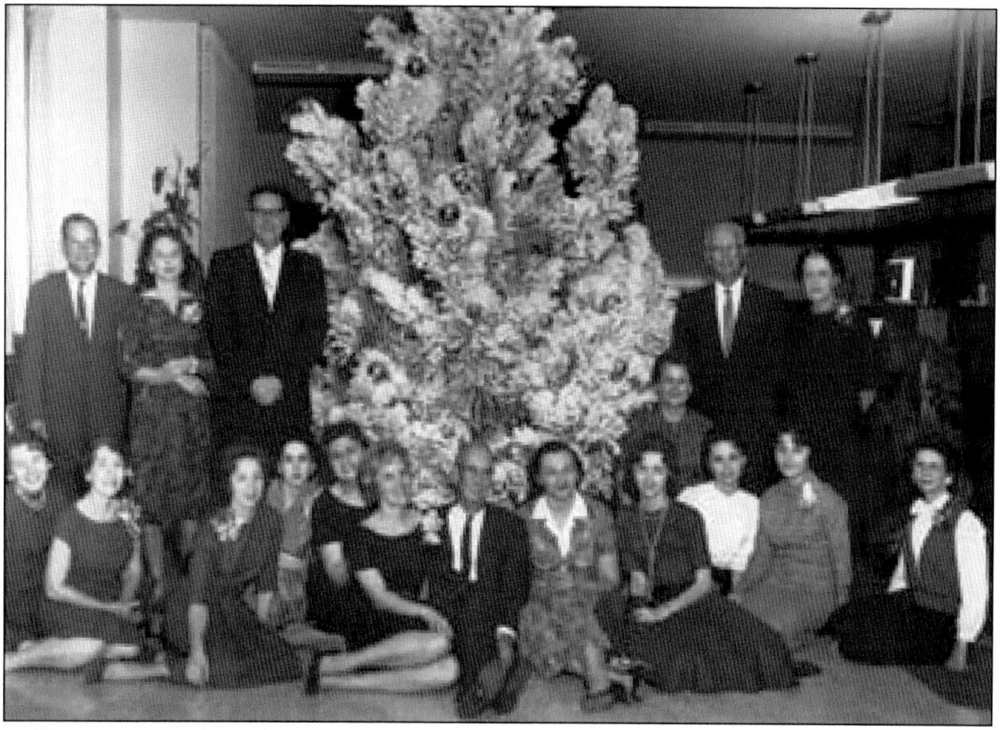

William J. Rogers (seated on the floor) came to Tavares in 1911. His banking career began in 1918 when he became cashier at the Bank of Tavares. In 1923, he became vice president of the bank; in 1938, executive vice president; and in 1961, chairman of the board of directors. Rogers had a 52-year career as an executive officer with the Bank of Tavares. He married Dolly Duncan in 1913. The employees of the Bank of Tavares are pictured above in the new bank building, which opened in July 1961. Executives standing in the second row are, from left to right, Osler Adams, unidentified, Joe Duncan, W.G. Fleming, and Frances Lovell. In the photograph below, Rev. George Kroff (left), former officer of the German Army, buys the first US Savings Bond sold at the Bank of Tavares from Rogers. (Both, courtesy of the Lake County Historical Society.)

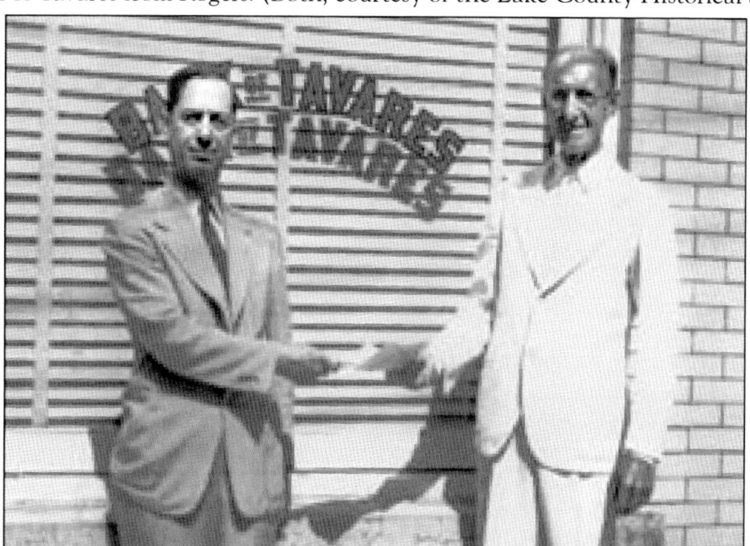

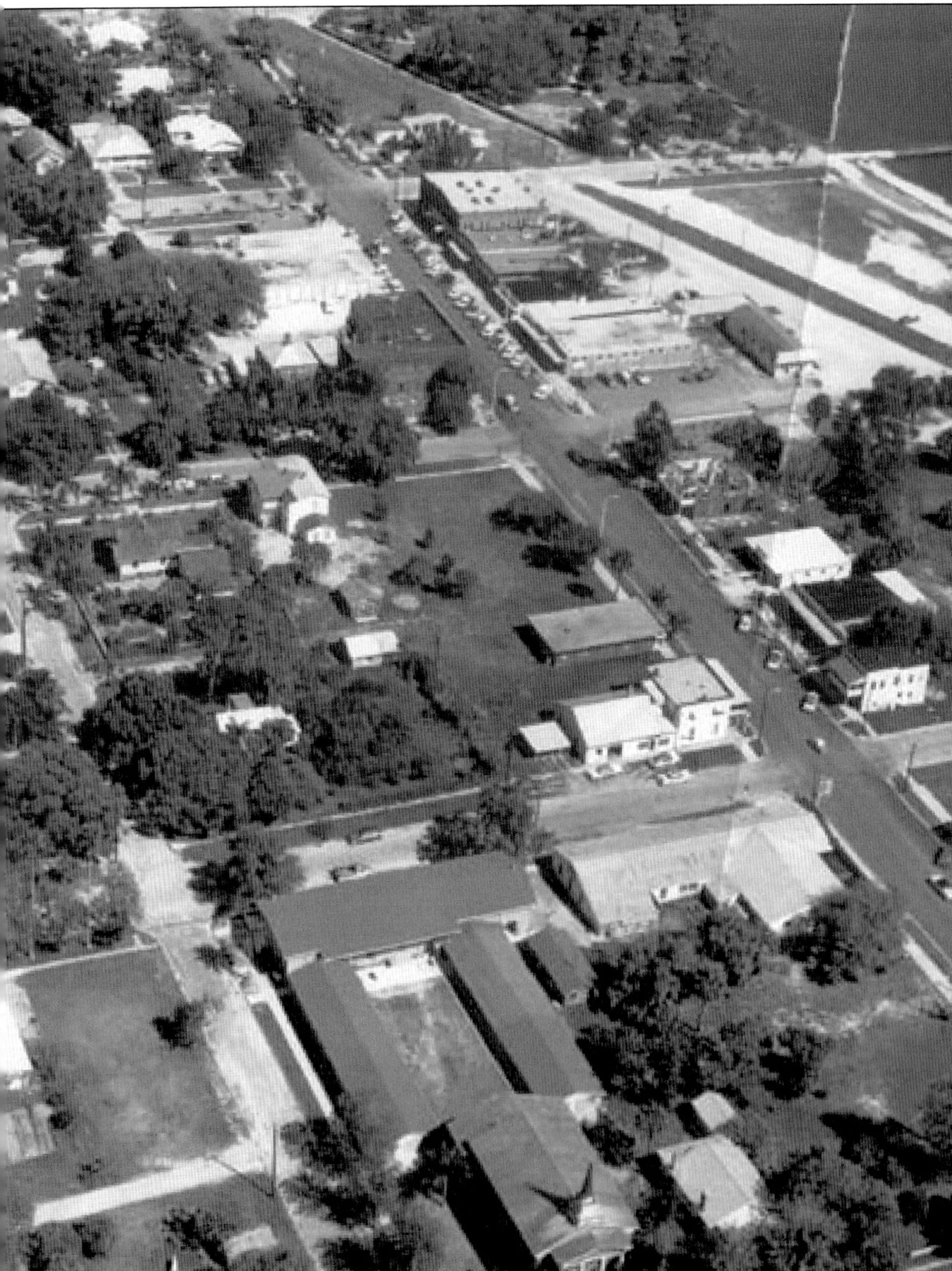

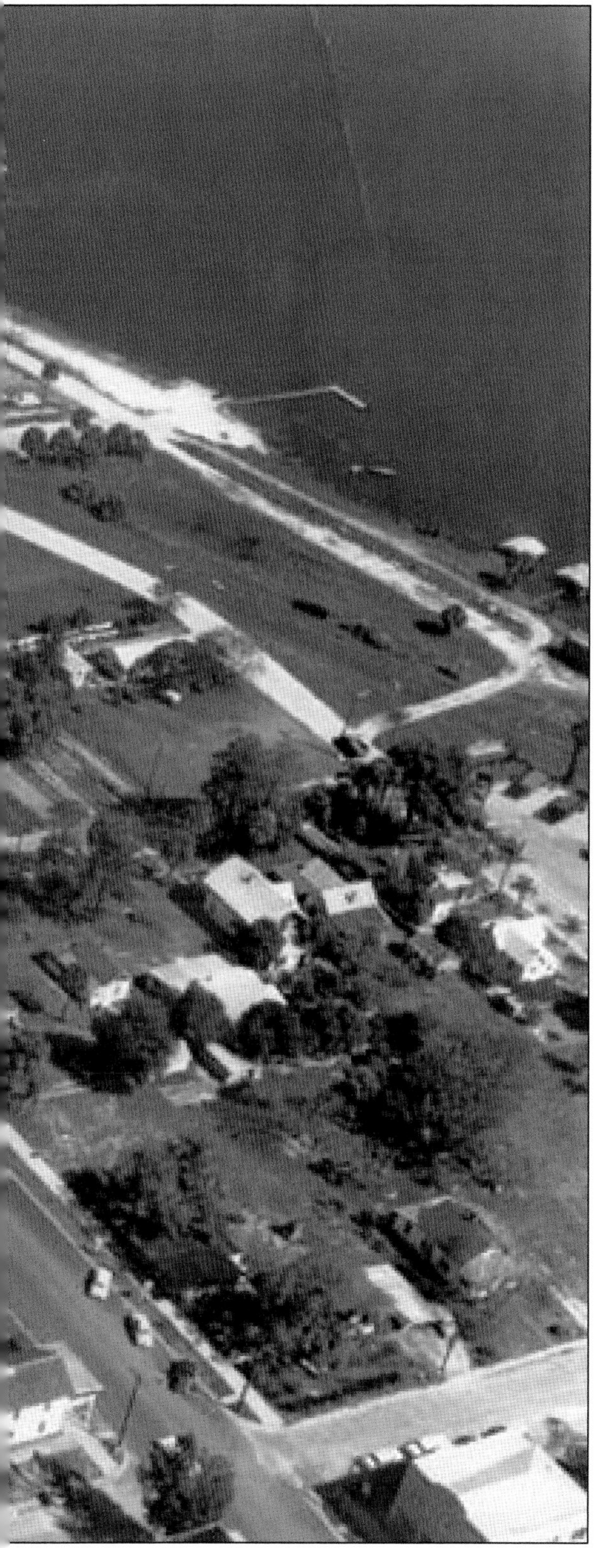

This 1960 aerial of Main Street in downtown Tavares features the Pavilion on Lake Dora. The Pavilion was razed in 1961. Other famous historical structures shown here that are no longer standing include the old Atlantic Coastline Railroad depot and the Lake Building at the intersection of St. Clair Abrams Avenue and Main Street at the top of the photograph. The Osceola Hotel on the corner of Main Street and Rockingham Avenue has given way to today's Tavares City Hall. Gardner's Garage (which later became the Ace Hardware), the First Baptist Church, and the Tavares Masonic Lodge buildings are among several structures in this photograph that are still part of the Tavares skyline. (Courtesy of the Lake County Historical Society.)

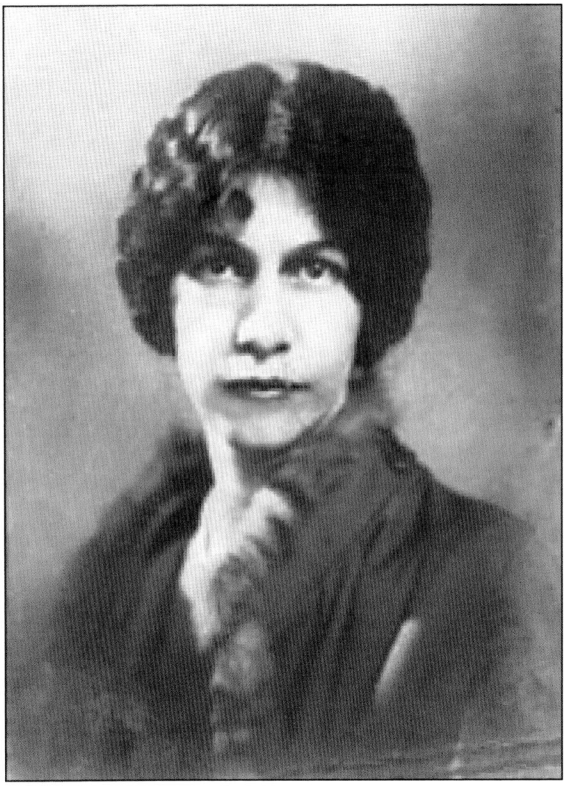

Marie Cox King (pictured) was born in 1896 along the Pee Dee River in North Carolina. She arrived in Tavares in the 1920s as a home demonstration agent. Over the next six decades, Marie was an active, prominent, and beloved person in the Tavares community. She did monthly reports for the agriculture department in Gainesville and had a weekly article in the local newspaper. Marie married railroad telegraph operator Jack King in 1927. In 1931, the Kings purchased a 1920s inn built by W.P. Floyd on North Rockingham Avenue. It was called the Tavares Inn (below). The inn had 11 bedrooms and five baths and became a popular attraction. (Both, courtesy of Charlene Nichols King.)

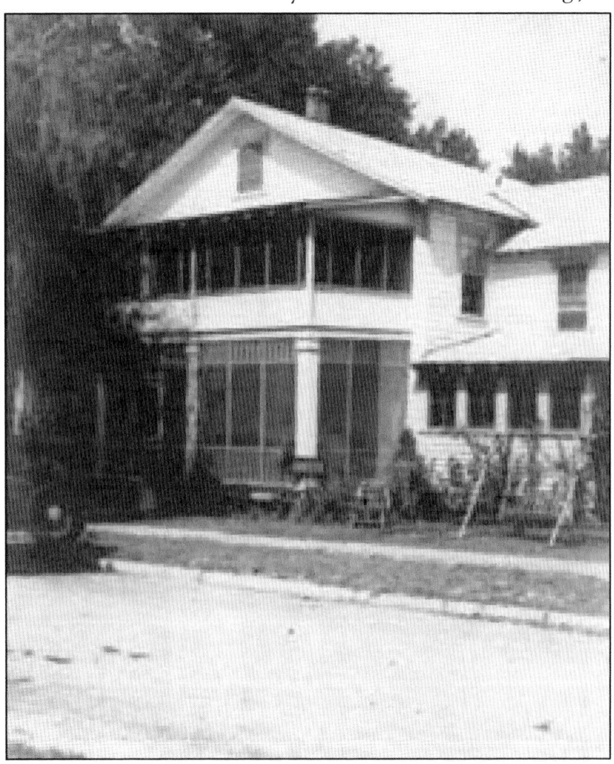

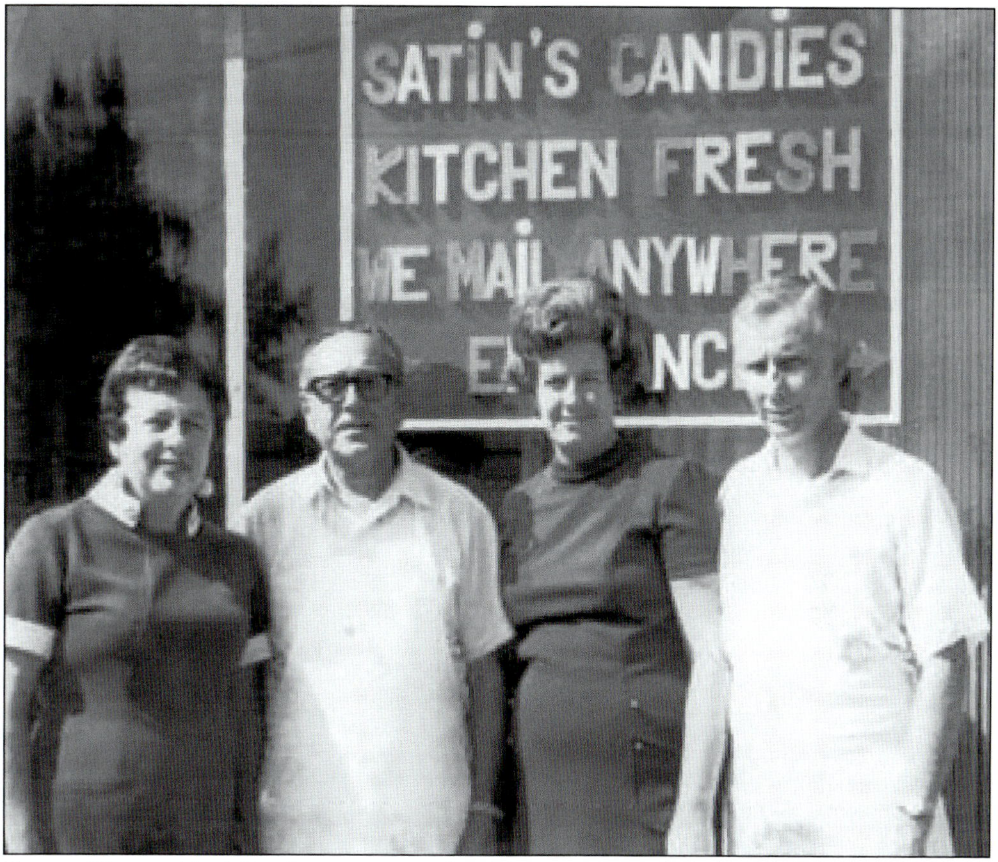

Orange Blossom Trail Candies was opened in Tavares in the 1940s by Sybil and George Satin (above left). The candy factory, located on Alfred Street, was known as Satin's Candies. In 1970, Kathy and Bob Cook (above right) purchased the factory from the Satins. The Cooks made many varieties of candy including coconut patties, Heavenly Mallo, Mint Pecan Feast, and Chocolate Gofer. The Cooks opened an outlet shop on Highway 27 to take advantage of tourist travel. A regular customer was Mrs. Alonzo Decker, wife of the power tool innovator. Also, Jacqueline Kennedy ordered regularly by mail. In 1980, the Cooks sold the company to new owners, who moved the business to Polk County. The photograph below shows the cooking room on Alfred Street. (Both, courtesy of Bob and Kathy Cook.)

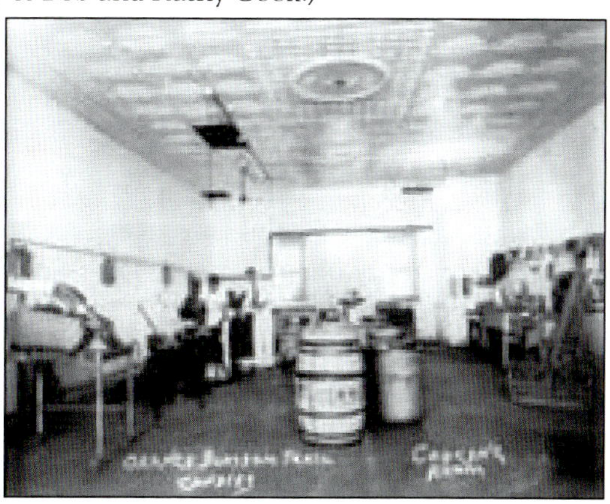

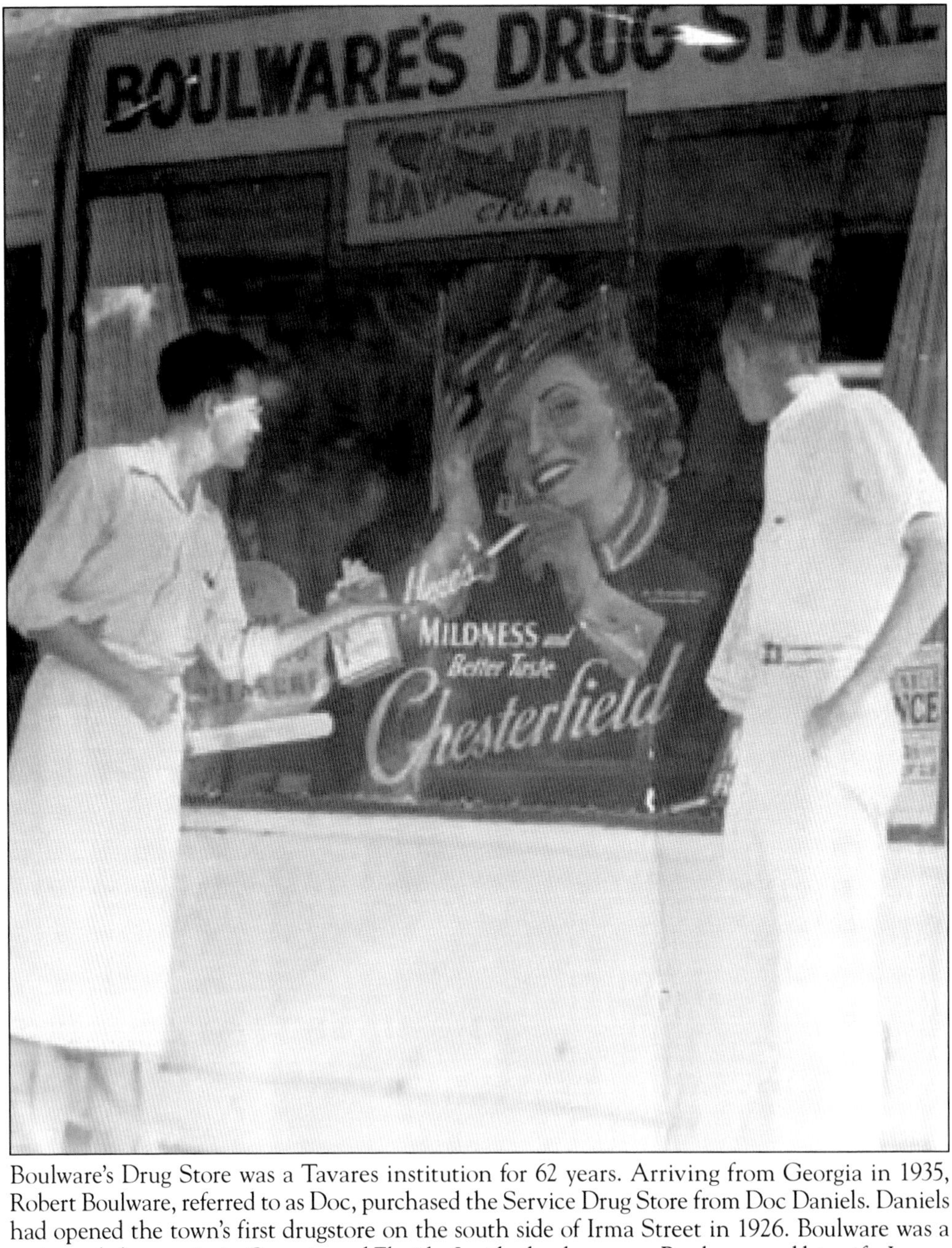

Boulware's Drug Store was a Tavares institution for 62 years. Arriving from Georgia in 1935, Robert Boulware, referred to as Doc, purchased the Service Drug Store from Doc Daniels. Daniels had opened the town's first drugstore on the south side of Irma Street in 1926. Boulware was a registered pharmacist in Georgia and Florida. Inside the drugstore, Boulware and his wife, Laura, had a popular fountain service offering root beer floats and ice cream sundaes. During World War II, Bettye Coven became Boulware's first girl soda jerk. Boulware's Drug Store became known as the "home of the 5 cent cup of coffee." In 1955, the Boulwares moved their pharmacy across Irma Street but continued to operate at the old location as the Tavares Soda Shop. (Courtesy of the Tavares Historical Society.)

The Tavares Hardware store built in 1924 on Main Street originally was a filling station and garage. During the Depression, owner E.D. Gardner bought out the lumberyard and hardware store and incorporated it into one store. Ken Reutebuch, pictured here in 1973, purchased the store in 1964. In 1979, Tavares Hardware became a franchise of Ace Hardware. (Courtesy of the Tavares Historical Society.)

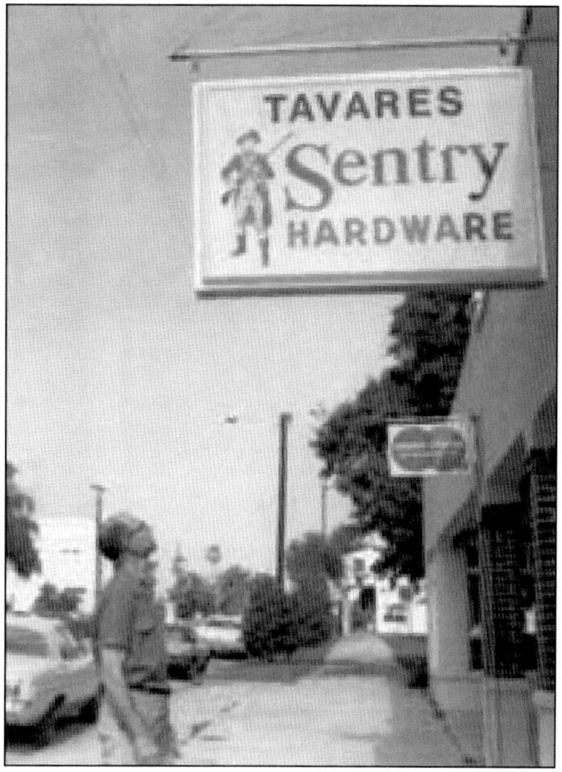

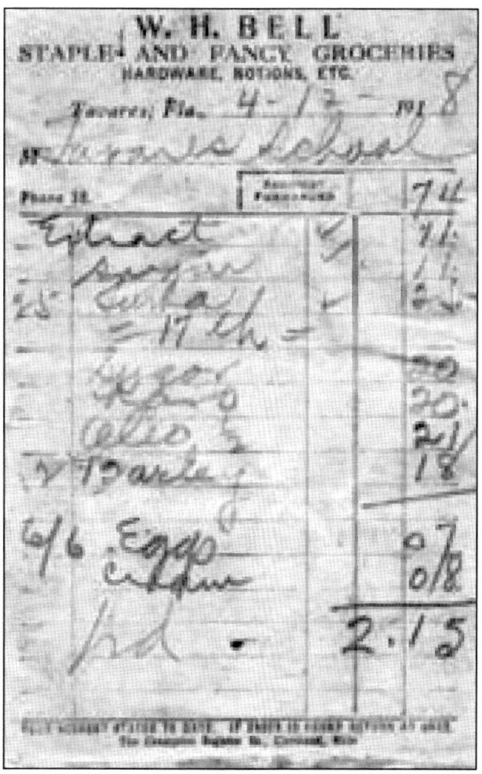
W. H. BELL
STAPLE AND FANCY GROCERIES
HARDWARE, NOTIONS, ETC.
Tavares, Fla. 4-12-1918
Tavares School
Eggs
2.15

The mission statement for W.H. Bell's Staple and Fancy Groceries, Hardware, Notions, Etc. reads, "OUR IDEA is that at all times you shall have the very best goods at the lowest possible price." Pictured is an April 12, 1918, shopping bill made out to Tavares School. (Courtesy of the Tavares Historical Society.)

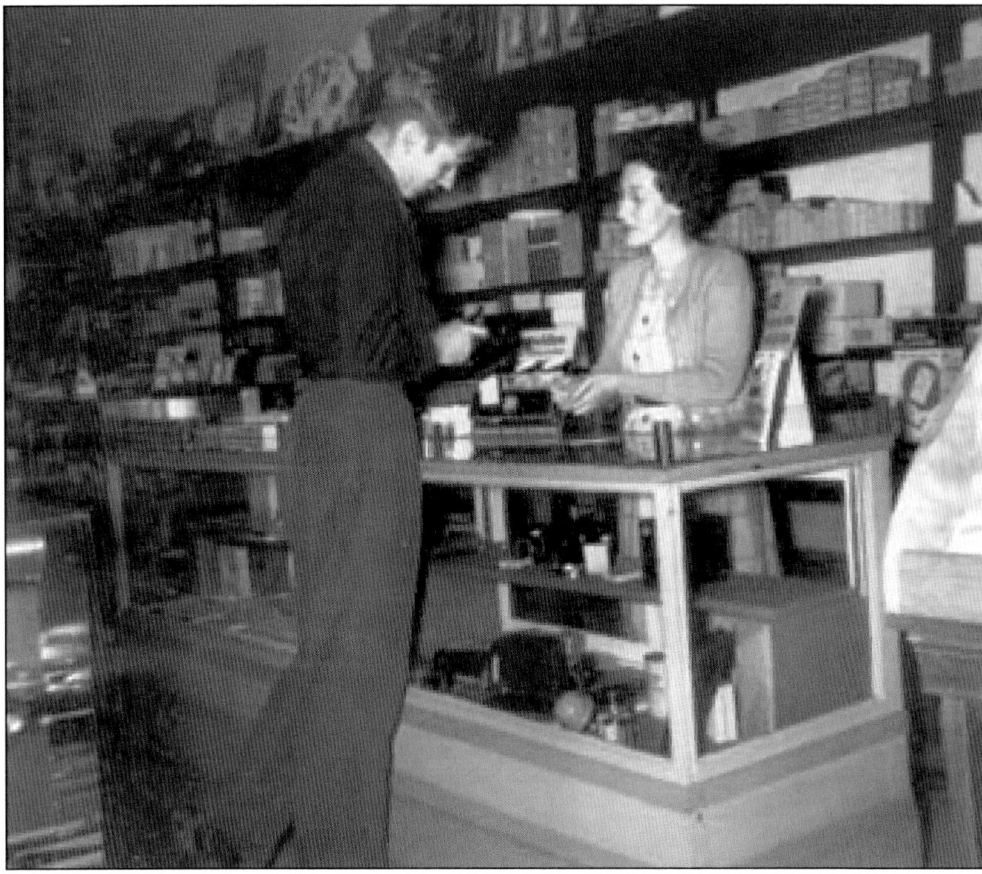

Peggy Keys Duncan Roth, seen here in 1945 assisting a customer with the purchase of a camera, was the owner of Peggy's Department Store. Peggy's was located on the south side of Irma Street for many years. Peggy would later become a paying and receiving teller at the Bank of Tavares. (Courtesy of the Tavares Historical Society.)

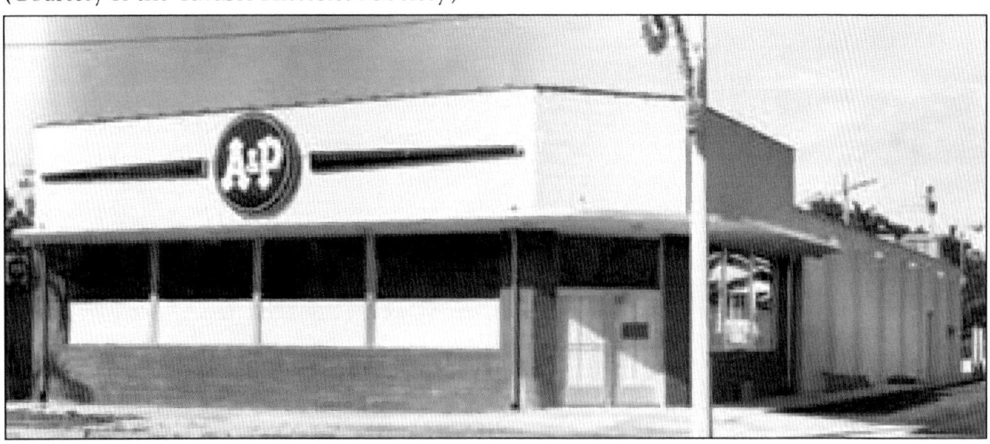

Around 1930, the Great Atlantic & Pacific Tea Company, better known as A&P grocery store, opened on Alfred Street but soon moved into the Lake Building on Irma Street. The store eventually relocated into this building on Irma Street. In the 1970s, when A&P moved out of Florida, the building housed Foodway and then IGA. (Courtesy of the Lake County Historical Society.)

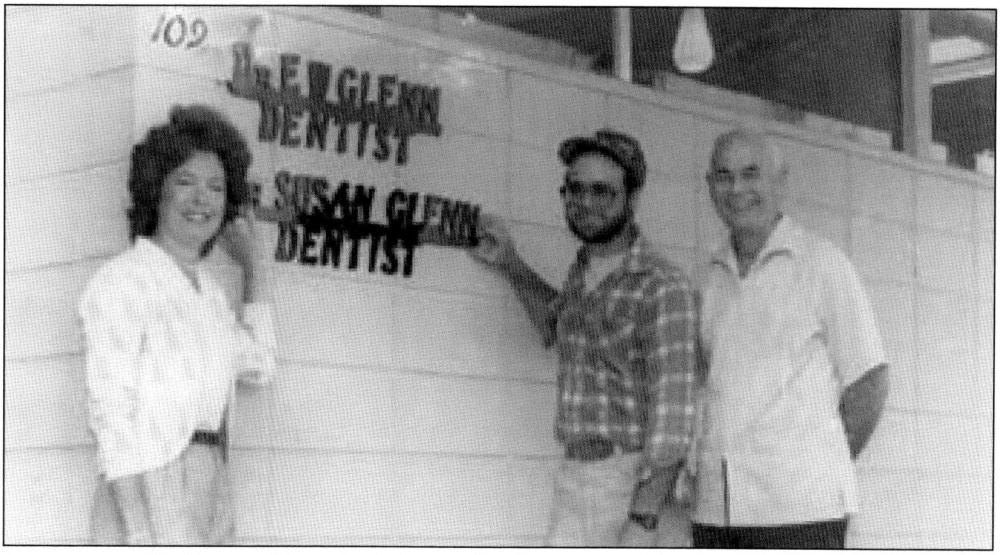

Tampa native Dr. Eugene Glenn (right) arrived in Tavares in 1962. That same year, Doctor Glenn became the first dentist to open a dental practice in Tavares. An adventurer and pilot, Doctor Glenn served as the Tavares mayor from 1974 to 1994. Glenn's daughter Susan (left) became a dentist in 1982 and joined her father's practice. Today, Dr. Susan Caddell still practices dentistry in the same office on Main Street. (Courtesy of Susan Glenn Caddell.)

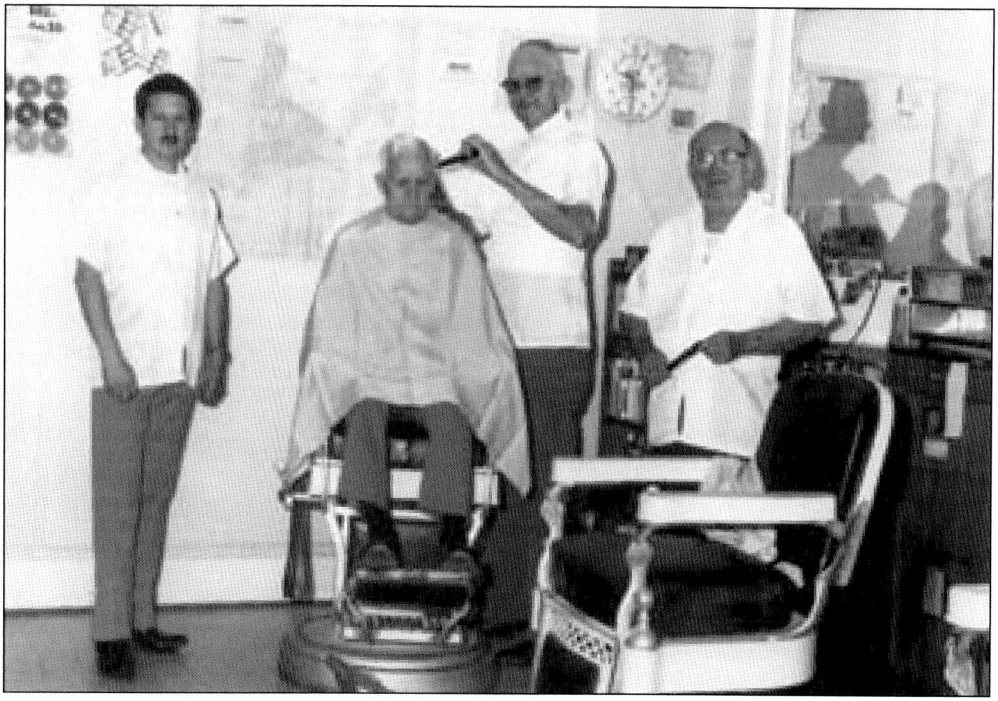

William W.H. LeVar (right) came to Tavares from Georgia in 1931 to find work, a condition his fiancée, Isabelle, insisted on before they married. LeVar asked Tavares barber Mr. Morgan for a job, though he had no experience. Morgan had him cut a customer's hair as a test. LeVar was hired, bought the shop from Morgan, and was a barber on Main Street for 51 years. (Courtesy of Lurlene LeVar Lawton.)

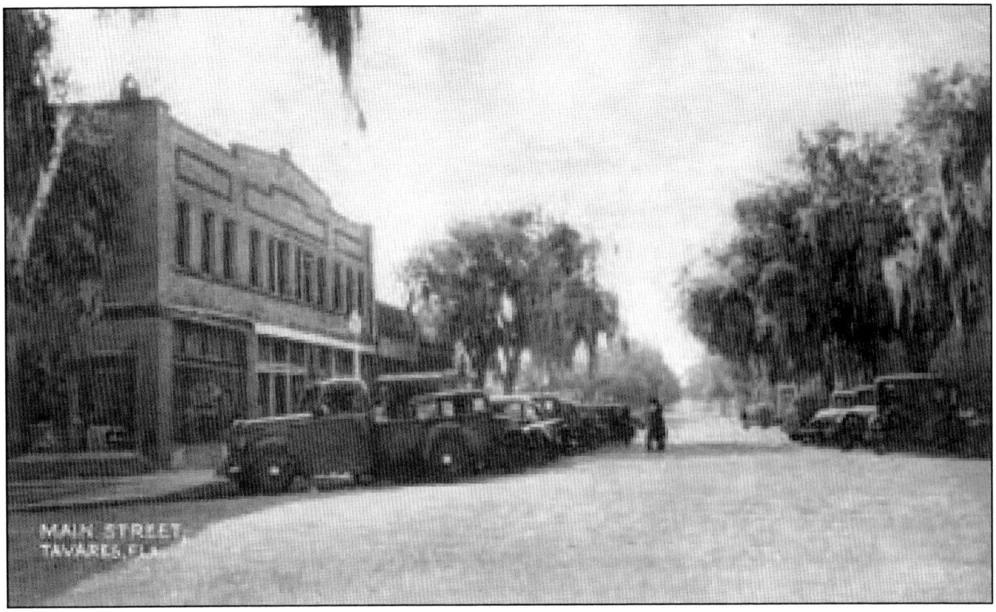

These photographs, looking west at slightly different angles, depict Irma Street (Main Street) during two different eras. The photograph above shows the east side business district in the 1930s, featuring the Lake Building and Doc Daniels Drug Store, where a large Coca-Cola sign hangs. The photograph below shows an active business district in the 1950s. Kesler's, Mac's Variety five-and-dime, the Hitching Post Tavern, and the Gulf filling station can be seen on the north side of Irma Street. Peggy Roth's store is on the south side. The traffic signal at Irma Street and Rockingham Avenue is no longer there. (Both, courtesy of Clayton Bishop.)

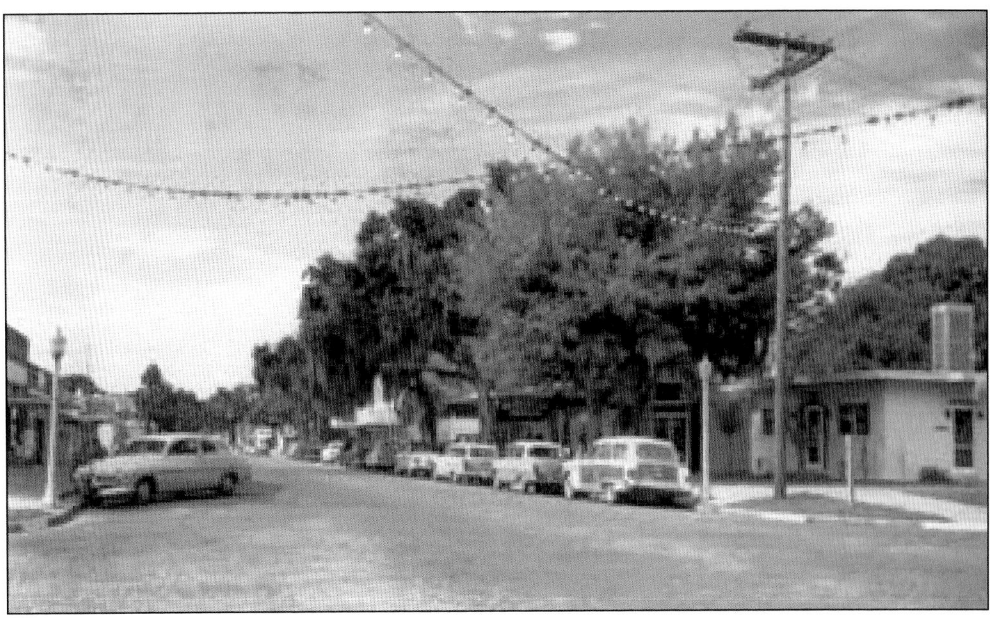

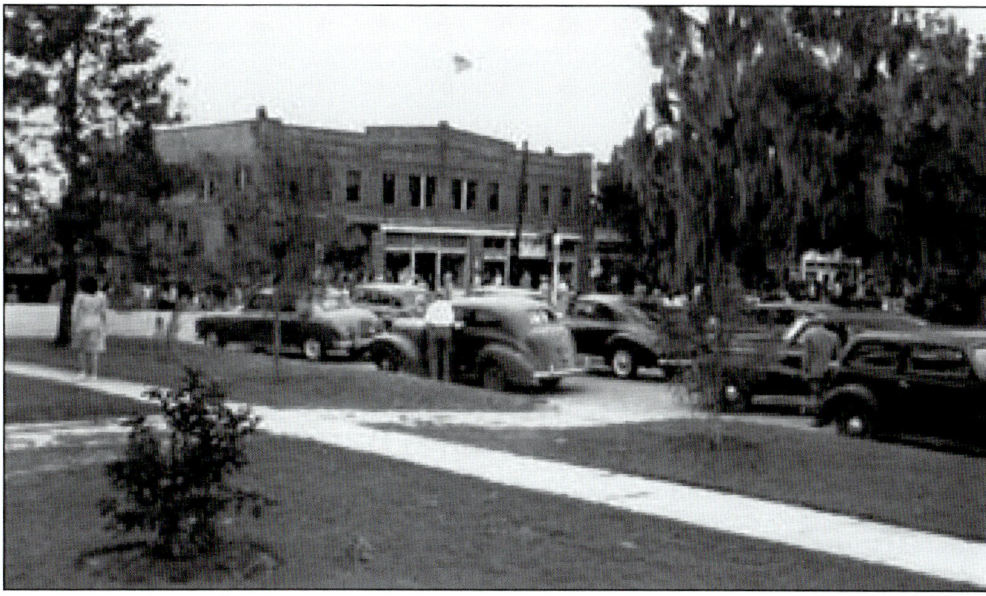

Tavareans gather in front of the Lake Building and along Irma Street for a special event in 1948. The A&P Store, the Tavares Post Office, and Peggy Roth's Department Store were all located inside the Lake Building. The sign over Peggy Roth's store announces a "selling out sale" in preparation for her move to a new building. (Courtesy of the Lake County Historical Society.)

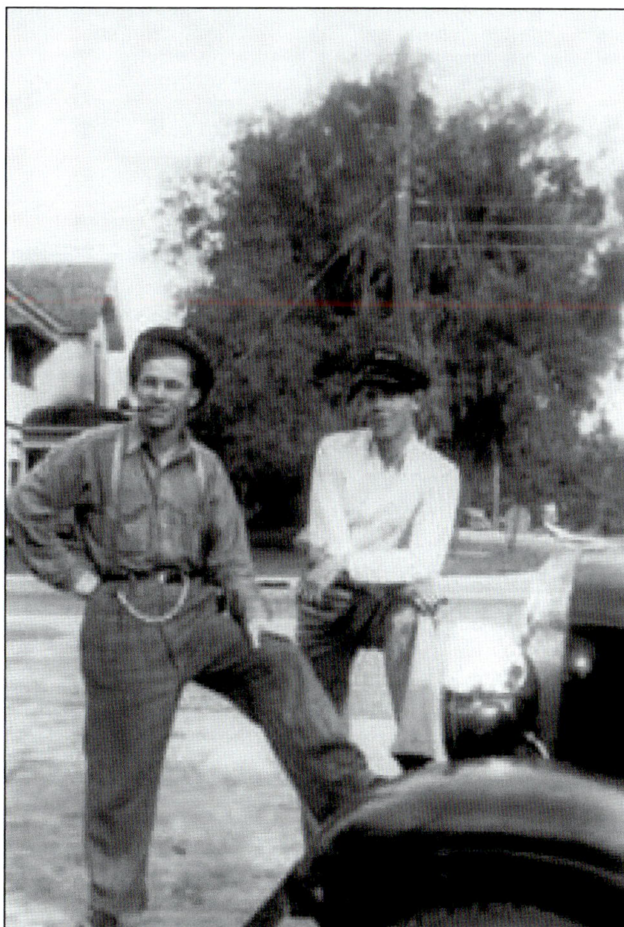

Sam Butler (left), pictured here in 1940 with Paul Foster Daniel Jr., worked at the Tavares Post Office while attending Tavares High School and after graduating. The Butler family lived on New Hampshire Avenue. Daniel, a Marine Corps veteran of World War II, was a building contractor. (Courtesy of the Tavares Historical Society.)

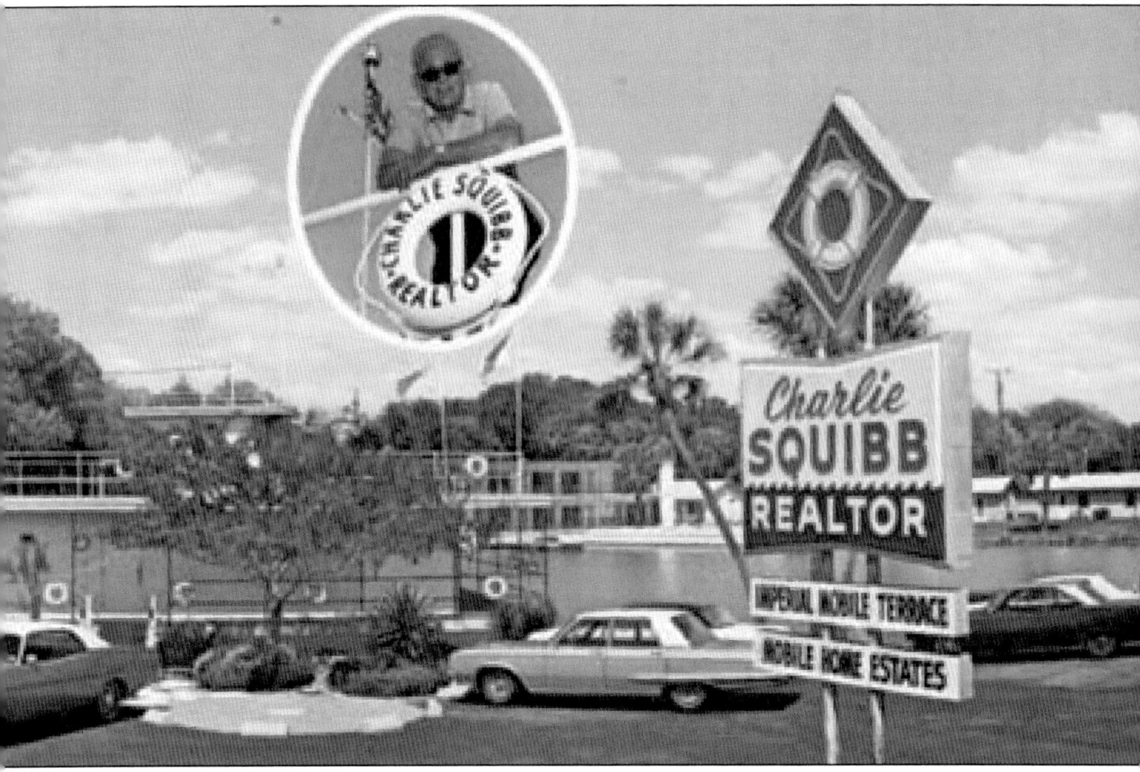

Charlie Squibb was a Lake County developer and realtor responsible for mobile home communities such as Imperial Terrace, Lake Saunders Acres, and Mobile Home Estates. Squibb moved to the area in 1954 from Tennessee. Squibb's company was one of the first in the country to create manufactured home communities where residents owned their homes. His familiar office, the SS *Squibb* pictured here, was located on Highway 441 on Lake Eustis. In 1988, Squibb and his wife, Gladys, donated 126 acres to Tavares for a nature park. The beautiful property located on Dead River Road is surrounded on three sides by water, including the Dora Canal. A Tarzan movie featuring Johnny Weissmuller and Maureen O'Sullivan was once filmed on this property with tree huts, vines, and cables for swinging. When Squibb donated the property, he said he and his wife wanted to give back to the city that did so much for them. (Courtesy of the Tavares Historical Society.)

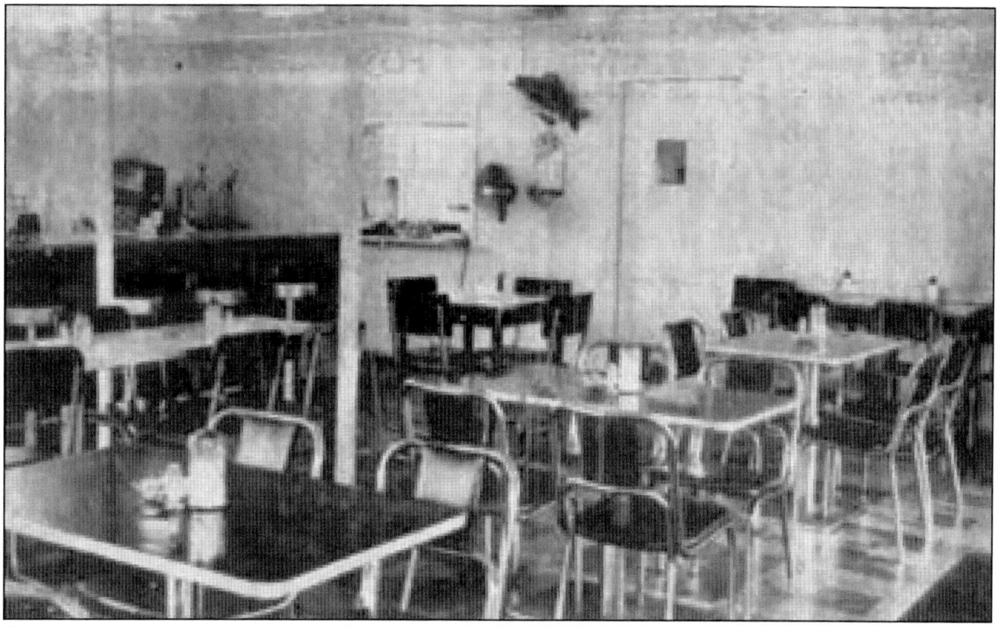

Brownie's Jungle Inn promoted itself as a place for fine foods: steaks, seafood, sandwiches, homemade pies, and ice cream. Lura Hall remembers Brownie's as a favorite hangout for the high school kids in the 1940s and 1950s. She also recalls that the owner and cook, a Mr. Brown, "was a big fella with a mustache who looked mean, but was quite gentle." (Courtesy of Clayton Bishop.)

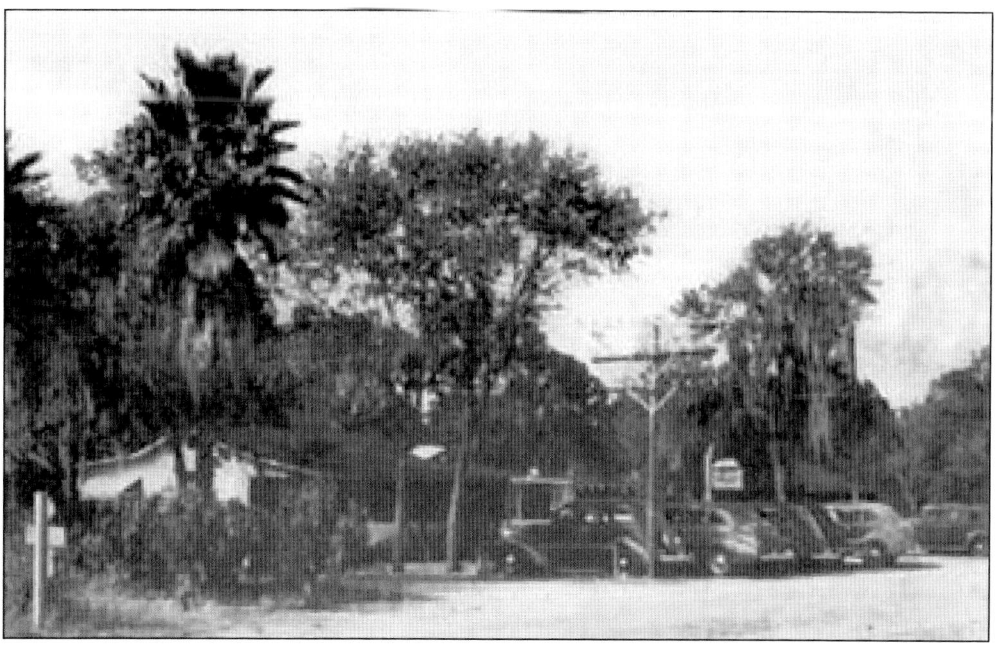

The Spinning Wheele, also called the Ye Olde Spinning Wheele Tea Room, was located on the Tavares-Eustis Road. The Spinning Wheele was owned and operated by Miss Dole since 1923. The restaurant, pictured here in the 1930s, featured "grand meals of New England style cooking." (Courtesy of Clayton Bishop.)

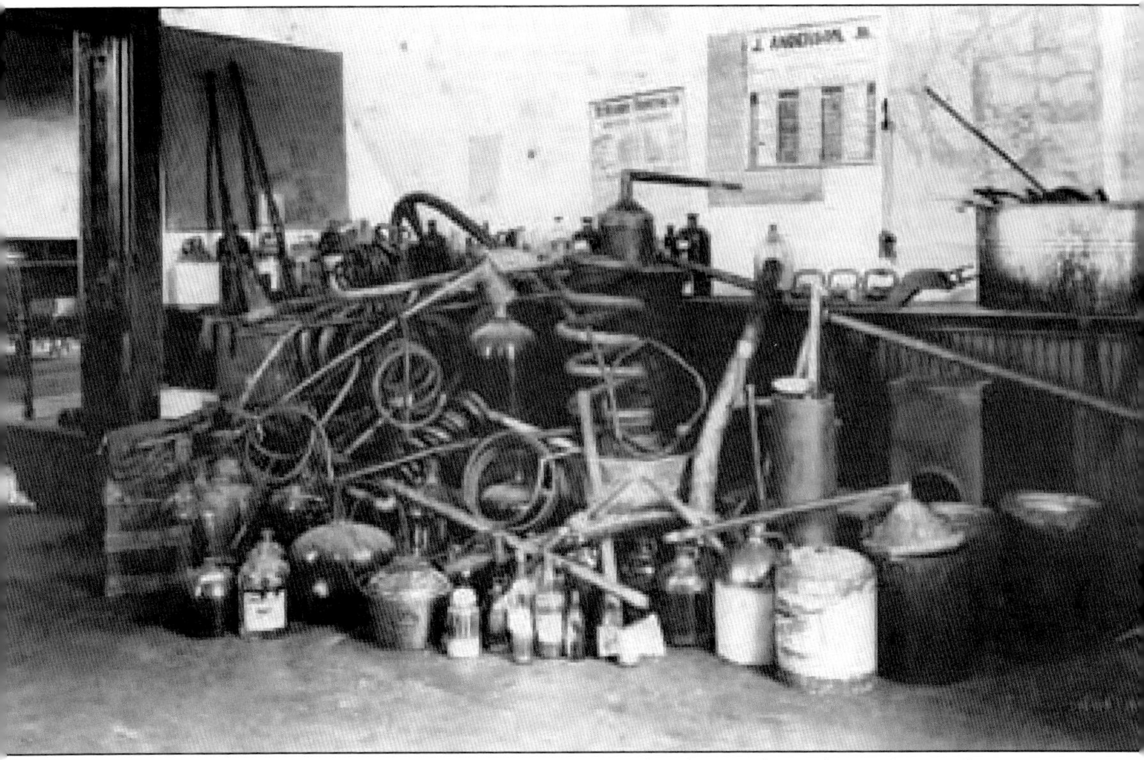

Not every business in Tavares and Lake County was a legal one. The making of moonshine—more commonly called white lightning, rot gut, or corn liquor—was a popular homemade concoction brewed out of Florida's backwoods and barns. Planters who experienced a bad year with their harvest offset their income by turning their corn into whiskey. The whiskey was also thought to be good for medicinal purposes. Backwoods brewers worked under the cover of night, which is why they were called moonshiners. Bootleggers were the men who transported the illegal liquor. Stock car racing had its roots with bootleggers. The moonshine stills, paraphernalia, jugs, bottles, and weapons seen here are in a storage room behind the courtroom at the old county courthouse. These stills were confiscated by Sheriff W.B. Gibson in 1924. Lawmen rarely arrested or charged moonshiners with making illegal liquor. (Courtesy of the Lake County Historical Society.)

Seven

Passing Time in Lane Park

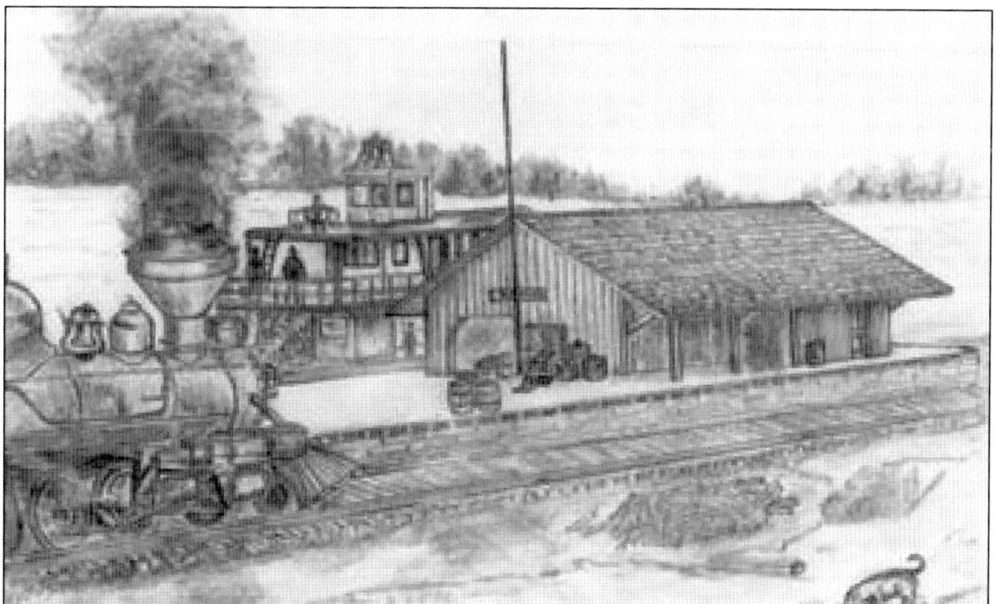

Lane Park is located three miles southwest of downtown Tavares. Before Lane Park received its name, after Capt. A.J. Lane, sections of the area went by the names of the various homesteads, such as Woodlea, Nithsdale, Oxmoor, and Esperance. Much of the land was owned by J. Traill Taylor. Lane Park was situated at the terminus of the St. Johns & Lake Eustis Railroad. (Courtesy of Bob Grenier Sr.)

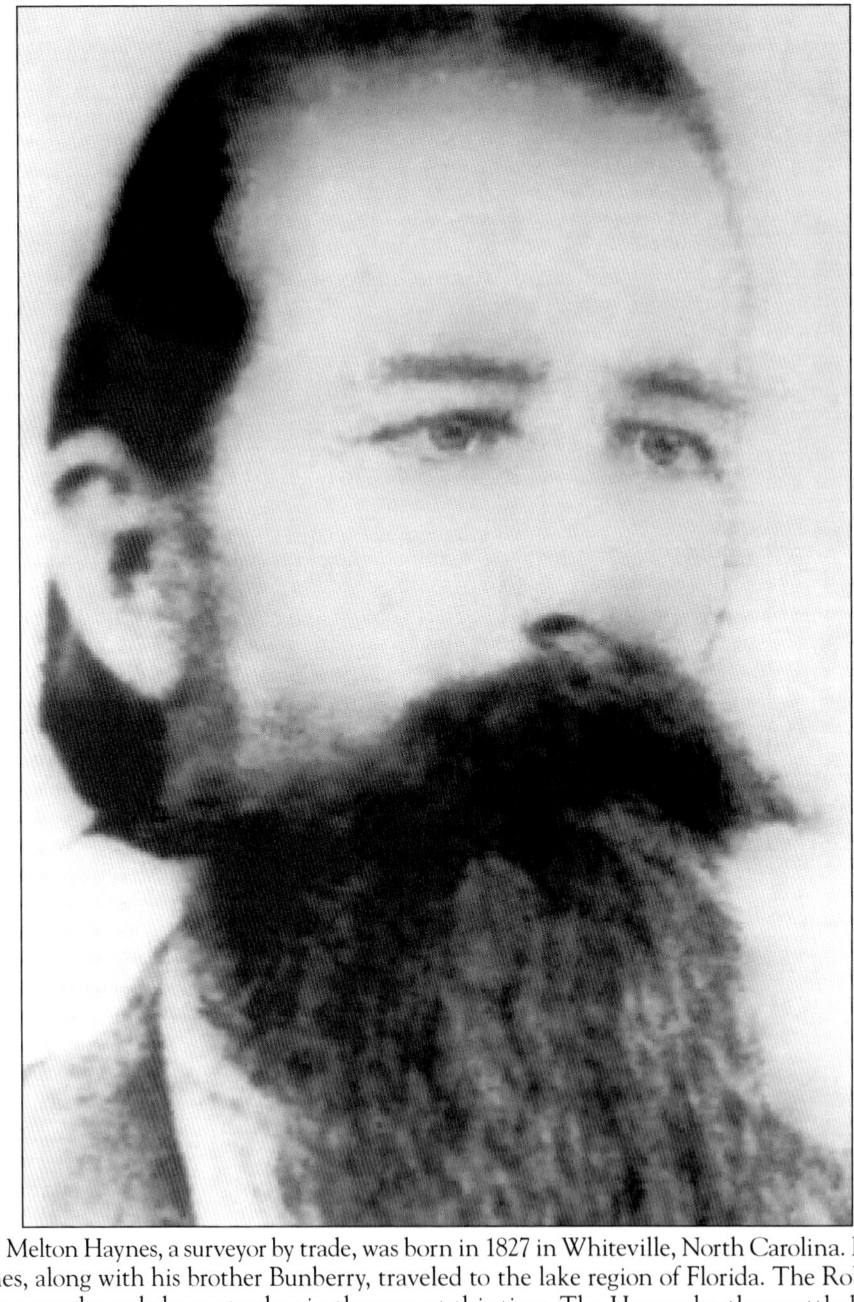

Capt. Melton Haynes, a surveyor by trade, was born in 1827 in Whiteville, North Carolina. In 1845, Haynes, along with his brother Bunberry, traveled to the lake region of Florida. The Robertson family were the only homesteaders in the area at this time. The Haynes brothers settled on the north side of Lake Harris and planted a quarter acre of seeds taken from the best imported sweet oranges Haynes could find in Charleston. These plantings became the birth of the citrus industry in the region. Haynes married Sarah Isabella Vaught in 1849. He was elected to the Florida House of Representatives in 1854 and the Florida Senate in 1866. During the War Between the States, he served as a Confederate cavalry officer in Florida. His commanding officer was Capt. J.J. Dickison, Florida's famous "Swamp Fox." In 1868, Haynes and his wife purchased land on the south side of Lake Harris, becoming the first settlers in the area of Lane Park. Captain Haynes died in 1883. (Courtesy of the Leesburg Masonic Lodge No. 58.)

Isabella May Haynes Keeling, pictured here around 1910, was the eldest daughter of Melton and Sarah Haynes. She was born in 1852 in Jacksonville, Florida. In 1868, when Isabella May's parents purchased the land at Lane Park, she was so inspired by the beauty of the property, she gave it the name Woodlea, which means "wooded meadow." (Courtesy of Rob and Gary Boone.)

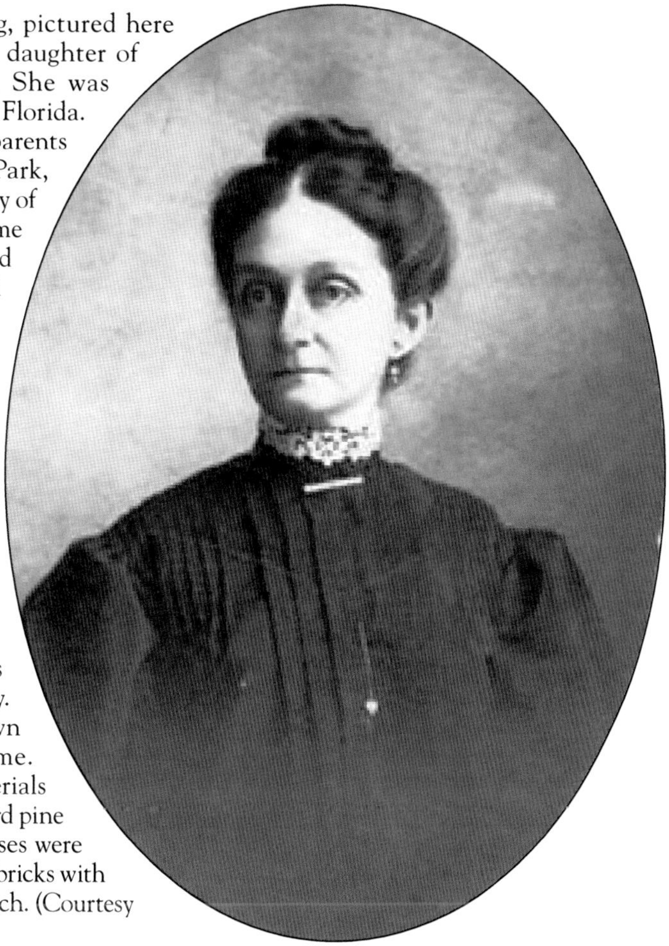

In 1871, Melton Haynes built his home on the Woodlea property. This style of structure was known as a double-pen cracker home. The home was built with materials supplied by the land, such as hard pine and cypress. Many cracker houses were set on foundations made of sand bricks with a shake roof and wraparound porch. (Courtesy of Bob Grenier Sr.)

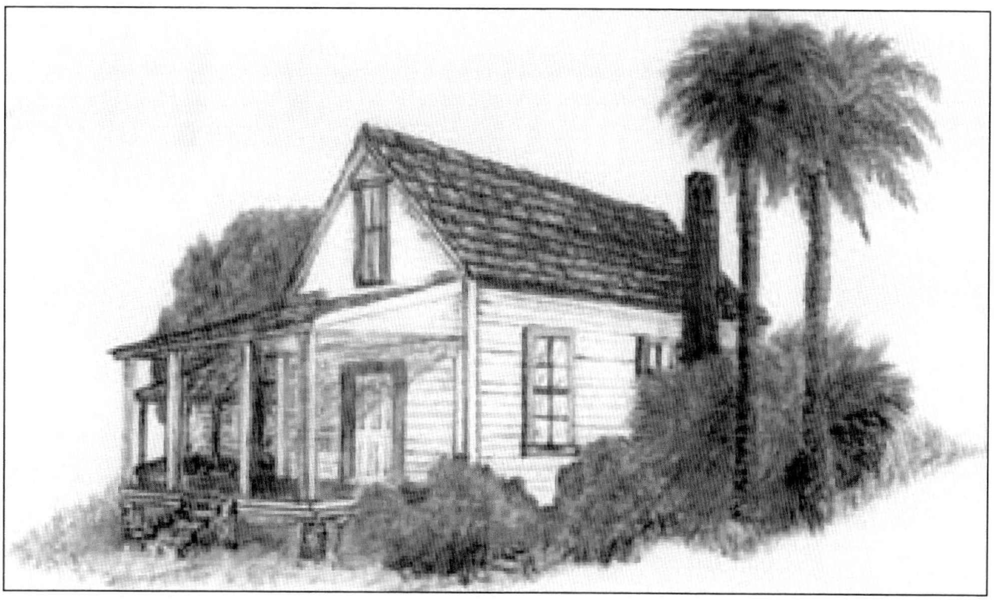

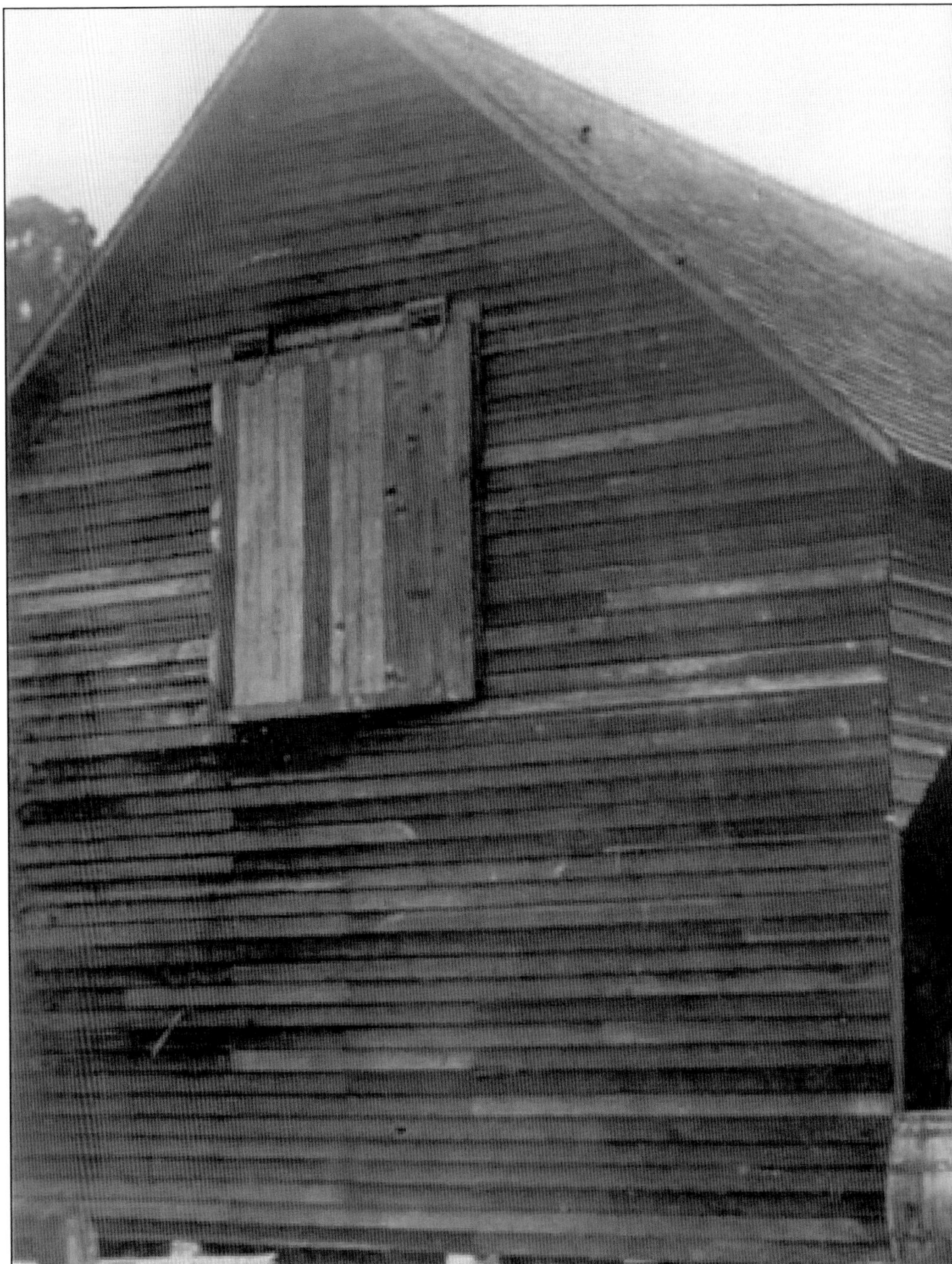

In June 1892, Amos Wakelin, a Philadelphia insurance agent, purchased the Woodlea property from Sarah Haynes. Captain Haynes had died in January 1883. In 1893, Wakelin and his wife, Ellie Morgan, restarted the orange grove operation at Woodlea but soon experienced the twin freezes of 1894 and 1895. The Wakelins established the Woodlea Company and then expanded

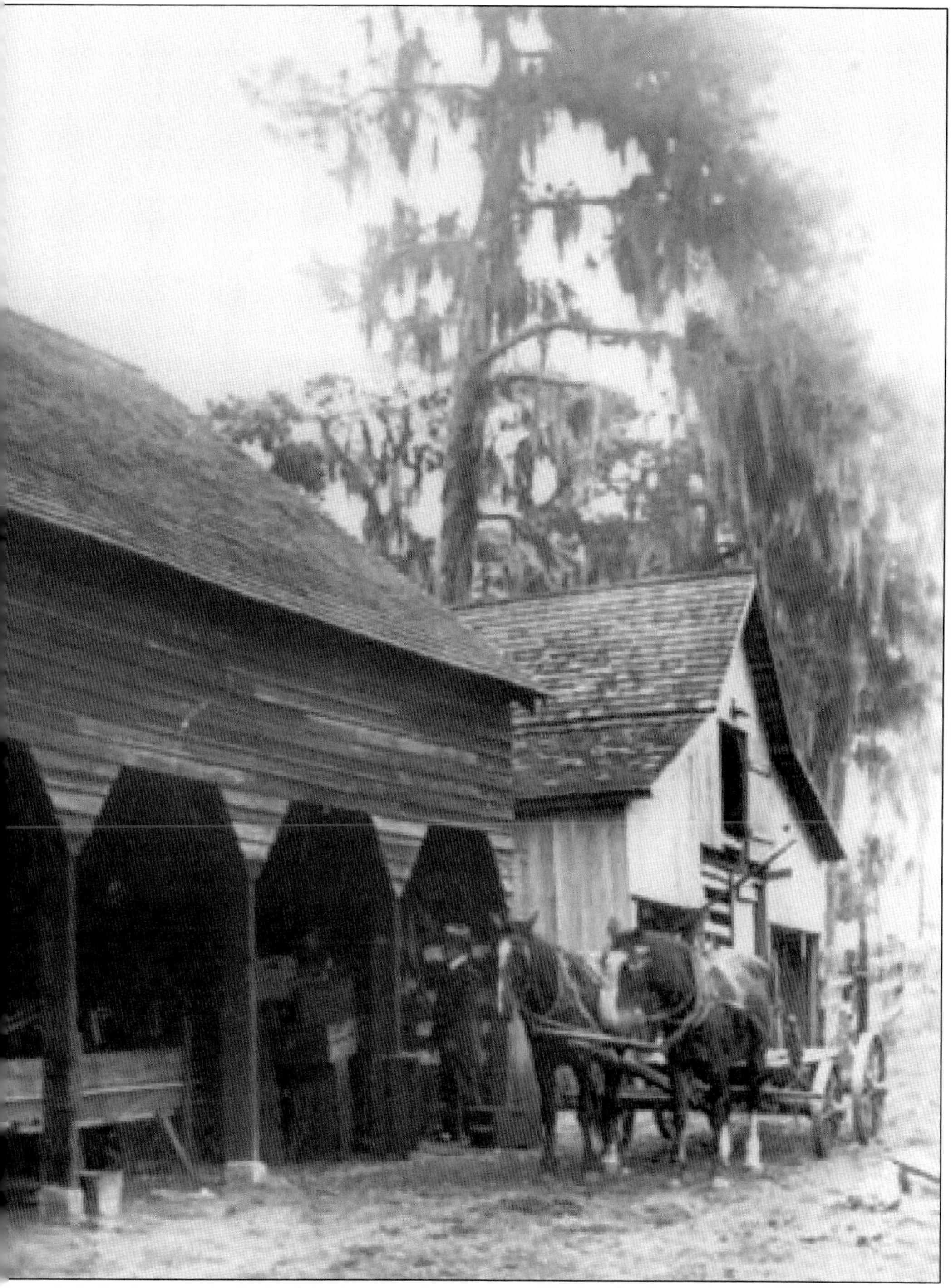

their business to include shipping navel oranges to England, where Amos Wakelin was born. In this 1916 photograph, Amos Wakelin is at his Woodlea packinghouse preparing to have a shipment of oranges loaded onto the wagon. (Courtesy of Jean Sims Miller.)

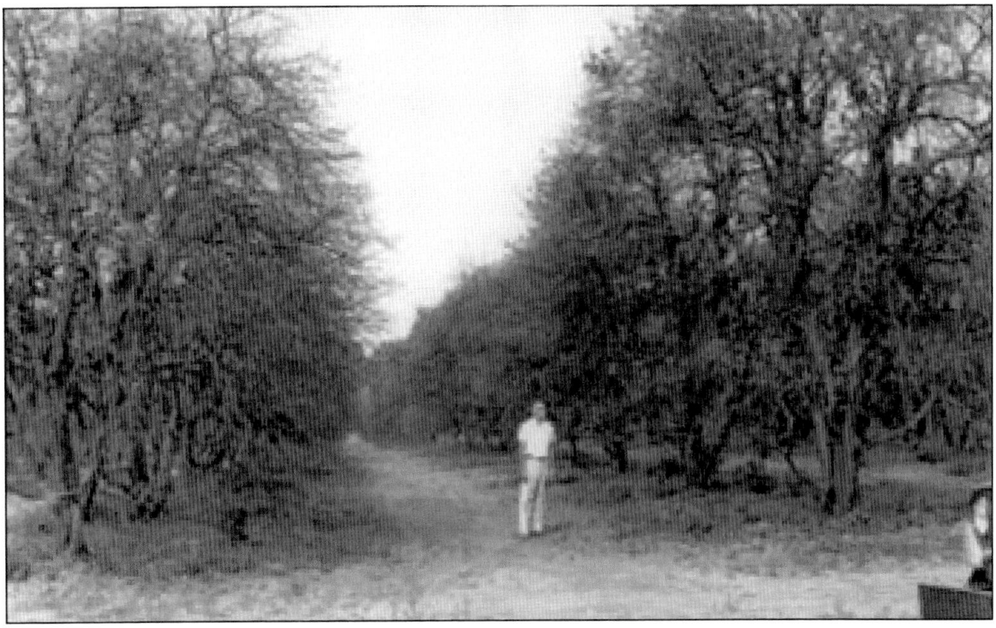

Guil Sims, nephew of Guilford and Maud Wakelin, inspects the citrus trees at Woodlea following a rare springtime freeze on April 1, 1963. Guil's sister-in-law Margaret Brown remembers a disheartened Guil saying, "One good overnight freeze could wipe out the lifetimes of four men!" Guil was referring to Captain Haynes, Amos and Guilford Wakelin, and himself. (Courtesy of Jean Sims Miller.)

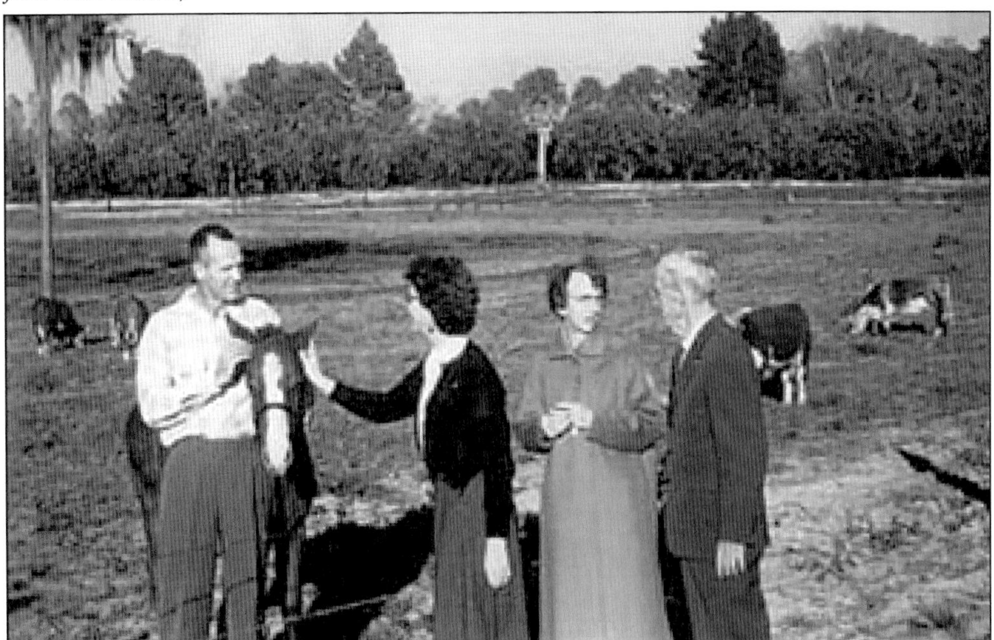

In 1945, Guil Sims arrived at Woodlea to live. Sims, along with his wife, Harriet, would advance Woodlea into the modern age of citrus growing. In this c. 1955 photograph taken at Woodlea are, from left to right, Guil Sims, Harriet Sims, Amabel Moore Taylor, and Guilford Wakelin. (Courtesy of Jean Sims Miller.)

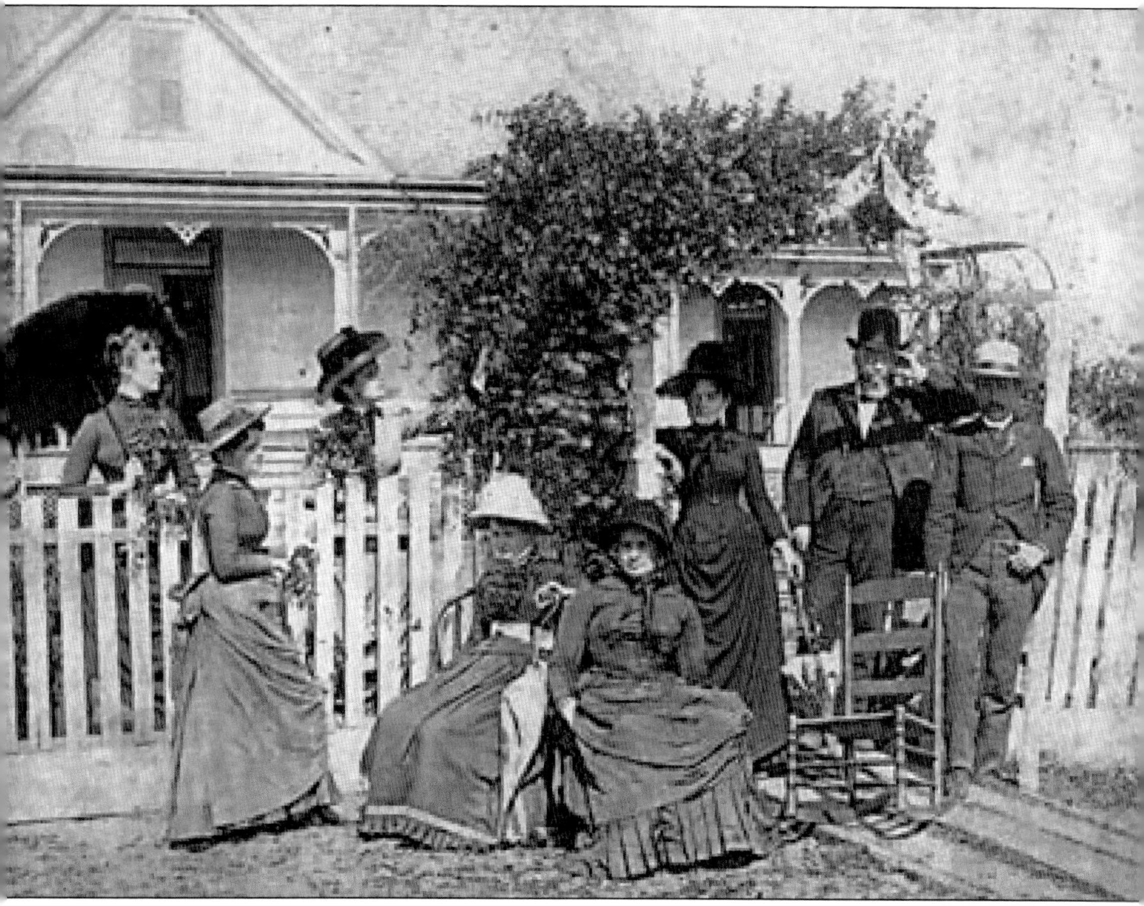

Daniel Shipman Troy of Montgomery County, Alabama, was a lieutenant colonel for the 60th Alabama Infantry during the War Between the States. In 1862, Troy was wounded leading a charge at Drewry's Bluff, Virginia. Lying on the field, he was captured and nursed back to health in a Union hospital. In the 1880s, Colonel Troy, a lawyer and businessman, built a home at Lane Park that he called Oxmoor (above). This photograph shows the Troy family and friends at Oxmoor. From left to right are Mrs. Robert London, Kate Finley Troy, Clara Lee, Irene Semple, Mrs. D.S. Troy, Cecile Baldwin, Daniel Shipman Troy, and Robert London. (Courtesy of the Lake County Historical Society.)

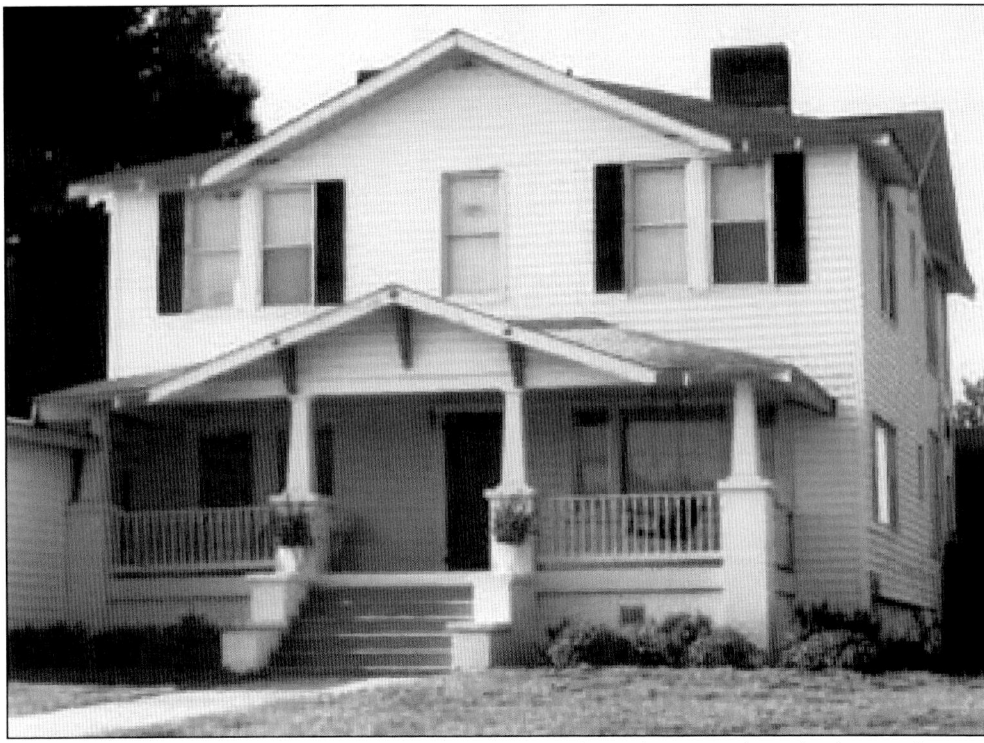

Alonzo Franklin Herndon, born in 1858, was a former slave who trained as a barber. He became one of Atlanta's most successful and wealthiest African American business leaders. In 1893, Herndon married Adrienne McNeil. Their son Norris Bumstead was born in 1897. Pictured is the Herndon vacation home in Lane Park. (Courtesy of the Tavares Historical Society.)

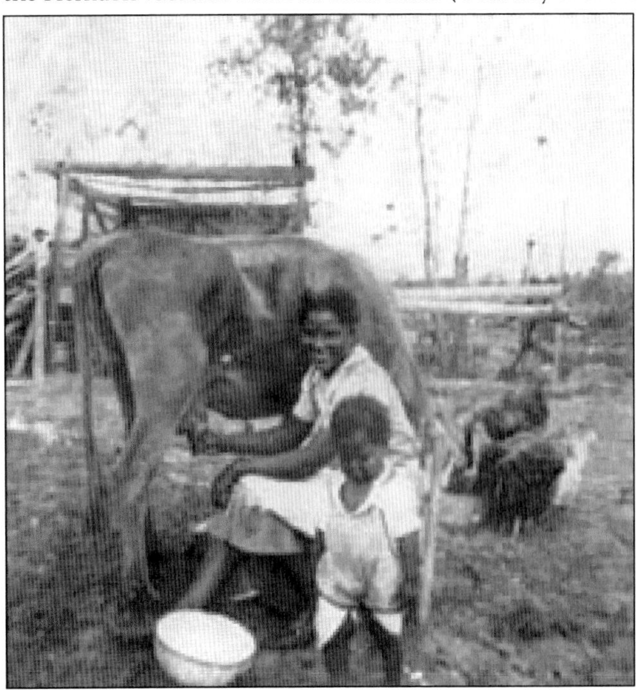

Mary Wiggins Shorts, pictured here in 1945 at their home near County Road 561 called Bayhead Plantation, came to Lane Park from Georgia in the early 1920s. She was married to Fred Shorts, who arrived from Georgia with his brothers, Sidney and Samuel, around 1916. Pictured with Mary is her granddaughter Carolyn Shorts. (Courtesy of Bernice Shorts Odums.)

The Leroy Kenon family lived near State Road 19 in Lane Park. Pictured in this c. 1960 photograph with Kenon are, from left to right, his granddaughter Sylvia Kenon, his daughter Lou Ethel Kenon, and son Joseph Kenon. Lou Ethel was a home health care worker and is very active in the Tavares community and her church, Shiloh Missionary Baptist. (Courtesy of Lou Ethel Kenon Jenkins.)

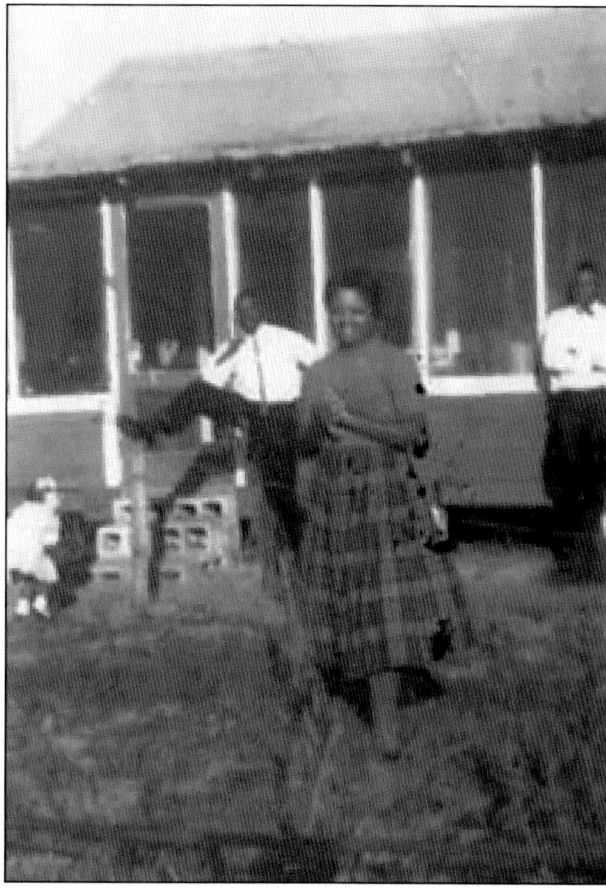

Pictured in this c. 1960 photograph taken at Mount Moriah Church are, from left to right, Mary Wiggins Shorts, Fred Shorts, and Ruby Shorts, Mary and Fred's daughter. When Fred arrived in Lane Park in 1916, he found work in the turpentine industry. He also planted and harvested citrus on his Lane Park farm. In later years, Fred owned his own lawn and garden service, which he operated until his retirement. (Courtesy of Bernice Shorts Odums.)

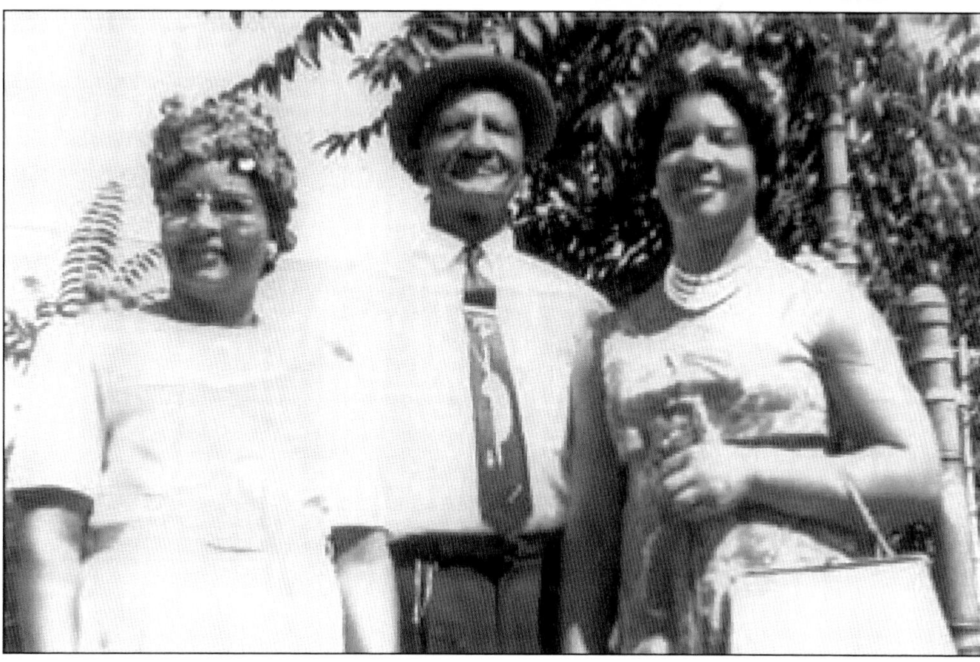

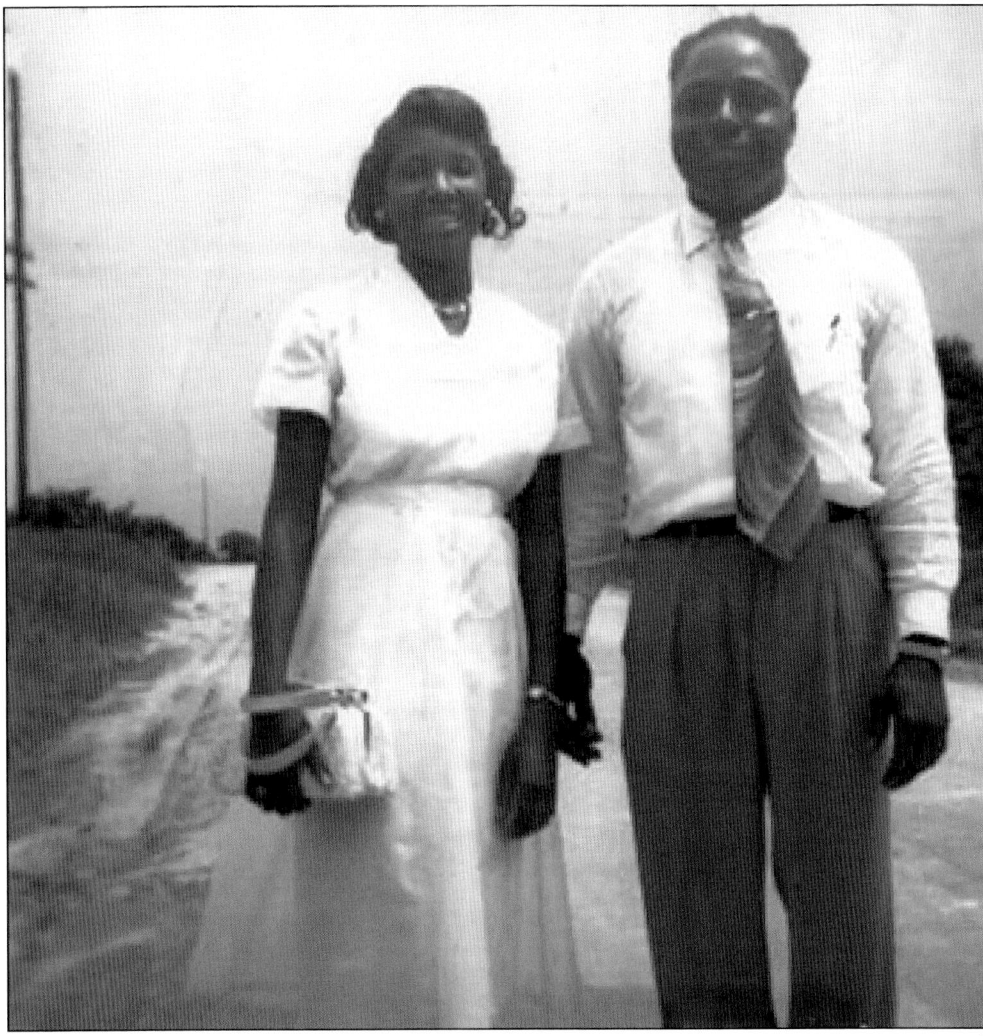

Bernice Shorts Odums—pictured here in 1951 with her cousin Samuel Parker at Mount Moriah Church—was born and raised in Lane Park. She attended Harrison Academy in Tavares and went on to graduate from Eustis Vocational High School. She attended the National Business College in Nashville, Tennessee, and Boston College for Business. Bernice stayed in Boston and worked at John Hancock Mutual Life Insurance before returning to Lane Park in 1964. She worked for the Lake County School Board as a teacher's aide and then as an assistant purchasing agent. She retired from the school board in 1998 after 34 years. Bernice has four children: Kevin, Karen, Kenton, and Keith. Bernice recalls that everyone in Lane Park looked out for each other. If a family had chickens, they shared their eggs. If they had cows, they shared their milk. And if they grew fruits and vegetables, they shared their harvest. (Courtesy of Bernice Shorts Odums.)

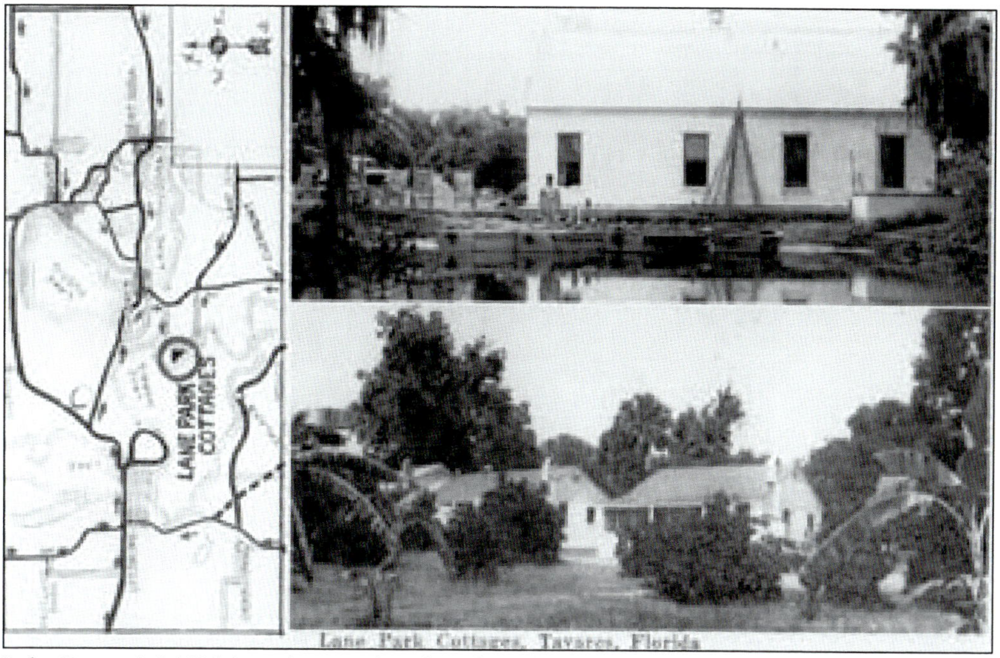

Lake County's 1,400 lakes, plus its miles of creeks and canals, make for excellent freshwater fishing. Tavares, bordered by Lake Harris, Lake Dora, and Lake Eustis, is at the heart of Lake County's sport and recreational fishing. Florida fish camps became very popular with tourists in the early 1900s, well before high-rise resorts or man-made attractions. The camps attracted visitors from all over the world. The state's beautiful tropical scenery enhanced the tourists' enjoyment while they fished for bass, bream, perch, or crappie. Though most of the old-time fish camps are gone, Tavares and Lane Park still feature fishing camps that have been around for more than 50 years, such as Palm Gardens on the Dead River and the Lane Park Cottages on Lake Harris (pictured here), owned by W.C. Willingham. (Courtesy of Glenda LaRoe.)

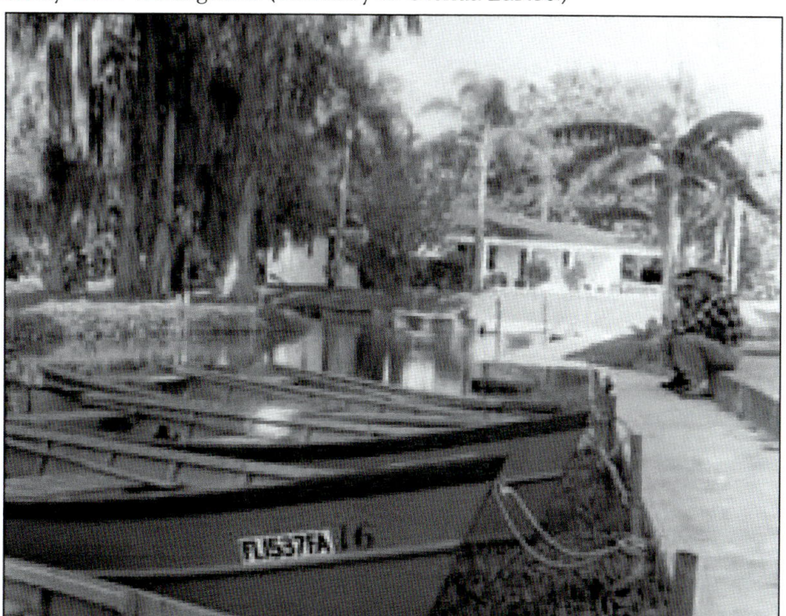

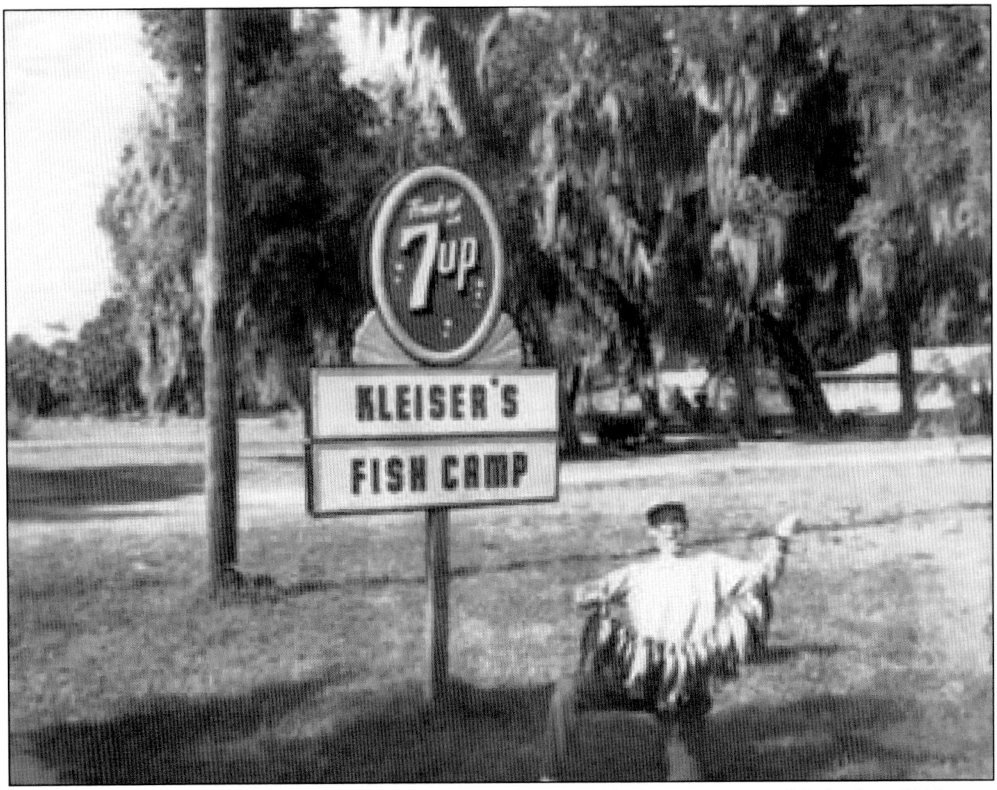

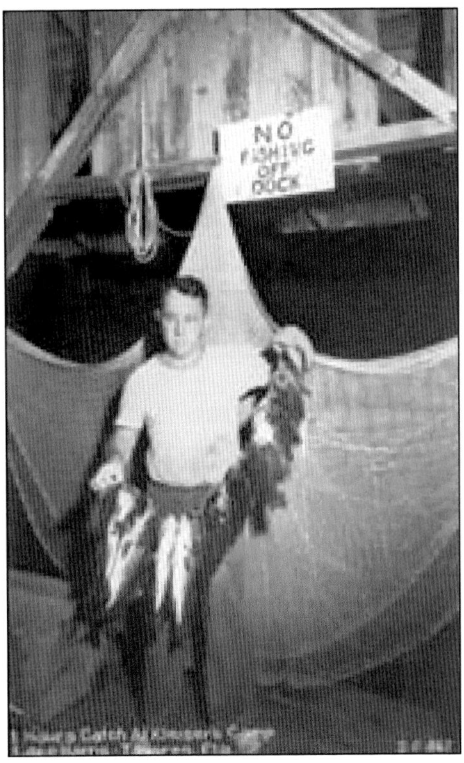

Kleiser's Fish Camp was established in 1918 on an island located in the middle of Lake Harris. Robert Forest Kleiser acquired the island and built six cottages, several boat sheds, and a pier. Several years later, Kleiser disassembled the cottages and moved the camp to Lane Park. Pictured is Kleiser's grandson George Kleiser Jr. in 1967. (Courtesy of Jane Kleiser Whaley.)

George Kleiser, pictured here in 1948, was born in 1919. His mother, Eva May Mattison, had come to Tavares around 1916, staying at Marie King's Tavares Inn. Eva May soon met George's father, Robert Forest Kleiser, at the "Flowing Wells" in Lane Park while he was on his 50-foot fruit boat loading containers with water. (Courtesy of Jane Kleiser Whaley.)

At Lane Park, Robert Forest Kleiser reassembled one cottage, brought over from the island, up on a hill for his family to live in. All the other cottages were placed near or along the Lake Harris shoreline. The Kleiser Fish Camp became more accessible and very popular. Pictured are Frances and Clayton Innes of Cleveland, Ohio, who were regular winter guests. (Courtesy of Jane Kleiser Whaley.)

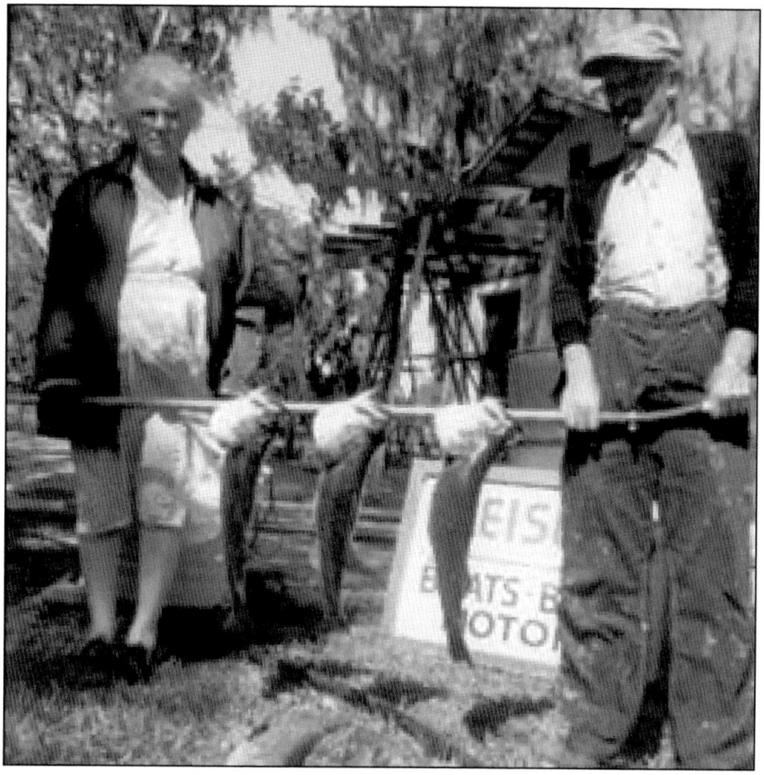

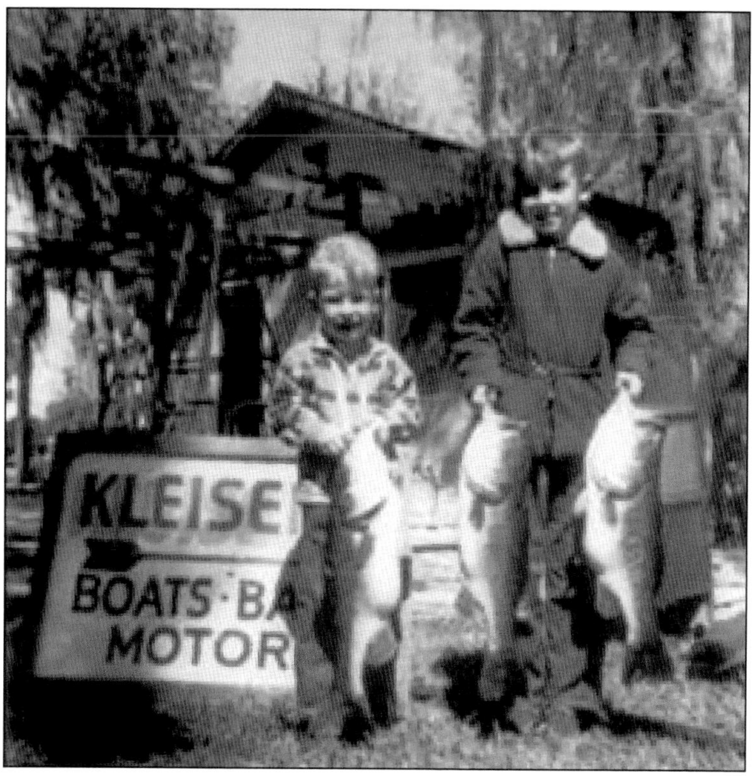

Freida and George Kleiser raised five children at Kleiser's Fish Camp in Lane Park: Opal, George Jr., Forest, Wilma Jane, and Jason. In this 1959 photograph, experienced fishermen Forest (left) and George Kleiser Jr. are holding largemouth bass they caught in Lake Harris. (Courtesy of Jane Kleiser Whaley.)

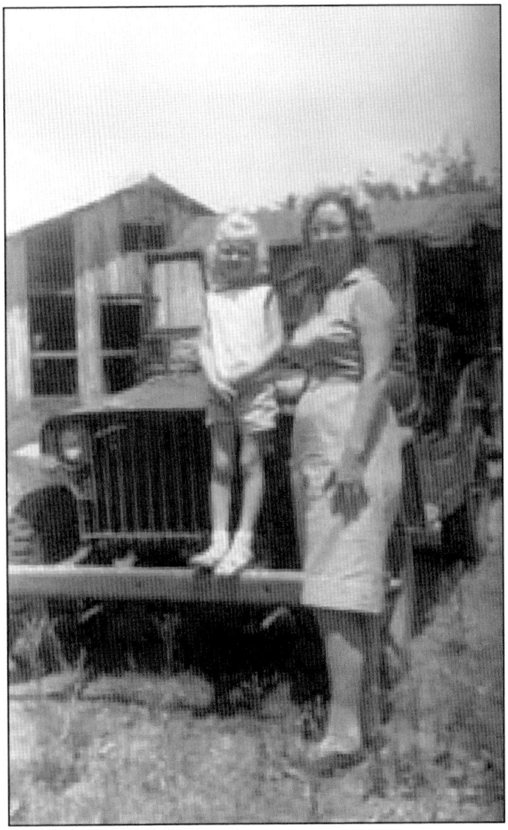

Freida Smith Kleiser was 15 when her family moved from Tennessee to Mount Dora in 1944. In 1948, while working at Nelson's Milk Bar in Mount Dora, Freida was introduced to George Kleiser, whom she married that year. The couple lived in a houseboat at the Kleiser Fish Camp. Kleiser's daughter Wilma Jane is pictured here with Freida in 1964. (Courtesy of Jane Kleiser Whaley.)

The Lane Park Road Prison was operating from the 1930s into the 1960s. The prisoners spent long hours in the hot Florida sun clearing trees and brush for roads. The Lane Park prison was one of the models for the 1967 motion picture *Cool Hand Luke*, starring Paul Newman and George Kennedy. Remnants of the prison are still standing today. (Author's collection.)

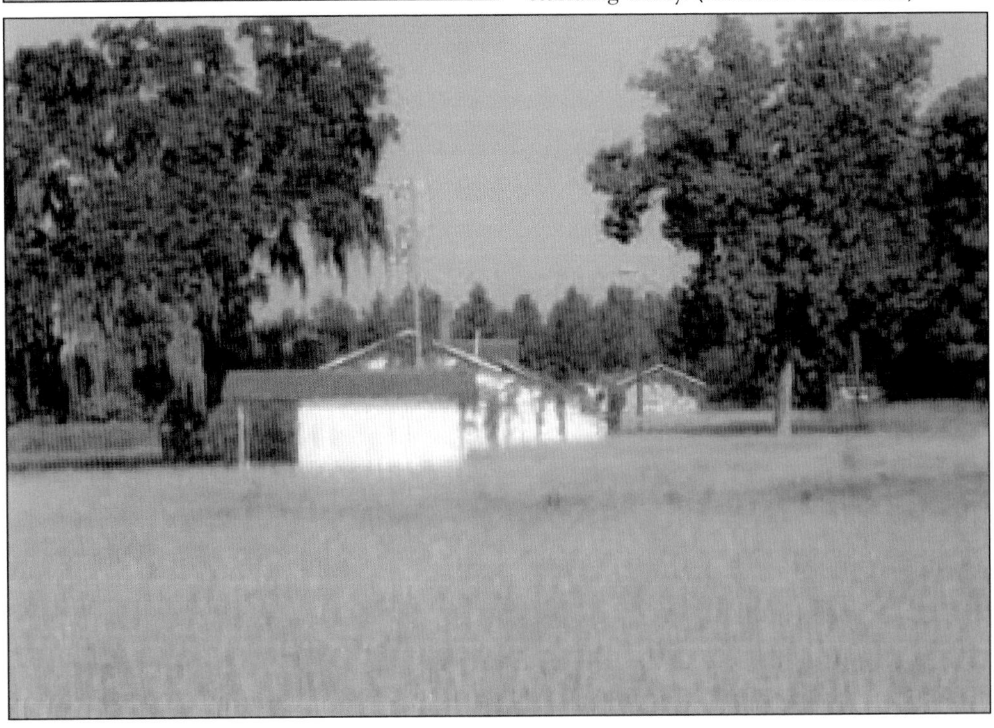

Eight

Building on a Historic Foundation

A series of "town hall" meetings began in 2006 to establish a plan for Tavares's future. The meetings resulted in the creation of a vision statement that begins, "Tavares, the Capital Waterfront City of Lake County, building on a historic foundation . . ." In 2007, Tavares began implementing its plan. Reaching back in time to the dawn of aviation, Tavares created its new brand as America's Seaplane City. (Courtesy of the City of Tavares.)

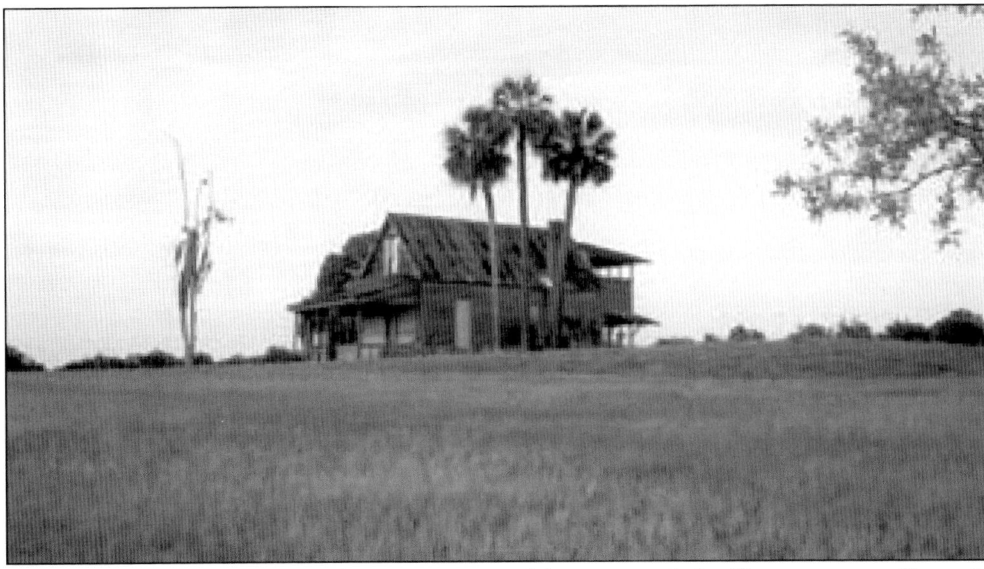

The 1871 Woodlea House, seen here at its original location on Lake Harris, was significant in Tavares history. In 2005, Tavares moved the historic home from its original location on private land to a new location on city-owned property. Though the plan called for Woodlea to be refurbished, the house sat unattended to. (Author's collection.)

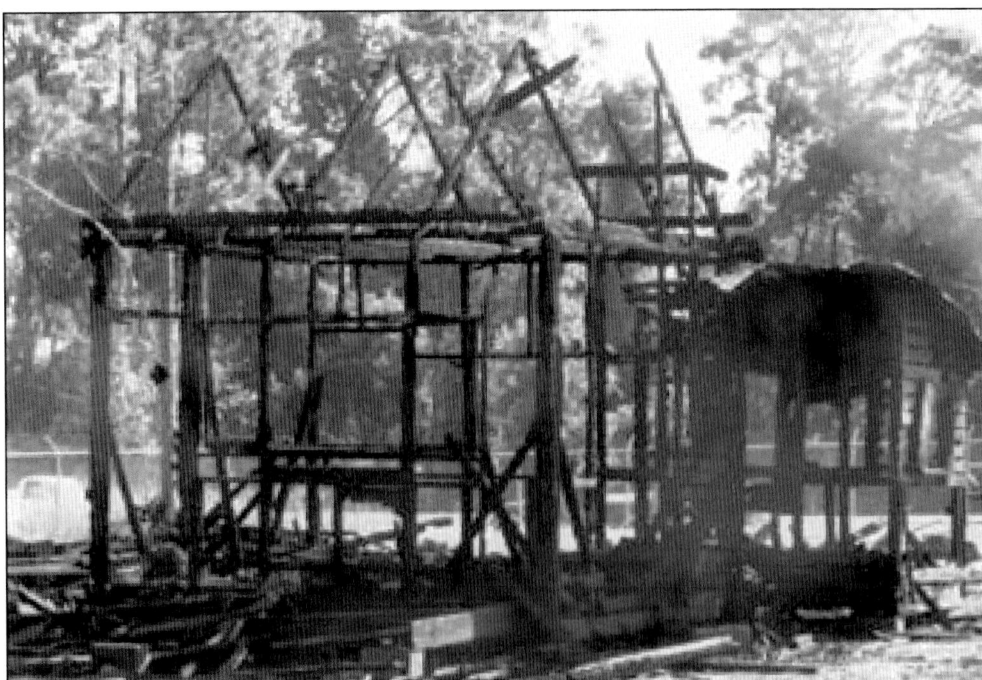

In September 2007, two arsonists burned down the Woodlea House, ending its 136-year history. Because of the popularity and special attraction this historic home held, the fire and its aftermath made newspaper headlines locally, statewide, and nationally, as well as television newscasts. An archeological dig followed shortly after the fire to salvage any relics. (Author's collection.)

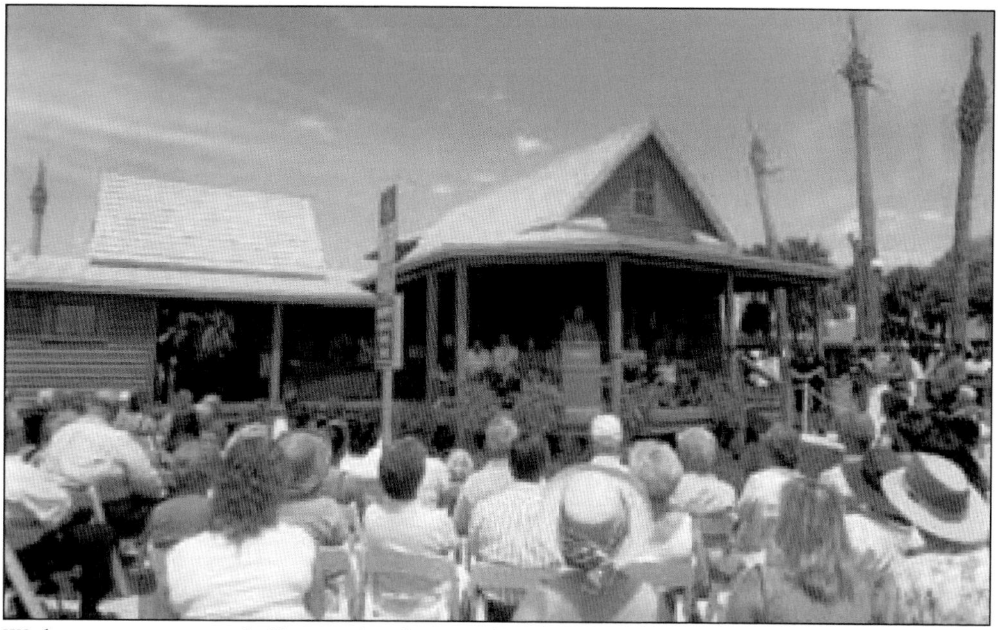

With an outpouring of affection for the Woodlea House, Tavares reconstructed the house at Wooton Park as part of the city's vision to build on a historic foundation. In 2010, at the opening dedication of Tavares's new Marina and Seaplane Base, hundreds of people gather to witness the ribbon-cutting ceremony of the new Woodlea. The Prop Shop at Woodlea serves as an airport terminal and gift shop. (Author's collection.)

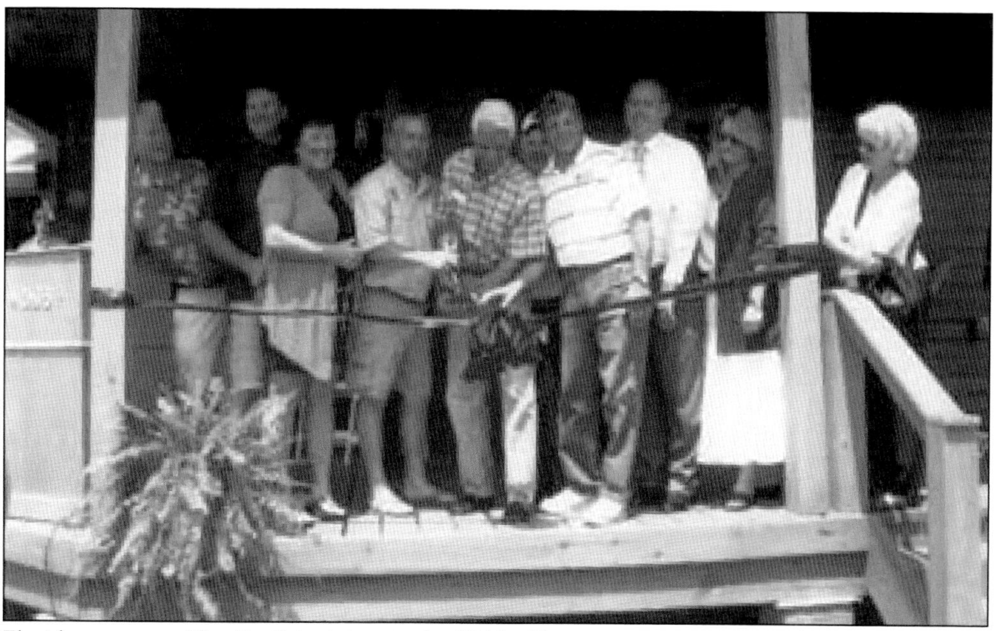

Florida governor Charlie Crist joins in the 2010 ribbon-cutting ceremony of the new Woodlea House. From left to right are City Administrator John Drury, Councilman Kirby Smith, Vice Mayor Lori Pfister, Mayor Robert Wolfe, Gov. Charlie Crist, Sen. Alan Hayes, Councilman Bob Grenier, Councilman Sandy Gamble, former mayor Nancy Clutts, and Tavares Historical Society secretary Brenda Smith. (Author's collection.)

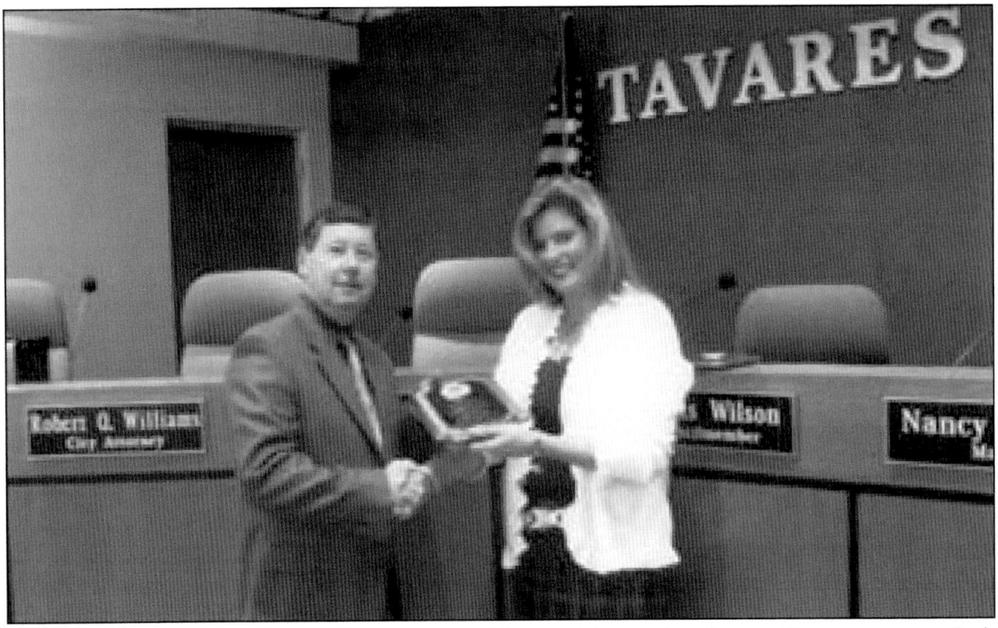

Former Tavares mayor Nancy Clutts, pictured here with another former Tavares mayor, Bob Speaks, launched the series of "town hall" meetings in 2006 that established the historic plan for Tavares's future. Clutts had been appointed by Mayor Leo Vaughn to fill a vacancy on the city council, though it took three attempts for her to finally accept Leo Vaughn's request. (Courtesy of Nancy Clutts.)

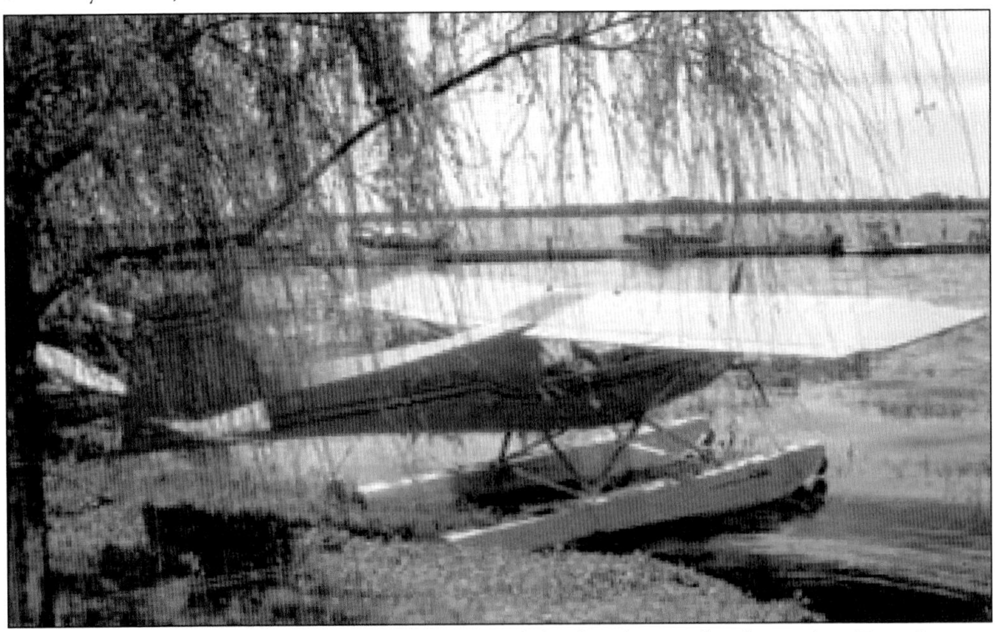

In 1914, record-setting aviatrix Clara Adams and the first licensed airline pilot, Tony Jannus, made historic flights into the lakes surrounding Tavares in aircraft such as the Thomas Flying Boat and the Benoist XIV. Today, there is a virtual east-west runway on Lake Dora, and the Federal Aviation Administration has issued Tavares's new seaplane port the identifier number FA1. (Author's collection.)

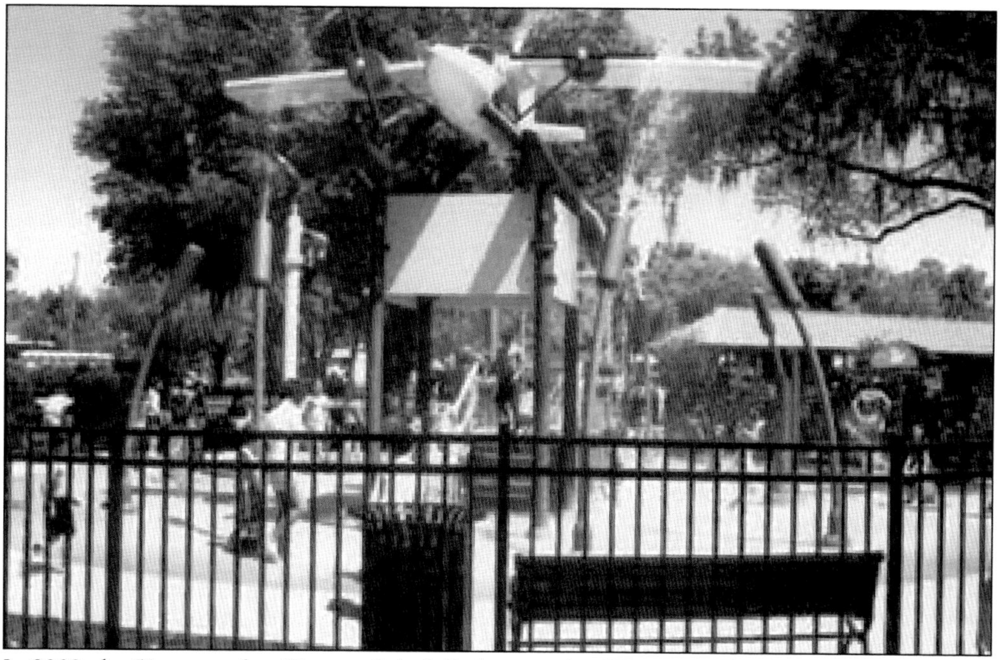

In 2009, the 50-square-foot Tavares Splash Park opened in Wooton Park. The splash park, which has become a popular children's attraction, features a seaplane with working propellers called the Rain Plane, cattails, water cannons, wet slides, aquatic-themed animals, and an array of water-spouting devices. (Author's collection.)

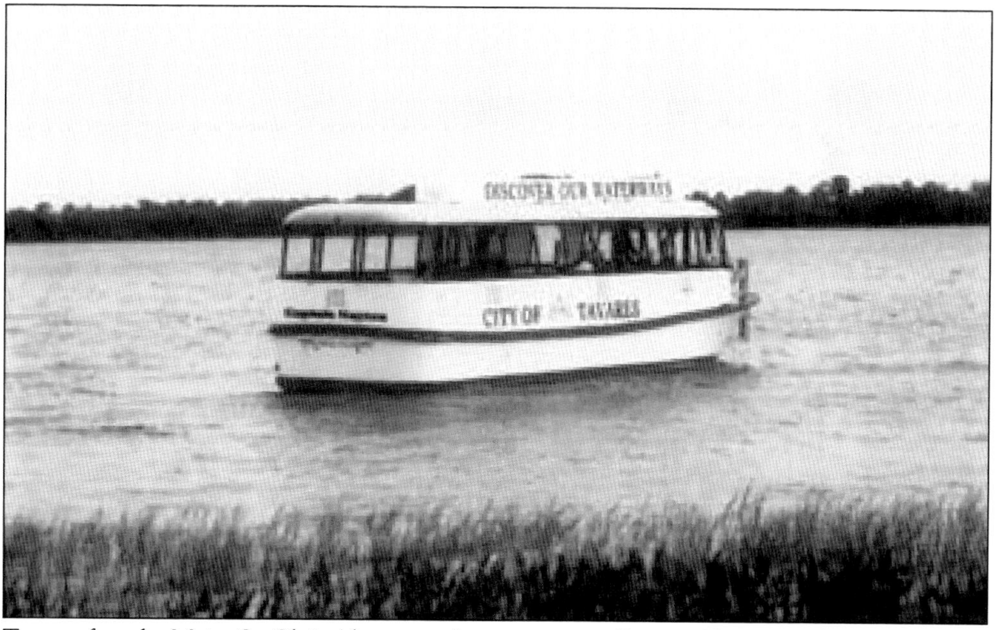

Tavares founder Major St. Clair Abrams and citrus pioneer Captain Haynes each operated water taxi services through Florida's waterways in the late 19th century. In 2008, the City of Tavares purchased and refurbished two water taxis to shuttle visitors across Lake Dora to and from Mount Dora during special events. The water taxis were named to honor Major St. Clair Abrams and Captain Haynes. (Author's collection.)

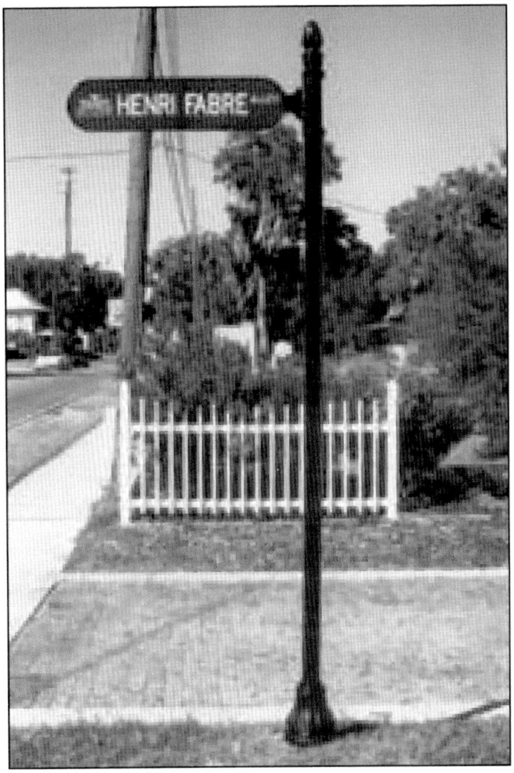

In 2010, Tavares began improvements of its 15 downtown alleyways, with each alleyway receiving a name for identification. The Tavares Historical Society provided a list of names for the alleyways (approved by the city council) that featured 11 well-known family names from Tavares history, such as Marie King (below), and four from seaplane history, including Henri Fabre, the inventor of *Le Canard*, the first seaplane in history. Other Tavares family names honored with alleyways include Cromartie, Gardner, Blanche Sperry, Boulware, T.A. Hux, J.N. Flowers, Talley, Bennye Kinsler, Shorts, and Coven. Seaplane pioneers include Clara Adams, John Cyril Porte, and Glenn Curtiss. (Both, author's collection.)

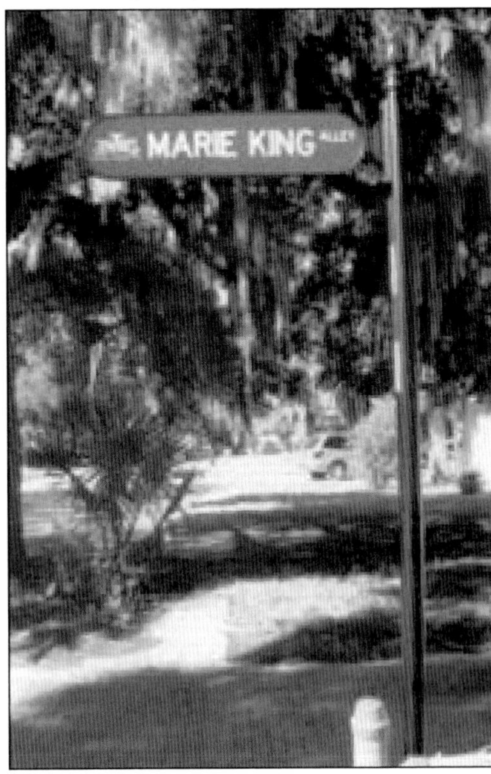

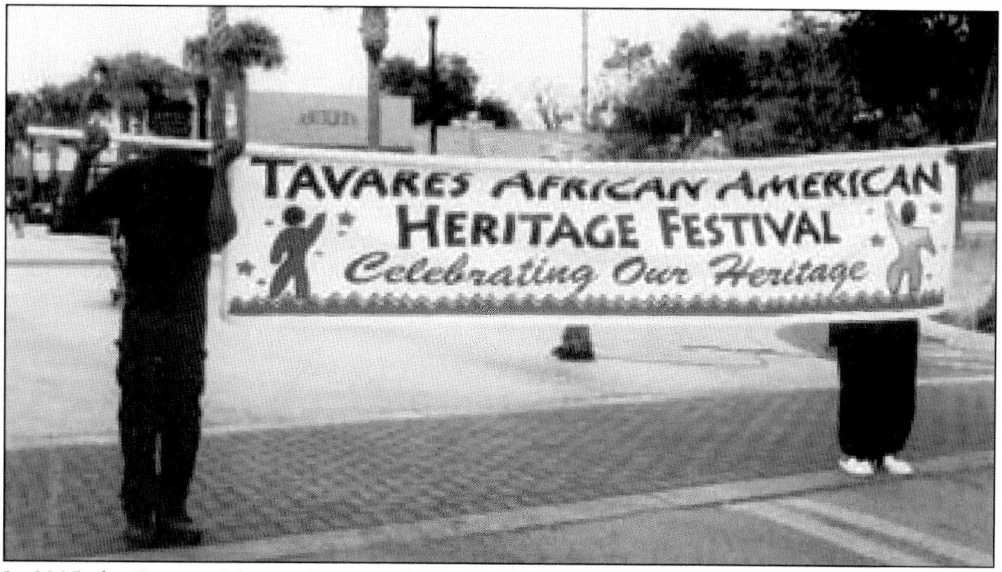

In 2005, the Tavares African American Heritage Organization was established to provide cultural, educational, religious, civic, and charitable contributions to the community. In February 2005, this organization, under the leadership of its president, Rev. Michael Watkins, held the first Tavares African American Heritage Festival at Wooton Park. Each year, the festival pays special tribute to the contributions of Tavares's African Americans. In the first year, the oldest African American citizens of Tavares were honored. The festival has also honored church pastors and military personnel. In 2011, the festival paid tribute to educator Bennye Kinsler. The festival begins with a parade down Main Street. (Both, author's collection.)

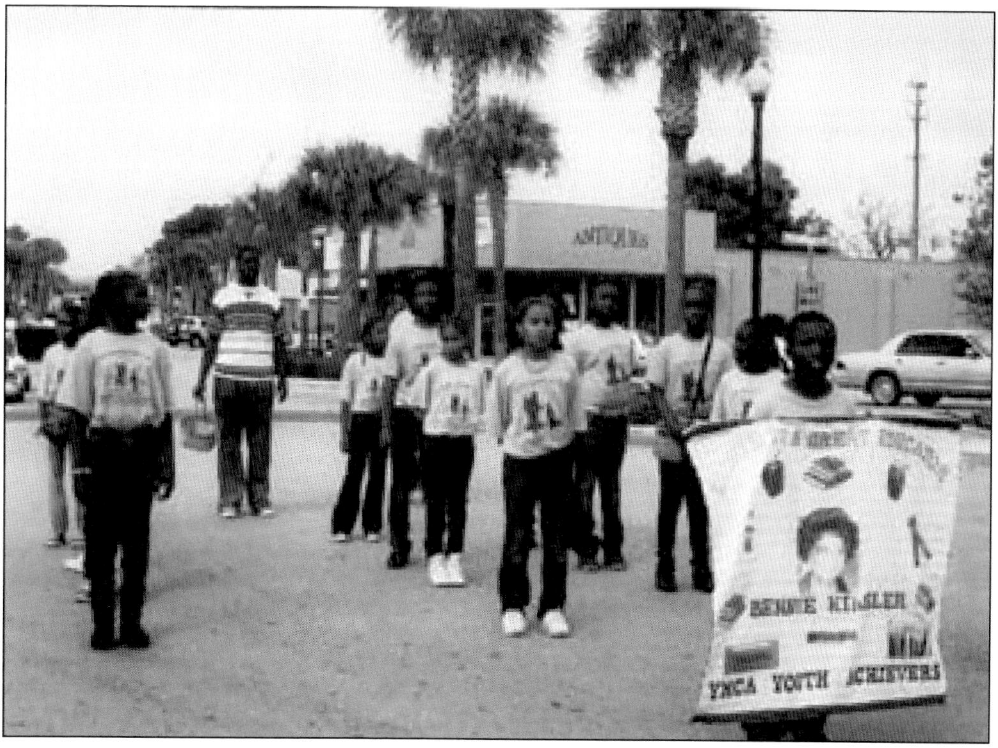

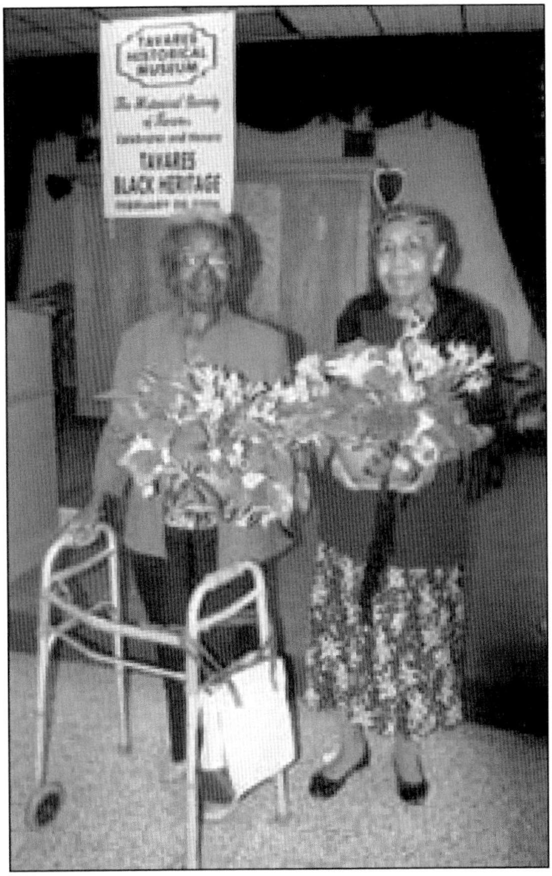

In February 2006, the Tavares Historical Society inaugurated the first African American Heritage luncheon at the Tavares Civic Center to celebrate Tavares's black heritage. In partnership with the Tavares African American Heritage Organization, the luncheon has become an annual event. Pictured at the heritage luncheon are Keturah Brodus (left), who passed away in 2010, and Lois Manigault, who passed away in 2011. (Author's collection.)

In Florida's pioneer days, the orange tree first served as a yard ornament that supplied fresh fruit and juice for the family breakfast, a tradition that carried through generations of Florida families. Bob Cook continues that tradition today by reaching out the window of his Banning Beach home to pluck a sweet navel orange for his morning juice. (Courtesy of Bob and Kathy Cook.)

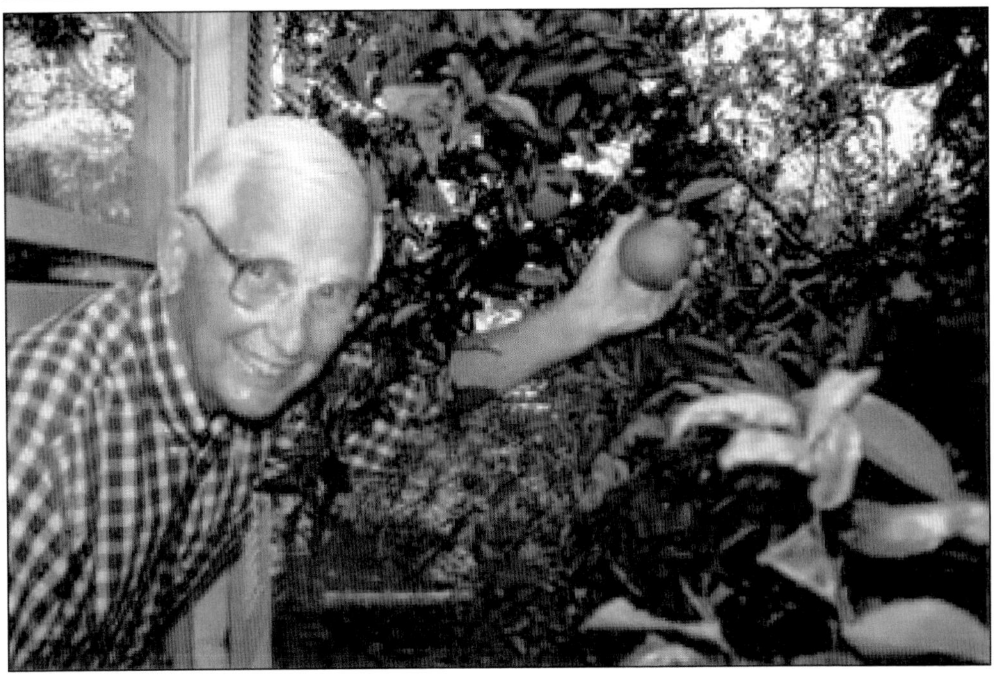

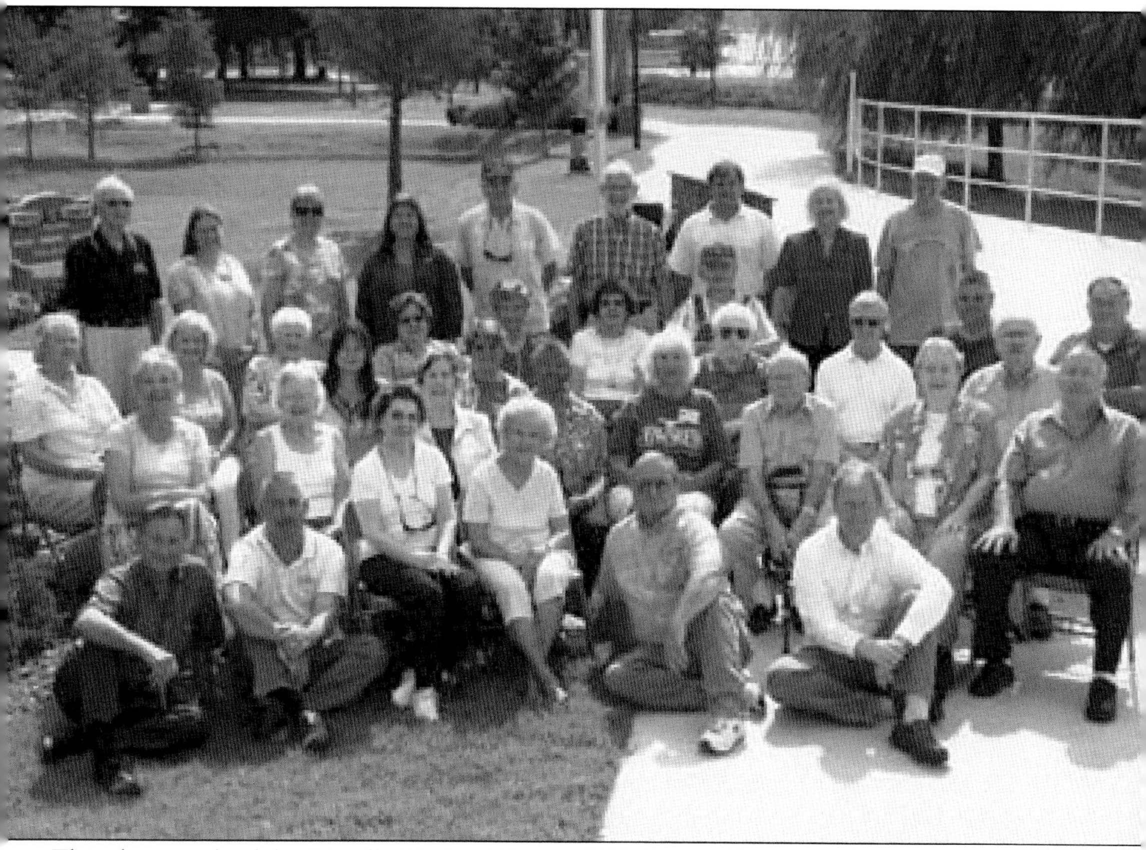

This photograph of the Friendly Circle of Tavares 2011 features Tavareans from yesterday and today, as well as those who have contributed to this Images of America: *Tavares* book. From left to right are (first row) Gene Smith, Mayor Robert Wolfe, Yvette Young, Doris Ragan, Mike Coven, and city administrator John Drury; (second row) Brenda Smith, Bettye Wilcox, Harryette Anne Duncan, Bernice Odums, Betty Burleigh, Ralph Custar, Bobbie Rees, and Leo Vaughn; (third row) Betty Ann McClellan, Patsy Umlauf, Lura Hall, Lavonda Morris, Geneva Vaughn, Judy Rainey, Imogene Wigglesworth, Kathy Cook, Bruggs Kennedy, Charlie Kennedy, Rick Reed, Tom Russ, and Billy Powell; (fourth row) Bill Burleigh, Kathy Carter, Lurlene Lawton, Debbie Stivender, Robert Young, Bob Cook, author and Vice Mayor Bob Grenier, who is proudly standing behind Clayton Bishop (seated), Charlene King, and Jim Nichols. (Photograph by Bonnie Whicher.)